Good News Babylon

Good News Babylon

The Mysteries, Miracles, and Secret Prophecies of 9/11

Dr. David Randolph

iUniverse, Inc.
Bloomington

Good News Babylon
The Mysteries, Miracles, and Secret Prophecies of 9/11

iUniverse books may be ordered through booksellers or by contacting:

iUniverse
1663 Liberty Drive
Bloomington, IN 47403
www.iuniverse.com
1-800-Authors (1-800-288-4677)

ISBN: 978-1-4697-4435-3 (sc)
ISBN: 978-1-4697-4436-0 (hc)
ISBN: 978-1-4697-4437-7 (e)

Library of Congress Control Number: 2012900553

Printed in the United States of America

iUniverse rev. date: 01/09/2012

Contents

Good News Babylon - Introduction Page

Gods self-expression, His Miracles, have always been intriguing. Most have made the declaration, "It's a miracle". Those read about in ancient scripture and others more recent, such as the apparitions of Our Lady in Fatima, Portugal in 1917, have already been declared True Miracles by the Holy See, and accepted as true. Many people report miracles of their own, little happenings that are better explained as attributable to the Lord God, those too far outside the boundary of chance. Knowledge of such instances and believing a miracle has taken place, makes one aware of those that occur in daily life through personal experience. They are often a benefit for which people will spontaneously give thanks to God, while others are regarded as a sign. We recognize them when we see them. Proving events are True Miracles to the general public may be a challenge, the supporting facts must conclusively eliminate the possibility of chance. The evidence in this book is meant for this purpose, to prove that the two recent signs we observed, the devil in the smoke of the burning World Trade Center towers during 9/11, and the Cross of Jesus Christ that was left standing atop the rubble after the WTC towers had fallen, are in fact True Miracles, signs intended for the world to see. They do carry a message and it's urgent to understand them. Most Americans already agree both were a miraculous sign, the question is just exactly what must we learn from them that God would need to send them with

9/11. The mystery has been solved, the secret meaning has been found. See and read the dramatic and conclusive evidence that these two signs were miraculous, and in truth a 911 call to the world from God.

You are invited to travel on an adventure into the reality of miracles, of prophesy fulfilled, one briefly transporting you in time, back to ancient Babylon, the birthplace of civilization, to review a lesson since forgotten. From Babylon, review ancient then modern day prophesies of 9/11 and pick up the trail to arrive at and see the true prophesy of September 11, 2011. Using it, examine the range of tangible miraculous evidence that prove the very existence of God, Resurrection of Jesus Christ and the Divinity of Our Lady, the Blessed Virgin Mary. This true adventure sought the purpose of God's message to a successful conclusion. After a science degree and a doctorate, it is ineffective when those who claim the appearance of the devil in the smoke and the Cross of Christ standing atop the rubble of the fallen WTC towers, were manifest by a random act of physics. Many want to dismiss the miracles of 9/11, but evidence will make you certain, these true miraculous symbols shown us, were an act of God. The signs hint there is a message to us involving the devil, and Jesus Christ, and that God had a hand in creating the symbols. You will discover that 911 was an emergency call for assistance, our help is needed.

The devil vanished into thin air. The Cross of Christ was spontaneously recovered by the knowing rescuers and placed on a pedestal for the world to see. The meaning of it all has been quietly speculated upon many, yet others strangely ignore them entirely. Having experienced 911, we have all become active participants in the adventure of unveiling the mystery and finding the true meaning of these miracles. The world is waiting for the spiritual explanation for the symbols received on 911, and the reason they were sent. The image in the smoke needs identification, while the Cross belongs to Jesus Christ. Knowing this is a start, but by themselves, only empty consolation until the details of the messages is discovered. The mystery has remained unsolved, until now.

Chapter 1

God Reveals Himself to the World on September 11, 2001

Figure 1[1]

The cross of Jesus Christ found standing in the rubble of the fallen World Trade Center towers

Photo taken by Anne M. Humphreys Bybee

The cross of Christ standing on top of the rubble of the fallen World Trade Center and the image of the devil in the smoke coming from the burning towers of 9/11 (Devil in the smoke?, can be looked up on the internet, no reprint permission could be obtained for copyright

1 "A picture of Hope from 911", photo taken and provided by Anne M. Humphreys Bybee, All Rights Reserved. Used by Permission.

use): both are tangible visual miracles that should not be ignored. They are symbolic, carrying a message from the Lord God. These images He intended for the world to see, to help provide the answers to all our questions about Him and those concerning the root cause of 9/11. These signs have been embraced by the Christian faithful as miraculous affirmation, yet others willfully chose to deny them continuing to dismiss them as coincidental, even though doing so is unreasonable, if not altogether unwise. Respectful rescue workers recognized the cross in figure 1, as symbolic of Jesus Christ and thoughtfully retrieved it from the rubble. Soon, it was raised up to a platform, put on display for the world to see. It has become part of the 9/11 Memorial, and stands as a strong testament for Jesus Christ. Obviously the cross was recognized by some as worthy of contemplation.

Both miraculous images when taken together, for those accepting them as a sign, illustrate the very existence of God. Supernatural forces were at work on 9/11, serving notice to Christians and those overtly and covertly antichrist. The direct interpretation of these signs is this: there is an antichrist faction in the world today, who deny and oppose Jesus Christ, at work in efforts to discredit and diminish Jesus Christ and his Church. There are many known examples. In some Muslim countries, where Christianity has been made illegal all together by the government, Christians are being attacked and murdered simply for being Christian. In some countries, Christians have been forced to go underground to avoid imprisonment or worse. God knows of those willing to crush the cross of Jesus Christ under their foot. Even in America were religious freedom has long been accepted as a God given right, Christianity is under attack, no longer properly protected from persecution and oppression by those who methodically erode Christian religious rights and liberty, their identity revealed openly by their actions. These antichrist activities are what is represented by the Antichrist figure in the smoke of 9/11.

The Lord Jesus Christ is the subject of the cross. Christians must in unity with one another, become active participants in defending their faith, particularly Catholics. The cross is your queue, a sign from God our Creator, to relieve your fear of standing up for the rights he alone endowed. Seen together on 9/11, these signs were also necessary because they are the key to recognizing, knowing and confirming the details of an urgent message. The discovery of the message was made possible only by the grace of our Lord and Savior Jesus Christ. The training in dental school, to arrive at conclusions only after comprehensive examination and attention was given to fine details, was a significant help in recognizing it for what it is. Finding it was simply a gift from the Lord.

There is much more to learn about the miraculous signs left behind at ground zero than their identity, they urge contemplation to understand the full content of the message being sent. Having biblical signs show up at the WTC disaster, should prompt observers to check scripture and prophecy to see if it was predicted. They may hold the reason and meaning of the signs in this catastrophe. Experience with prophesy, logic and theology, make preposterous the claims the devil's image, the images of angels, and those of the multitude of other faces and creatures that appeared in the smoke were of no meaning or consequence. They are in fact compelling testimony of prophesy. When combined with the cross of Christ left standing on the rubble of the towers, they could not possibly have been just the product of random acts of physics. They far transcend chance into the miraculous and therefore worthy of a prophecy. We all believe messages have come from God when they can be found in prophesy. The images in the smoke and the cross are most likely an orchestrated display arranged by the divine power of God, shown to the world for a true and serious purpose. The sheer number of pictures available on the Internet of all the images found in the smoke has sparked great interest. There are so many it is virtually impossible to attribute them to anyone but God and many fully believe they were an act of the Lord God of all, their faith has no need for a prophesy. The interpretation of the biblical signs has been speculated upon by many American individuals and several religious groups who have concluded the signs are miraculous, with one notable exception: major public broadcast media. They refuse to bring the issue into the public domain and discuss the differential opinions offered by religious groups and Christian representatives. Reason beyond doubt is needed for some to believe that it was indeed the hand of God that sent a message for us on 9/11, that it was a warning for Christians and non-Christians that Christianity is under attack in America and elsewhere by antichrist factions in the world. This accusation needs evidence, even though it seems obvious God is outraged and has shown it. Yet things will not change without more proof, for steadfast is the beast.

The initial evidence to prove this notion comes from prophecy, and begin with the physical similarities between the events of September 11, 2001, and the historical events that took place in ancient Babylon, and as recorded in the book of Isaiah. The prophecy of Joel is then examined and restated in modern language, to demonstrate how closely it resembles the events taking place on 9/11/2001, the fall of the twin towers, and the means by which it took place.

Finally and more important than the Joel prophesy, is the presage of 9/11 that has been discovered in twentieth century documents. Amazingly, these recent documents actually provide the techniques necessary to decipher the hidden secrets and the meaning they possess, the code for translation actually written in. Then by following one series of the clues, arrive at the prescribed destination they lead and verify the message in the document is authentic, to see the prophecy of 9/11 come to life firsthand. There you will find the Lord's message all around and the prediction of the event, describing the scene, providing the date, the place, and even jets were going to be involved in the catastrophe known now as 9/11. The evidence mandates that a specific action, a task must be undertaken at our Lord's request. The interpretation of this message is not tainted opinion. Instead, it is visual and thoroughly convincing. God's message revealed is real and tangible evidence; Jesus Christ has been raised from the dead and is Lord of all people, now and forever. Alleluia! It is in trying to destroy the Church of Jesus Christ that brought about 9/11. The catastrophe came with an emergency warning for the world of the serious nature of the antichrist— the cause and the reason for 9/11.

There is much to decipher and interpret in the signs and symbolism shown to the world on that fateful day. There can be no doubt that God was sending a message to us. The mystery that remains unknown is just what exactly does the Lord God want us to know, learn, and do? The objective is to take action based upon the knowledge gained, after accurate interpretation. In deliberately choosing to ignore the miraculous symbols displayed during 9/11 and the lessons that can be found in related prophecy, many have closed their eyes to God's instructions for us. Make no mistake, there was chastisement in 9/11 for a reason, and therefore it behooves us to understand and act upon these miraculous signs, beginning with a review of old and new prophecies to determine the true cause of 9/11 and what should be done about them. When we finally understanding the message, we will need to modify the way we conduct ourselves, if only to prevent such a catastrophe from happening again. If you are not part of the cause, you are requested to be part of the solution.

Surely, God spoke on September 11, 2001. For thousands of years, God has offered words of wisdom and guidance. Many times in history He has delivered rebuke and administered justice to those who refuse to repent and knowingly go against His Will. He has before and He will again if need be. If we had lived as He said we should, this catastrophe could have been prevented.

Consider the venue at which God chose to make His voice heard. The catastrophe of September 11, 2001, which we have come to call 9/11, took place at perhaps the most recognizable center of world trade, appropriately named the World Trade Center. Curious and noteworthy, the World Trade Center towers were right down the street from the United Nations center, where the nations of the world assemble to discuss and iron out their differences and unify as one global people. At the UN, all nations are expected to respect all others and provide the opportunity for each to present the conditions under which they live and the position and concerns their respective governments have in a forum where they can make a plea to the rest of the world for help or even mercy. It is expected by the citizens of all nations that their Diplomats and Ambassadors put history behind them and work for a better world; it is the reason and the foundation of the institution. Unfortunately, the spirit of this institution has faded; world peace hangs in the balance, and we are failing miserably. We can try harder, but as you will see, we cannot do it ourselves—God knows we have tried. 9/11 should be viewed as a new opportunity for peace.

The catastrophe of 9/11 grabbed the undivided attention of the entire world. Many chose a side to defend; but there is plenty of blame to go around for everyone. America was host to the World Trade Center and remains the home to the United Nations. God chose this global venue, and in doing so has given America a divine gift. He seems to be making America His own, His home. Consider this possibility: God in His own way, took the floor of the United Nations, struck the gavel, and spoke to the world. The Commandments for living were struck long ago and have been made available to everyone; the world members should have read them and minded God. "Treat your neighbor as you would treat yourself" would go far on an international peace scale. The way things are, few see peace happening soon, but an effort made by diplomats to promote mutual respect would be nice start.

Unfortunately, many innocent American men and women, police officers, and firemen sacrificed their lives in this catastrophe. Some are martyrs by most standards—willing, faithful heroes whose metal was tested in the furnace when they put the lives of strangers before their own. Their sacrifices were the ultimate show of unselfish love; they knew the potential consequences, especially after the first tower collapsed, yet they displayed the heroism in service to their fellow man in acts of bravery beyond the norm, exhibiting the very model Jesus Christ set for us. We may entrust their souls to the Lord for mercy, kindness, and eternal life.

For a person of faith, there is a strong feeling that there is still a message to be learned. It simply must be an emergency call from God Himself. It is our duty to find the specifics in God's message. It is our global and personal responsibility to do so—acting upon it, our proper obligation to God. It is time to learn and respect God's signs to know we are being warned or punished and for what reason, examining what transpired before catastrophic events of all kind.

Chapter 2

The 9/11 Attack Recapitulates Ancient Babylon[2]

The New York City World Trade Center towers were the signature symbolic towers of American ingenuity and prosperity. In scripture they share the same fate as the ancient city of Babylon: total destruction.

Babylon, the "gateway of God," was located between the Tigris and Euphrates Rivers, considered the birthplace of civilization and widely accepted as the same region in which Abraham lived.

---

2 Wikipedia; Babylon, Nineveh, Nebuchadnezzar. Wikipedia.com, 2011. (Albert Houtum-Schindler, "Babylon," *Encyclopædia Britannica*, 11th ed.)

- I.L. Finkel, M.J. Seymour, Babylon, Oxford University Press, 2009 ISBN 0195385403
- Joan Oates, Babylon, Thames and Hudson, 1986. ISBN 0-500-02095-7 (hardback) ISBN 0-500-27384-7 (paperback)
- The Ancient Middle Eastern Capital City — Reflection and Navel of the World by Stefan Maul ("Die altorientalische Hauptstadt — Abbild und Nabel der Welt," in Die Orientalische Stadt: Kontinuität. Wandel. Bruch. 1 Internationales Kolloquium der Deutschen Orient-Gesellschaft. 9.–1 0. Mai 1996 in Halle/Saale, Saarbrücker Druckerei und Verlag (1997), p. 109–124.
- Chisholm, Hugh, ed (1911). "Babylon". Encyclopædia Britannica (11th ed.). Cambridge University Press

Located about fifty-five miles south of Baghdad, all that remains of ancient Babylon now is a "tell" just a mound of mud-brick buildings. It is the equivalent to what remained of the twin towers—a mound of rubble, only a "tell" of that terrifying day of destruction.

Babylon was first established by the Amorites, semi-nomadic Semitic invaders from the west. It was then invaded by the Hittites, and then conquered by the Kassites, which resulted in a dynasty that lasted for 435 years until 1160 BC.[3] They were eventually overrun by the Assyrians and King Tukuliti-Ninurta I, who reigned in 1235 BC. The Assyrian domination continued until 608 BC, when in a constant state of turmoil and revolt by competing factions, the city was reduced to ruins and rubble before it was thrown into the sea. The act of totally destroying Babylon so angered the religious consciousness of the Babylonians, Assyrian King Sermcherib was killed in retaliation—not unlike the fate of Osama bin Laden for his part in the terrorist attack in New York City and Washington, DC. Upon Sermcherib's death, his elder son, Assyrian prince Shamash-shum-ukin ruled Babylon. In time, he began a civil war in 652 BC against his own brother Ashurbanipal, who was ruler in nearby Nineveh, a city famous for its scriptural heritage. Ashurbanipal prevailed and celebrated a "service of reconciliation" to God. After his death, the Assyrian Empire began to unravel in more civil war, the result of which was the Babylonian people finally freeing themselves from Assyrian rule. The fall of the Assyrian Empire was seen as an act of divine vengeance against the Assyrians for ruining Babylon.

The events of and consequences for the act of terror that led to the destruction of the World Trade Center on 9/11 are much like the history of Babylon including the sequence of events involving the Assyrians. The Islamic extremists who attacked America declared a Holy War against the United States with stated intentions of conquering the

---

3 Ibid.

world, and forcing everyone to become Muslim. Therefore, the militant Islamic extremists have acted anti-Christ. For the act of terror alone some consider the war in Afghanistan, just consequence, justified in the eyes of God, it being right vengeance, similar to the sentiments of the citizens of Babylon after it was destroyed. In any case, the reality of the situation now is both we and they were at war. We have lost four aircraft with passengers and crew, the Trade Center towers, and suffered damage to the Pentagon. There have been countless related deaths. The man-hours of work destroyed, number in the millions, maybe billions, with a financial cost of hundreds of billions of dollars, just to recover—not including what it will take to rebuild. In return for the extremists attack, the terrorists brought war to their nation of refuge, destruction, and hundreds of billions of dollars in damage of their own. There is no doubt the damage done and the cost of war has seriously harmed the global economy and the sooner it comes to a peaceful end, the sooner the world economy will recover. The truth could be we have both received our due in divine justice. There is strong evidence to support it.

What have we both done to receive divine chastisement? Was the terror of 9/11 God's just due or does He have a goal in mind? He did engage us with a divine warning using the signs presented at the scene at ground zero on 9/11. We cannot reason away the devil in the smoke and the cross standing in the rubble as random. God's cause appears to be defending His Son, Jesus Christ and that Our Lord is under attack. His warning signs could be considered to be a message going out to all Christians of a need to defend Christianity, while the act of terror remains as punishment for those who are antichrist, those who actively oppose Jesus Christ and deny His Gospel message. It is reasonable to conclude then, that as soon as Christianity is allowed its peaceful place as a faith whose religious liberty is respected by governments, the world may actually experience a period of true and lasting peace.

The lessons learned in Nineveh

Nineveh, assessing the potential of its own destruction, was spared the vengeance of God during the days of the prophet Jonah. Jonah instructed the people of Nineveh that God was going to destroy the city because of their behavior. The king heard this warning, and his response was to act and instruct all people to repent and change their ways. He called for a fast and dressed in sackcloth. He sat in ashes for three days as an act of penance and reconciliation, praying that this great disaster Jonah predicted would not befall his city. For this God relented and spared the city. He acted upon the warning he was given through Jonah to spare his people catastrophe. They admitted their guilt to God; they repented, and He relented. This is part of what we are all called to do.

Is it cleansing and reconciliation with God that is called for today? Consider the terror attack at the World Trade Center, the Pentagon, and flight #93; if 9/11 was an act of God—divine vengeance—America and the rest of the world have not been as compliant with God's teaching and warnings to reconcile with him and change our ways as did the people of Nineveh. Repentance is not optional but made mercifully easy and available through Jesus Christ and the Holy Church to those willing. With it God has been shown to be relenting in punishment a blessing well worth the effort.

The signs are there, it is inescapable; 9/11 is a catastrophe of Biblical proportion. God indicated through the devil in the smoke of the burning WTC towers and the cross of Jesus Christ left standing on top of the remains of the twin towers what the problem is. He used the event to send a message. The antichrist caused the catastrophe. In essence, God used it and left behind a blessing, providing the signs, the reason and solution for our problem. Prophesy tells us catastrophe's of this magnitude often come with due warning and 9/11 was no exception.

Chapter 3

The Prophecy of Isaiah

God is merciful! He has provided warnings to prophets to pass on to everyone for as far back as they were ever needed. You may ask, "Where and when did you tell us of 9/11, Lord?" There are prophecies that may have foretold 9/11; in fact, two are the same prophecies given to warn Babylon in the Book of Isaiah. In these, the imagery clearly recalls the day of 9/11 comparing the World Trade Center towers to Babylon. The word of God proclaimed through the prophets informed us long ago catastrophes like these can occur if we are indifferent to God's Word and warnings. It's happened before and likely to happen again, if not, God would have had no need to provide these Old Testament prophesies, there would be no prophet or record of God providing them. His warnings given on September 11, 2001, are no exception. In 9/11 he sent a new warning out to everyone with the image of the devil in the smoke and with identifying himself as Jesus Christ, the only Son of the God of Israel, using the cross of Jesus Christ standing in the rubble, as seen in the photo, *A Picture of Hope from 9/11.*[4] 9/11 was only the wake-up call, prophetic in its own right of further greater catastrophe.

---

4 "A picture of Hope from 911", Photo by Anne M. Humphreys Bybee, All rights reserved, Used by permission.

Is there any particular behavior in the world being brought to our attention needing immediate change today? As a precaution, it falls upon all people of the world to give the idea some contemplation—not just Americans. By reflecting on how we should hold our respect for God above all else, we can discover how the way we treat one another needs to be modified. It is time for global self-examination and realignment, the signs to do so have arrived. Terror and war are not a solution. As many try, there are serious stumbling blocks to ending war by mutual agreement, for some people their greed is greater than their respect for your life, and they make a ton of money during war, a real killing. It may in fact be the greater cause of war, causing a financial drain on the national economy and resources, for the profit of few. This greed alone has most assuredly instigated, encouraged and re-started war many times over.

Why restrict ourselves to God's rules anyway? Why listen to the warnings? If there were no known consequence for misbehavior, no rules given by God, there could be no such thing as misbehavior or sin. Our pious citizens originally established the law and administered justice based on God's moral standards. America's founding fathers are prime examples, but today the Antichrist promoters are living as if there is no such thing as sin, the Constitution or God, and have taken it upon themselves to actually legislate against both, rescinding religious principles in favor of immorality and secularism, not for principle but profit. It is happening around the whole world, especially in America, and in direct defiance of our founding fathers, who, had gone out of their way to guarantee religious freedom. It is as though Satan has blinded some people from seeing the evil behind sinning. People have become desensitized to immorality. Some people spend their time promoting sin for profit and attacking the Christian faith at the ultimate expense of all citizens. The consequence for dismissing God's guidance is severe, that for demeaning his Son Jesus Christ, the end all. Infrequently, over millennia man has seen the negative results of sin, of them some of these events such as war, have been outlined in catastrophic prophecy. The following evidence will show one of the most recent consequence of sin is 9/11.

Most of us were once taught the general rules of morality, those laws grounded in faith we need to live by to stay in favor with God. God knows if we have successfully circumvented the rule of law unjustly, and it is guilt in His court that really matters at day's end. Even unjust law will be judged by God. We have been warned in prophecy and you can try to deny there is a divine message for us in 9/11, but in your heart you know it is true. There is a need to change our collective behavior. The world has been served notice for our own protection. Our leaders and power brokers must lead by example, putting God above temptation and greed. By living Jesus' teaching, by his Word the Gospel, there is no harm, nor offense to any one. His way is empirically fair, moral, just, uncorrupt, and honest. Sure, we are all allowed free will to do as we please, but the rules of God remain; we obey God's rules or disregard them with indifference. According to the St. Maria Lucia of the Immaculate Heart of Mary, the eldest of the three Fatima children who witnessed the apparitions of the Blessed Virgin Mary, Notre Dame, in Fatima Portugal in 1917, this indifference, is a major part of the world's problems: disregarding God's Word. We all know our sins against God. Only we and God know the full, real truth. It is why the words "so help you God" spoken before testimony in court are so very important. By saying those few words, you recognize your responsibility to God for your testimony—and that real justice will prevail in the end, even if you lie on the stand. For the innocent made guilty, God is comfort; for the guilty deemed innocent by trickery of law, God looms large and self-guilt burns. An example of this rejection of Gods law came when God was removed from the courtroom. How could this happen in a country that professes to be "one nation under God"? Secularism is separating us from God, the foundation of America.

How were we to know when this antichrist behavior pressed us beyond Gods tolerance, when did we cross the line? The answer is, some time ago, and the consequence was 9/11. Where then was the prophetic warning for 9/11, and how did we miss it? How were we supposed to know this would happen? Someone is responsible for this tragedy—who? And where are they? We lash back at the obvious, the terrorists and their sympathizers, but we may be missing the point. For many of us, powerlessness and fear has kept us silent about the meaning of the signs of 9/11. But it is time to gather our collective courage and challenge the influence of evil in our society. Boycotting those who are anti-Jesus and their anti-Christian agenda is a first step. Why should we vote for or invest in or provide financial gain for those who promote the antichrist agenda? 9/11 says we should do so no more.

Christians have wondered how the notion of God could be pushed away from a nation of our background. It is because of the apparitions of Our Lady in Fatima that one should view the world and examine prophecy from a Catholic perspective if only to be aware of what it offers. This examination of scripture prophecy involves a dissection of it into parts to allow for analysis of each word or phrase individually, extracting the meaning using the broad-spectrum vocabulary found in any dictionary and applying them to 9/11 to establish that it can be one of the catastrophe's intended by the prophetic message. It may seem a bit unorthodox at first but will eventually defend itself with evidence. Imagery is critical in prophesy. It is used to understand the ancient prophecies and apply them to a modern catastrophe like 9/11. Rewording and reexamining them converted into a modern translation using terms from today's language, was thought an appropriate approach given the need.

Proving a prophecy was intended to predict 9/11 specifically is difficult, as many consider the imagery to be too abstract. When

9/11 took place, the symbolism indicated God decided to use it to remind us that we need to live within the guidelines He told us. When God has to reveal his power over us to make us change, He is no longer making a suggestion—He is demanding change. We have to change. We should consider ourselves blessed that God would put on such a display of power as 9/11 and show us supernatural signs to deliver his message. Jesus is the subject of the 9/11 message God presented by virtue of the cross standing in the rubble and was God's irrefutable statement that Jesus truly is his Son and the Christ. 9/11, as the fulfillment of prophecy will defend and confirm this as part of God's message.

Take a new view of these words from the prophet Isaiah in the Old Testament. You are the watchman, stationed to remain constantly vigilant. You with trained eyes are appointed to recognize the signs of approaching trouble, the early warning signal for everyone. The Catholic Church headed by the Holy Father and knowing the rules of God has served as watchman for everyone. Now it is you, the watchman, assigned to your post in one of the twin towers. You see signs of trouble and report your concerns, having done your duty, you return to your post. You become worried; no preparations are being made, no changes in defense, no changes in behavior. You warn them again. You tell them it's urgent, making certain they understand, asking not to be held accountable should something happen, and then you return to your post. Then, in a flash, from over the horizon comes your worst nightmare. Unable to speak, all you can do is watch as this transpires before your eyes.

Isaiah 21[5]

The fall of Babylon

1 Oracle on the wasteland by the sea:
Like whirlwinds sweeping in waves through the Negeb,
there comes from the desert, from the fearful land,
2 A cruel sight, reveled to me; the traitor betrays, the
despoiler spoils. "Go up, Elam; besiege, O Media; I will
put an end to all groaning!"
3 Therefore my loins are filled with anguish, pangs have
seized me like those of a woman in labor; I am too
bewildered to hear, too dismayed to look.
4 My mind reels, shuddering assails me; my yearning for
twilight has turned into dread.
5 They set the table, spread out the rugs; they eat, they drink.
Rise up, O princes, oil the shield!
6 For thus says my Lord to me: Go, station a watchman, let
him tell what he sees.
7 If he sees a chariot, a pair of horses, someone riding an ass,
someone riding a camel, Then let him pay heed, very
close heed.
8 Then the watchman cried, "On the watchtower, O my Lord,
I stand constantly by day; and I stay at my post through
all the watches of the night.
9 Here he comes now: a single chariot, a pair of horses; He
calls out and says, 'Fallen, fallen is Babylon, and all the
images of her gods are smashed to the ground.'"

---

5 *"New Revised Standard Version Bible: Catholic Edition, copyright 1989, 1993, Division of Christian Education of the National Council of the Churches of Christ in the United States of America. Used by permission. All rights reserved."*

10 O my people have been threshed, beaten on my threshing
floor! What I have heard from the Lord of Hosts, the God
of Israel, I have announced to you.

Isaiah 47[6]

The fall of Babylon

1 Come down, sit in the dust, O virgin daughter Babylon; Sit
on the ground, dethroned, O daughter of the Chaldeans.
No longer shall you be called dainty and delicate.
2 Take the millstone and grind flour, remove your veil; Strip
off your train, bare your legs, pass through the streams.
3 Your nakedness shall be uncovered, and your shame be
seen; I will take vengeance, I will yield to no entreaty,
says our redeemer.
4 Whose name is the Lord of Hosts, the Holy One of Israel.
5 Go into darkness and sit in silence, O daughter of the
Chaldeans. No longer shall you be called sovereign
mistress of kingdoms.
6 Angry at my people, I profaned my inheritance, and I gave
them into your hand; but you showed them no mercy,
and upon old men you laid a very heavy yoke.
7 You said, "I shall remain always, a sovereign mistress
forever!" But you did not lay these things to heart, you
disregarded their outcome.
8 Now hear this, voluptuous one, enthroned securely, saying
to yourself, "I, and no one else! I shall never be a widow
or suffer loss of my children."

---

6 Ibid

9 Both these things will come to you suddenly, in a single day:
Complete bereavement and widowhood shall come upon you for your many sorceries and the great number of your spells;
10 Because you felt secure in your wickedness, and said, "No one sees me." Your wisdom and your knowledge led you astray. And you said to yourself, "I, and no one else!"
11 But upon you shall come evil you will not know how to predict; disaster shall befall you which you cannot allay. Suddenly there shall come upon you ruin which you will not expect.
12 Keep up, now, your spells and your many sorceries; Perhaps you can make them avail, perhaps you can strike terror!
13 You wearied yourself with many consultations, at which you toiled from your youth; let the astrologers stand forth to save you, the stargazers who forecast at each new moon what would happen to you.
14 Lo, they are like stubble, fire consumes them; they cannot save themselves from the spreading flames. There is no warming ember, no fire to sit before.
15 Thus do your wizards serve you with whom you have toiled from your youth; each wanders his own way, with none to save you.

This may not be meant directly for 9/11 but it sounds familiar and does provide evidence the Lord God will act when He deems it is needed. The imagery includes catastrophic ruin, an empire brought down. Chariots and horses, the vehicles of those days carried it out. The Prophet messenger imparts the lessons to be learned, not to be quickly forgotten. It is written as an example for future generations to learn.

Over and over you try to understand 9/11. Initial thoughts were, was this accident or error. The reflex of fear brought people to their knees, knowingly and spontaneously calling upon the Lord for understanding. The image of the devil and the cross of Jesus Christ—what could it mean? The involvement of biblical scripture combined with the physical evidence indicates the supernatural, God is involved. With an open mind, the imagery is there to interpret Isaiah and visualize something similar to 9/11. As a prophetic description of Babylon, Isaiah is unmistakable since it mentions Babylon directly. It is directly a catastrophic Prophesy for Babylon. The imagery leaves this prophesy open to interpretation, as are most others, by virtue of its abstract description, such as referring to Babylon as a woman, a daughter with her nakedness (her sins), uncovered. This sounds like 9/11 in a way, though New York City or the World Trade Center towers are of course not mentioned specifically, they too have been referred to as she, just as ships and buildings often are. With this in mind, prophesy can have its imagery reinterpreted and applied to multiple catastrophe's. Not only could they be but probably ought to be tried for a possible fit when imagery dictates.

A point of interest in the Isaiah Prophesy is this: the destruction of Babylon took place with Assyria as the unconscious instrument of God, meaning God used them to punish, but ending with words of warning, telling them not to try to use His justice, to advance themselves.

Does the word *Media* in the prophecy—used in reference to an ancient city in Isaiah 21:2—ring a bell, hint at another meaning in this case? How often since 9/11 have you seen the image of Satan in the smoke at 9/11, broadcast on TV? How often has the cross of Christ in the rubble of 9/11 been contemplated in documentaries? "Suspicion arises when media intentionally neglects the obvious. We have yet to hear one public broadcast discussion of the meaning of the evil face in the smoke or the cross of Jesus Christ. There have not been any to recommend Jesus, the Son of God be recognized for what he is believed to be. Scores of witnesses along with video evidence documented the facts, yet mainstream media has no need or apparent desire to show the Antichrist or the cross of Christ, instead focusing only on telling the whole world how the catastrophe was an act of terror and a cause for revenge, the reflex response of blaming someone else. Ignoring these biblical signs altogether however, is a conscious decision by those who own media, when in retrospect the signs were the biggest news story of all for many observers. There has been no denial of biblical signs appearing on 9/11, it's what these particular signs represent, that continue to be selectively denied or entirely ignored by media. Was there a message for us when the antenna towers on top each WTC tower remained astonishingly vertical until they disappeared into the dust?

The problem for those who choose to ignore catastrophic prophecy and these obvious signs of 9/11 is that they are a necessary part of prophecy and only come from God. Ignoring or even refuting them, shows an indifference to God's law. They are God's own messages, not just words of a prophet; they have a purpose and God will make good on his promises to prophets. We can interpret prophecy, but we cannot change them. They are inherently good. They are an aid to keep us morally straight, to help us believe in God and remain in the grace of God. They tell us that abiding by His law is in our best interest and insulates us from harm. They also show us that when we have strayed too far, is when we will be brought to suffer the consequences of our own action. God's tolerance of our collective behavior must have limitations, with works directed at eliminating Him at or near the top of the list. Offending and harming each other daily does not seem to be enough to cause fulfillment of catastrophic prophesy, because it is happening all the time. The case of 9/11 is different. Signs indicate the harm being done is aimed at the reputation of His Son and damaging His Holy Church. Those who continue to do it are not about to point it out for you. With this in mind as the reason, were the terrorists the unconscious instrument of God once again and the war resulting from the attack just reprimand for the same reason?

We must have all disobeyed the rules of remaining in grace with God and misused the friendship with our fellow man or world resident nations more than once with full knowledge it was wrong for things to have gotten so out of hand. We were not hit by God, but by our fellow man, in the name of spirituality and morality no less. Consider the cross of Jesus Christ standing on the top of the fallen World Trade Center towers as the message, so everyone can agree to stop promoting harm against the Holy Church. This is one activity going on today that directly goes against Gods Will.

There are other prophecies that are pertinent, but for now, these two chapters of Isaiah are enough at least to spark an interest. It is written in the Holy Scriptures, the Old and the New Testament with the Gospel of Jesus Christ, that the knowledge of prophecy can be learned and its wisdom applied to prevent problems. All faiths have their own book of scripture; it does not matter really how or where we find prophecy or what we call the book that contains them, so long as God was the true source. God validates His Word when prophecy becomes fact. It would not surprise me if other scriptures hold prophecy of 9/11, since it is of global significance. The presence in other scriptures' prophecies would not change the facts or meaning of the cross of Christ at ground zero, only add to its significance for others on a broader global scale.

These readings from the Book of Isaiah strike as a visual of 9/11. These past prophetic passages came from the Old Testament of the Holy Bible, from the God of Israel, and they do resemble the terrorist attack of September 11, 2001, on the World Trade Center towers and the United States Pentagon, home of the US Defense Department.

Perhaps the inclusion of the Pentagon holds the key to the date 9/11. The emergency call goes out for us to defend ourselves from the expected and least expected. The way things are proceeding, we need to be concerned with an attack and domination from within our own borders.

Chapter 4

The Prophesy of Joel

For it to be established that there was a divine message in 9/11 to a steadfast atheist, there would need to be more to back it up than a devil in the smoke and the cross of Christ. If a prophecy could be found that more closely resembles 9/11, perhaps media might give the meaning of the devil in the smoke and the cross of Jesus Christ standing on top the rubble some credence and airtime and report what it means. Even though the prophesy of Isaiah has some imagery of 9/11, even if they were actually intended by relative conception to contribute to a greater understanding of 9/11, the call for proving it would arise. Furthermore, a warning without any indication of what to do holds no real value, especially if you're a nonparticipant in faith.

The message of the cross in the rubble should immediately have drawn the attention of all Christians. The first qualification to speak for the cross of Jesus is being Christian. If there is some message, we should be the first to recognize the solution. What is needed to prevent further catastrophic prophecy from becoming reality is having Christians answer the emergency call and take action. This 9/11 was not a call to be taken lightly; it is a life and death message. The world needs to respond. When the miraculous arrives on our doorstep with a warning of this magnitude, some behaviors must change. Otherwise, we will bring upon ourselves the consequence of catastrophe again. Quite frankly we cannot afford another catastrophe, there must be corrective action. The Lord God has given the reason for His outrage. The damage was self-inflicted. The faithful hope someday everyone will believe in God, to worship and do His Will the best they can.

The Book of Joel

It was composed about 400 BC. Its prevailing theme is "A Day of the Lord," much like September 11, 2001. It is said to describe the Passion and death of Jesus Christ. His death is reiterated as the death of His Body and Blood. The Catholic Eucharistic celebration of the Holy Mass uses bread and wine. Both are referred to in Joel as failing or languishing. If antichrist actions, activity to take down Jesus and His Church, are Gods reason to give the signs in the catastrophe of 9/11, the book of Joel should somehow have a connection.

This prophecy is disaster at the hand of the Lord God, imagery of what things might be like if it came to pass. A terrible invasion of insects was envisioned—devouring insects that in adult maturation, can fly. Some Bible versions use the imagery of locust to describe the invading army. In the face of this threatened catastrophe, the prophet summoned the people to repent, to turn to the Lord with fasting and weeping. They were ordered to convoke a solemn prayer and in return, the Lord promised to drive away the plague and bless the land with peace and prosperity. To these material blessings would be added an outpouring of the spirit on all flesh. St. Peter, in his first discourse before the people at Pentecost spoke about Joel in (Acts 2: 16–21), and tells of the coming of the Holy Spirit.

The concluding passages of Joel picture the nations gathered in the Valley of Jehoshaphat, where the Lord is about to pass judgment. Enemies are present as well, to hear the solemn indictment: their evil deeds are at last requited. The tumultuous throng assembled in the valley of decision is made up of all the enemies of God, and they face inevitable destruction, if … . God is both the vindicator of his people and the source of their blessings (Joel 4, 1–21). The miracles at ground zero mean to draw everyone's attention to the God of all people and Jesus Christ, God's Son, who he has come to defend. If we will try to defend His Son, He promises to help us relieve us of the plague. Since Joel is all about the Passion and death of Jesus Christ, the analogy of the fallen cross at ground zero of 9/11, can be looked upon as due to the antichrist actions of those working to bring down Christianity through some misunderstanding. Joel could be the prophetic message that has relevance to 9/11. See for yourselves if the prophecy of Joel could be about 9/11.

Joel 1-2:16

The book of Joel[7]

1 The word of the LORD that came to Joel son of Pethuel:

Lament over the Ruin of the Country

2 Hear this, O elders,
give ear, all inhabitants of the land!
Has such a thing happened in your days,
or in the days of your ancestors?
3 Tell your children of it,
and let your children tell their children,
and their children another generation.

4 What the cutting locust left,

7 *"New Revised Standard Version Bible: Catholic Edition, copyright 1989, 1993, Division of Christian Education of the National Council of the Churches of Christ in the United States of America. Used by permission. All rights reserved."*

the swarming locust has eaten.
What the swarming locust left,
the hopping locust has eaten,
and what the hopping locust left,
the destroying locust has eaten.

5 Wake up, you drunkards, and weep;
and wail, all you wine-drinkers,
over the sweet wine,
for it is cut off from your mouth.
6 For a nation has invaded my land,
powerful and innumerable;
its teeth are lions' teeth,
and it has the fangs of a lioness.
7 It has laid waste my vines,
and splintered my fig trees;
it has stripped off their bark and thrown it down;
their branches have turned white.

8 Lament like a virgin dressed in sackcloth
for the husband of her youth.
9 The grain-offering and the drink-offering are cut off
from the house of the LORD.
The priests mourn,
the ministers of the LORD.
10 The fields are devastated,
the ground mourns;
for the grain is destroyed,
the wine dries up,
the oil fails.

11 Be dismayed, you farmers,
wail, you vine-dressers,

over the wheat and the barley;
for the crops of the field are ruined.
12 The vine withers,
the fig tree droops.
Pomegranate, palm, and apple—
all the trees of the field are dried up;
surely, joy withers away
among the people.

A Call to Repentance and Prayer

13 Put on sackcloth and lament, you priests;
wail, you ministers of the altar.
Come, pass the night in sackcloth,
you ministers of my God!
Grain-offering and drink-offering
are withheld from the house of your God.

14 Sanctify a fast,
call a solemn assembly.
Gather the elders
and all the inhabitants of the land
to the house of the LORD your God,
and cry out to the LORD.

15 Alas for the day!
For the day of the LORD is near,
and as destruction from the Almighty it comes.
16 Is not the food cut off
before our eyes,
joy and gladness
from the house of our God?

17 The seed shrivels under the clods,
the storehouses are desolate;
the granaries are ruined
because the grain has failed.
18 How the animals groan!
The herds of cattle wander about
because there is no pasture for them;
even the flocks of sheep are dazed.

19 To you, O LORD, I cry.
For fire has devoured
the pastures of the wilderness,
and flames have burned
all the trees of the field.
20 Even the wild animals cry to you
because the watercourses are dried up,
and fire has devoured
the pastures of the wilderness.

Chapter 2

1 Blow the trumpet in Zion;
sound the alarm on my holy mountain!
Let all the inhabitants of the land tremble,
for the day of the LORD is coming, it is near—
2 a day of darkness and gloom,
a day of clouds and thick darkness!
Like blackness spread upon the mountains
a great and powerful army comes;
their like has never been from of old,
nor will be again after them
in ages to come.

3 Fire devours in front of them,
and behind them a flame burns.
Before them the land is like the garden of Eden,
but after them a desolate wilderness,
and nothing escapes them.

4 They have the appearance of horses,
and like warhorses they charge.
5 As with the rumbling of chariots,
they leap on the tops of the mountains,
like the crackling of a flame of fire
devouring the stubble,
like a powerful army
drawn up for battle.

6 Before them peoples are in anguish,
all faces grow pale.
7 Like warriors they charge,
like soldiers they scale the wall.
Each keeps to its own course,
they do not swerve from their paths.
8 They do not jostle one another,
each keeps to its own track;
they burst through the weapons
and are not halted.
9 They leap upon the city,
they run upon the walls;
they climb up into the houses,
they enter through the windows like a thief.

10 The earth quakes before them,
the heavens tremble.
The sun and the moon are darkened,

and the stars withdraw their shining.
11 The LORD utters his voice
at the head of his army;
how vast is his host!
Numberless are those who obey his command.
Truly the day of the LORD is great;
terrible indeed—who can endure it?

12 Yet even now, says the LORD,
return to me with all your heart,
with fasting, with weeping, and with mourning;
rend your hearts and not your clothing.
13 Return to the LORD, your God,
for he is gracious and merciful,
slow to anger, and abounding in steadfast love,
and relents from punishing.
14 Who knows whether he will not turn and relent,
and leave a blessing behind him,
a grain-offering and a drink-offering
for the LORD, your God?

15 Blow the trumpet in Zion;
sanctify a fast;
call a solemn assembly;
gather the people.
16 Sanctify the congregation;
assemble the aged;
gather the children,
even infants at the breast.
Let the bridegroom leave his room,
and the bride her canopy.

For copyright reasons, a maximum of 36 verses may be displayed. A further 45 verses have been omitted. Numbers were added to aid in comparing to other Bible translations.

King James Version of the Bible completes the book of Joel[8]

Joel 2:17 Let the priests, the ministers of the LORD, weep between the porch and the altar, and let them say, Spare thy people, O LORD, and give not thine heritage to reproach, that the heathen should rule over them: wherefore should they say among the people, Where [is] their God?

18 Then will the LORD be jealous for his land, and pity his people.

19 Yea, the LORD will answer and say unto his people, Behold, I will send you corn, and wine, and oil, and ye shall be satisfied therewith: and I will no more make you a reproach among the heathen:

20 But I will remove far off from you the northern [army], and will drive him into a land barren and desolate, with his face toward the east sea, and his hinder part toward the utmost sea, and his stink shall come up, and his ill savor shall come up, because he hath done great things.

21 Fear not, O land; be glad and rejoice: for the LORD will do great things.

22 Be not afraid, ye beasts of the field: for the pastures of the wilderness do spring, for the tree beareth her fruit, the fig tree and the vine do yield their strength.

---

8 *The Holy Bible of the Old and New Testaments, Translated out of The Original Tongues.* New York: American Bible Society, 1850.

23 Be glad then, ye children of Zion, and rejoice in the LORD your
God: for he hath given you the former rain moderately, and
he will cause to come down for you the rain, the former
rain, and the latter rain in the first [month].
24 And the floors shall be full of wheat, and the fats shall
overflow with wine and oil.
25 And I will restore to you the years that the locust hath
eaten, the cankerworm, and the caterpillar, and the
palmerworm, my great army which I sent among you.
26 And ye shall eat in plenty, and be satisfied, and praise the
name of the LORD your God, that hath dealt wondrously
with you: and my people shall never be ashamed.
27 And ye shall know that I [am] in the midst of Israel, and
[that] I [am] the LORD your God, and none else: and my
people shall never be ashamed.
28 And it shall come to pass afterward, [that] I will pour out my
spirit upon all flesh; and your sons and your daughters
shall prophesy, your old men shall dream dreams, your
young men shall see visions:
29 And also upon the servants and upon the handmaids in
those days will I pour out my spirit.
30 And I will show wonders in the heavens and in the earth,
blood, and fire, and pillars of smoke.
31 The sun shall be turned into darkness, and the moon into
blood, before the great and the terrible day of the LORD
come.
32 And it shall come to pass, [that] whosoever shall call on the
name of the LORD shall be delivered: for in mount Zion
and in Jerusalem shall be deliverance, as the LORD hath
said, and in the remnant whom the LORD shall call.

Chapter 3[9]

1 For, behold, in those days, and in that time, when I shall
bring again the captivity of Judah and Jerusalem,
2 I will also gather all nations, and will bring them down into
the valley of Jehoshaphat, and will plead with them there
for my people and [for] my heritage Israel, whom they
have scattered among the nations, and parted my land.
3 And they have cast lots for my people; and have given a boy
for a harlot, and sold a girl for wine, that they might drink.
4 Yea, and what have ye to do with me, O Tyre, and Zidon,
and all the coasts of Palestine? will ye render me a
recompence? and if ye recompense me, swiftly [and]
speedily will I return your recompence upon your own
head;
5 Because ye have taken my silver and my gold, and have
carried into your temples my goodly pleasant things:
6 The children also of Judah and the children of Jerusalem
have ye sold unto the Grecians, that ye might remove
them far from their border.
7 Behold, I will raise them out of the place whither ye have
sold them, and will return your recompence upon your
own head:
8 And I will sell your sons and your daughters into the hand
of the children of Judah, and they shall sell them to the
Sabeans, to a people far off: for the LORD hath spoken [it].
9 Proclaim ye this among the Gentiles; Prepare war, wake
up the mighty men, let all the men of war draw near; let
them come up:
10 Beat your plowshares into swords, and your pruning hooks
into spears: let the weak say, I [am] strong.

9 Ibid

11 Assemble yourselves, and come, all ye heathen, and
gather yourselves together round about: thither cause
thy mighty ones to come down, O LORD.
12 Let the heathen be wakened, and come up to the valley of
Jehoshaphat: for there will I sit to judge all the heathen
round about.
13 Put ye in the sickle, for the harvest is ripe: come, get you
down; for the press is full, the fats overflow; for their
wickedness [is] great.
14 Multitudes, multitudes in the valley of decision: for the
day of the LORD [is] near in the valley of decision.
15 The sun and the moon shall be darkened, and the stars
shall withdraw their shining.
16 The LORD also shall roar out of Zion, and utter his voice
from Jerusalem; and the heavens and the earth shall
shake: but the LORD [will be] the hope of his people, and
the strength of the children of Israel.
17 So shall ye know that I [am] the LORD your God dwelling
in Zion, my holy mountain: then shall Jerusalem be holy,
and there shall no strangers pass through her any more.
18 And it shall come to pass in that day, [that] the mountains
shall drop down new wine, and the hills shall flow with
milk, and all the rivers of Judah shall flow with waters,
and a fountain shall come forth of the house of the LORD,
and shall water the valley of Shittim.
19 Egypt shall be a desolation, and Edom shall be a desolate
wilderness, for the violence [against] the children of
Judah, because they have shed innocent blood in their
land.
20 But Judah shall dwell for ever, and Jerusalem from
generation to generation.
21 For I will cleanse their blood [that] I have not cleansed: for
the LORD dwelleth in Zion.

The Book of Joel as a Presage of 9/11

Using contemporary language to discuss and interpret Joel, the prophecy could be used to depict 9/11 more than the other ancient prophecy of Isaiah. Selecting this prophesy, was done based on other evidence that points to it as having pertinence to 9/11. Word association and reducing the terms into their empirical form seems natural whenever interpreting prophecy.

The Word of the Lord, Which Came to Joel[10]

Joel was the watchman sent to bring a message to the people, a warning of catastrophic consequence if the message was rejected.

The Word of God coming to Joel could be interpreted as being about the end days for Christ, a description of the destruction of the Body of Jesus Christ during the Passion of Christ and the consequences for men that came with His death.

Within this prophecy could well be the imagery of the World Trade Center (WTC) twin towers being attacked and crashing to the ground. The fate of flight 93 that crashed on the farmlands of Pennsylvania might be part of this prophecy as well. How true is it of September 11, 2001, and the attack on the WTC towers? We were the land invaded. Take great liberty in deciding what this prophecy may mean to you.

> Joel 1:1 The Word of the Lord which came to Joel, the son of Pethuel.

10 "New Revised Standard Version Bible: Catholic Edition, copyright 1989, 1993, Division of Christian Education of the National Council of the Churches of Christ in the United States of America. Used by permission. All rights reserved."

Joel was to present this message as a warning of an impending catastrophe: a mistake would cause disaster, but it would be preventable if the warning was taken to heart. You will see the requirements necessary to gain protection and salvation.

Joel 1:2 Hear this, O elders,
give ear, all inhabitants of the land!
Has such a thing happened in your days,
or in the days of your ancestors?

Be it the life and death of Jesus Christ or the event of 9/11, the phrase applies. No one living today was there when Christ lived and died; what happened exactly is a mystery of faith. Pay attention to the description of 9/11 in the following passages. In 9/11, the ashes and smoke from the huge explosion from the impact of the aircrafts has never been seen or anything like it ever happened before. The events of 9/11 taken together as a whole will not be forgotten. Surely, it received global attention. The earth shook again as the towers tumbled to the ground.

Joel 1: 3 Tell your children of it,
and let your children tell their children,
and their children another generation.

The crucifixion of Jesus was documented in many ways in the New Testament. The Good Book has withstood the test of time. The Gospels of Jesus—His very words, the Word of God—the world will never forget. The events of Jesus' life, His miracles, His conviction and sentence of death, and then the gruesome death by crucifixion of Jesus Christ take place. The Gospels will be passed on to children forever as the message of Jesus Christ. It happened. Denying it is like denying the Holocaust.

After the September 11, 2001, attack in New York City, the same sight was seen: the phrase "We will never forget" was printed on flags and bumper stickers all over America. We will tell our children, and I expect they will tell their own children, of the horror experienced from the attack on the WTC. There are many books written about the events leading up to, during, and after the attacks on the WTC of 9/11, all with reason. People feared there could be many more attacks, and only time will tell if this fear will become a reality. America, it is said, is doing everything it can to prevent another attack. Has it included an interpretation of what we believe God wants us to do: repent like the prophecy states and moreover, stop offending God by harming the reputation of His Son and the Church? It is much easier to place blame than to accept responsibility.

Joel 1:4 What the cutting locust left,
the swarming locust has eaten.
What the swarming locust left,
the hopping locust has eaten,
and what the hopping locust left,
the destroying locust has eaten.

Scholars interpret these phrases as an invading army. This section of Joel describes the attack of the WTC from an invading outside army, the locust fly. The word "cutter" has several meanings. A cutter is also a ship powered by a motor or oars, similar to twin jet engines mounted on wings. This cutter generally carries cargo or passengers.

There is another reference to locust in Revelations: "Locusts came out of the smoke onto the land, and they were given the same power as the scorpions of the earth" (Revelations 9:3). Suddenly, the book of Revelation enters the picture.

The remark that these "locusts" came out of the "smoke" could explain the many creatures seen in the smoke from the WTC. The airships took a major toll and crushed the towers into the earth. The airliners are analogous to locusts and had the power of the scorpions of the earth. The sting of a scorpion burns and can result in death. Incoming aircraft caused the same.

The twin towers destroyed as if attacked by a huge invading army. These canker worms, locust and caterpillars can totally destroy a crop not unlike the physical destruction of the World Trade Center towers.

Joel 1:5 Wake up, you drunkards, and weep;
and wail, all you wine-drinkers,
over the sweet wine,
for it is cut off from your mouth.

The Blood of Christ, fruit of the vine, the sacrament of Communion, the Holy Eucharist, the true Body and Blood of Jesus, was instituted at the Last Supper. Jesus had been arrested and His future placed in the hands of those who plotted against Him. He was aware of His own fate. More likely, this could be indicative of the future held for those still refusing to repent. They were warned but pushed away the notion of acceptance and subservience to the Lord.

Some people were probably asleep at the time of the 9/11 attack. There were many tears shed and much weeping.

Joel 1:6 For a nation has invaded my land,
powerful and innumerable;
its teeth are lions' teeth,
and it has the fangs of a lioness.

When first read, this phrase from the prophecy of Joel could apply to 9/11. For Americans, images of World War II fighter aircraft with the mighty teeth of meat-eaters painted on the fuselage might come to mind. We have all seen them in movies, those fighter planes with the teeth and jaws of lions, sharks, and the like painted on the nose. The roar of the twin turbine engines sound would be those of the lion and lioness.

> Joel 1:7 It has laid waste my vines,
> and splintered my fig trees;
> it has stripped off their bark and thrown it down;
> their branches have turned white.

Here the twin towers with near the same image: the outer shell of the WTC towers are stripped away as they fall. Afterward, the outer walls and shards of the metal skin of the WTC buildings are made white, covered with ash. People are also the Lord's fruit of the vine. Stripping *them* may be an issue.

> Joel 1:8 Lament like a virgin dressed in sackcloth
> for the husband of her youth.

Losing the twin towers of the World Trade Center was like losing a member of the family, considered sacred by many. They were violated, causing painful grief. People cried and were devastated. In short, a virgin weeps over her loss.

> Joel 1:9 The grain-offering and the drink-offering are cut off
> from the house of the LORD.
> The priests mourn,
> the ministers of the LORD.

When Jesus died, His disciples temporarily lost the Lord, His Body and Blood. When He rose again, His Body and Blood lived again. The Eucharist is the grain and wine mentioned here, the living Body and Blood of Christ. Surely there was sorrow for days, even weeks following 9/11. The Catholic priests called on the faithful to pray at special prayer services. They offered counseling to parishioners who were upset and grieved over the unknown victims or those they knew, those somehow involved. Wanting to pray for the victims, many gathered to weekday Masses and prayer vigils. Most everyone knew someone involved or someone living in the area surrounding the twin towers: a cousin, friend, sister, or nephew. The event touched so many lives it could not be ignored by anyone. The buildings were gone forever. By trying to take down Jesus in today's world, the antichrist actions to abolish the Blessed Host and Wine, the sacrament of the Eucharist is repeating that fateful day on Calvary.

Joel 1:10 The fields are devastated,
the ground mourns;
for the grain is destroyed,
the wine dries up,
the oil fails.

This passage has more content if you look in the right places. The Body and Blood of Christ were ravaged during His Passion and Crucifixion. The grain can represent the Eucharistic Sacrament He instituted at the Last Supper. Discrediting and damaging the reputation of the Holy Church is doing the same to the Eucharistic celebration and Jesus Christ. The "must" used in other bible versions is wine, also used at the Last Supper. The Light of the World is being lowered. This in particular seems the warning sent on 9/11.

Too few mustard seeds, God needed to act. The Lord your God is calling his people back to the fold. He sent a cross and planted it in the rubble as a reminder, as a clear sign! It wasn't a random toss of physics. It is an open invitation from Him. It should be a celebration that God should speak to us.

The crash site of flight 93 in Pennsylvania provides another example. The impact of the aircraft ravaged the soil and caused the burning jet fuel to slowly smolder. The cross of Jesus Christ doesn't fall out of the sky for no reason; this is serious business. Those who have dismissed Jesus and notions of God as imaginable folly should reconsider what the faithful already know true.

Joel 1:11 Be dismayed, you farmers,
wail, you vine-dressers,
over the wheat and the barley;
for the crops of the field are ruined.

Men have become less diligent in nourishing the spiritual lives of their families. There is less encouragement provided. The Word of God drifting away or is unknown altogether. Spiritual neglect minimizes morality, the physical body becoming only a source of pleasure rejected as the fountain new of life. This leads to the next passage. It has gotten so that not only is the Church not thriving from the work of His disciples, it now has to contend with being publicly demeaned by those with an antichrist agenda.

Joel 1:12 The vine withers,
the fig tree droops.
Over the wheat and the barley, because the harvest of the field has perished.
Pomegranate, palm, and apple—
all the trees of the field are dried up;
surely, joy withers away
among the people.

Jesus said He is the Vine and we are the branches of the vine. His body, the church, is dying from attacks from the antichrist work of others, demeaning the Church, encouraging the abandonment of the moral fabric of faith and teaching the world to distrust the clergy. The clergy are losing their flock. The vinedressers are responsible for the care of the vine. We, the branches of the vine, are withering.

Call to Penance

Joel 1:13–16 Put on sackcloth and lament, you priests;
wail, you ministers of the altar.
Come, pass the night in sackcloth,
you ministers of my God!
Grain-offering and drink-offering
are withheld from the house of your God.

14 Sanctify a fast,
call a solemn assembly.
Gather the elders
and all the inhabitants of the land
to the house of the Lord your God,
and cry out to the Lord.

15 Alas for the day!
For the day of the Lord is near,
and as destruction from the Almighty* it comes.

16 Is not the food cut off
before our eyes,
joy and gladness
from the house of our God?

This as much as says that 9/11 was an act of God. The Church is being attacked, the Body and Blood of Jesus Christ—the Eucharist instituted at the Last Supper—is being mocked and scorned, and the Rosary of Mary is being referred to as just a string of beads for counting, not prayer.

The desire for a secular lifestyle has been chosen by some that goes against the Will of God. It is being promoting as a right, with the resulting sin for profit their benefit, leaving the teaching and wisdom of the Holy Church in their wake, determining it to be an obstacle.

Yes, before our very eyes on September 11, 2001, we were reprimanded for the ways of the sinful. The last line says ruin from the Almighty is yet to come. The best course of action would have been to satisfy the Will of the Lord God and give respect to His Son Jesus Christ, before the day "near" arrives. This is an emergency—a 911 call—placed to the world, hence, the World Trade Center. But it is only the call; it is a warning and request for attention and action concerning a life-and-death situation that may occur if unheeded. There is a catastrophe on the horizon, but what is it? How are we to avoid it? It was Joel's calling to illuminate the cause, and he has. Attacking the reputation of God's Son Jesus and His Church is where God draws the line in the sand.

> Joel 1:17 The seed shrivels under the clods,
> the storehouses are desolate;
> the granaries are ruined
> because the grain has failed.

Are Christians being encouraged to drift away from the Holy Church and fewer attending Mass regularly? If this refers to total numbers, the Church—the watchman—to its credit has fulfilled its role; everyone is aware scripture prohibits exploitation and abortion.

Children are a gift to be treasured. Those blessed enough have them are fortunate. Scripture says this: "Children too are a gift from the Lord, the fruit of the womb, a reward. Like arrows in the hand of a warrior are the children born in one's youth. Blessed are they whose quivers are full. They will never be shamed contending with foes at the gate" (Psalm 127: 3–5). The Church's lifeblood, children of the faithful, a blessing, is being discouraged by contraception and abortion.

People are falling away from faith. All of these people—the husbandmen, the vinedressers, the elders, the entire assembly, the priests and ministers—are responsible for the faithful. We have failed in apathy, beaten by the "beast", the devil. Living within the moral guidelines of faith should be enough to encourage others to join. Expressing the joy and happiness experienced when living with faith is constantly being discouraged and ridiculed in media. They claim Catholic Church teachings are outdated, when it is the rejection of the Word of God that is really getting old.

Joel 1:18 How the animals groan!
The herds of cattle wander about
because there is no pasture for them;
even the flocks of sheep are dazed.*

These are the people who suffer the most from September 11, 2001, the herd, ordinary people who were led astray to follow the way of the evil to profit from sin. Hopefully, they have observed and recognized the devil and the cross—the unmistakable signs of September 11, 2001—and it has struck fear. The evil do not wish to see these signs again, they do not want to believe what was presented on 9/11, because it is contrary to their agenda. They want you to deny Jesus too.

Joel 1:19 To you, O Lord, I cry.
For fire has devoured
the pastures of the wilderness,
and flames have burned
all the trees of the field.

Flight 93 went down in a Pennsylvania field on the edge of a reclaimed strip mine and literally burned the field. Is it divine evidence that nudity and stripping is an unacceptable behavior, and encouraging it is evil? Was where 93 crashed divine providence for purpose? It is time to walk away from the beast and return to the way of the Lord.

The vaults that locked away feelings of guilt have been opened by 9/11. People should be awakened and others confronted by the *real* truth and justice. They need to make a decision: continue or change. The beasts, large and small, operating dishonestly, are now stricken with the pain of guilt and are slowed by those not so anxious to continue serving them.

Joel 1:20 Even the wild animals cry to you
because the watercourses are dried up,
and fire has devoured
the pastures of the wilderness.

The fire from burning fuel at the crash site literally torched the nearby woods, the trees of the field.

The twin towers of 9/11 were peeled to the ground. Those with no faith are confused as to which road of faith to follow if they seek one. The resources of the beast—those who have been treated no better than animals—no longer want to be subjects of the beast, and they are walking away. Christianity is divided too. The faithful are being scattered by different denominations and so-called free Christian churches that offer fewer moral restrictions and no need to properly reconcile with God.

Chapter 2[11]

The Day of the Lord

Joel 2:1 Blow the trumpet in Zion;
sound the alarm on my holy mountain!
Let all the inhabitants of the land tremble,
for the day of the Lord is coming, it is near—

The trumpet is a biblical expression and announcement. The events of 9/11 were quite a Trumpet blast. Having the cross of Christ standing in the rubble is a noticeable artifact worthy of attention.

Is it that this 911 emergency call is the delivery of the prophetic message and *not* the coming catastrophe itself, only the initial call for help?

The Joel prophecy describes 9/11 pretty well and adds the need for repentance. If 9/11 is just the trumpet call to get our attention telling us to change our ways, holy fright! The future catastrophe the prophecy warns of must then be really serious, like nothing ever seen before, about the same words President Harry S. Truman delivered. We must be willing to repent, reform and return to showing respect for the Lord. To accept and live the way Jesus told us is a God given right and must not be interfered with. The least we can do is beg for forgiveness and mercy. Fair warning has been delivered.

11 Ibid

Joel 2:2 a day of darkness and gloom,
a day of clouds and thick darkness!
Like blackness spread upon the mountains
a great and powerful army comes;
their like has never been from of old,
nor will be again after them
in ages to come.

This passage begins the description of the catastrophe. Here comes a mighty army. 9/11 was only swarm of four aircraft with fuel, but the devastation they caused!

Joel 2:3 Fire devours in front of them,
and behind them a flame burns.
Before them the land is like the garden of Eden,
but after them a desolate wilderness,
and nothing escapes them.

Images of the devil and others reported could not be seen in the flames, or when all that remained was just flattened smoldering filth. There were no flames before the airliners hit. The creatures in the smoke were the only things that appeared after the flames but before the smoldering rubble of the towers. Seeing the faces and bodies of these creatures in the smoke brings biblical identity and supernatural forces into this catastrophe. This doesn't necessarily mean these creatures were responsible for 9/11, but they may very well be signs of how a next catastrophe will be delivered. The Garden of Eden, a biblical reference included in this passage, suggests this catastrophe takes place at the doorway to Eden, a bountiful paradise. America could be what is intended. The devil's face appearing in the smoke is a sign of pure evil and analogous to the snake in the Garden of Eden. Trickery and deception are at issue. Angels, who make up the army and defenders of the Lord and respond when He is attacked, are in the smoke also. Some say the face of God is looking on. A bear's face was captured on film. Many saw an eagle and a woman standing. Anyone can see them in the film and photos found on the Internet by keying in "Devil of 9/11."

Limited to the mortal domain as we are, we are no match for them or whoever put them there. Those who recognize the power of God in this catastrophe—the faithful—see the signs, some showing that there is valid reason to believe in angels. Nobody delights in the destruction, there must be a message.

Flying at top speed, the airliners caused an explosion strong enough to push flames through to the other side of the buildings. The flames continued burning and smoldering. The heat softens the damaged metal shell, and then the weight of the building above the point of impact collapsed onto the remaining tower below. What remained was a lifeless pile of rubble—a desert waste. There was no escape for those trapped inside or daring to stay behind. Into our front door, America—the helper of many nations, who regularly together with others help those who suffer disaster; this fertile land, the breadbasket of the world, blessed with resources, considered the land of plenty by the grace of God—came an unwanted intruder. We are not perfect, we have compassion on the needy of the world, so why us? Future catastrophes need to be prevented.

Joel 2: 4–5 They have the appearance of horses,
and like warhorses they charge.
As with the rumbling of chariots,
they leap on the tops of the mountains,
like the crackling of a flame of fire
devouring the stubble,
like a powerful army
drawn up for battle.

The passage can describe the airliners as modern day chariots with outer metal armor, as powerful as an army of many racing toward the twin towers. They are airborne, leaping like locust at the top of the towers, as tall as a mountain. The twin engines of each aircraft are the horses of the chariot, providing the "horsepower" needed to pull these new age chariots. The jet engines rumble loudly—whether inside the towers as they approached or riding inside the jets, the power could be felt, their noise up close shakes the earth. Both rescuers and terrorists rushed to the scene.

Joel 2:6 Before them peoples are in anguish,
all faces grow pale.*

On 9/11, think of the faces of those in the towers realizing a jet aircraft was aiming straight at them; with no time to act, paralyzed, knowing their fate, their faces must have turned ghost white in fear. Even our own feelings watching the broadcasts of 9/11 turned our faces ashen, our future suddenly did not look as bright as it may have moments before.

Joel 2:7 Like warriors they charge,
like soldiers they scale the wall.
Each keeps to its own course,
they do not swerve from* their paths.

Read this and see emergency vehicles driving down the street, still following the usual traffic lanes. With the destination destruction known, they ran their engines straight ahead to the flight path of destruction.

Joel 2:8 They do not jostle one another,
each keeps to its own track;
they burst through the weapons
and are not halted.

Shortly after the first tower was struck, it was decided that this was not an accident, but rather a deliberate act of terror. The command was made to land all aircraft to clear the sky to locate the intruders. The airspace normally crowded was clear. The hijackers turned off the flight transponders; the planes dropped off the radar screen. Air traffic controllers had no way to track them. The aircraft landing to clear the sky were not checked to identify the planes missing. They had to find them visually. It was impossible to find them.

Joel 2:9 They leap upon the city,
they run upon the walls;
they climb up into the houses,
they enter through the windows like a thief.

This is a perfect description of the aircraft crashing into the twin towers. As the expression goes concerning the uncertain day and hour of our death—that it will come upon us like a thief in the night—they entered through the windows, not the front door in a sneak arrival, and they took everything. This is a reminder to be vigilant and remain in the good grace of God at all times to protect your soul and your future. This could signify the meaning of the devil and the angels. All must decide of their own free will: live our lives in sin and go with the devil, or live by the Word of God and leave with the angels to heaven.

Joel 2:10 The earth quakes before them,
the heavens tremble.
The sun and the moon are darkened,
and the stars withdraw their shining.

The towers crashing to the ground and the billows of smoke and dust came pouring into New York like a giant title wave, blocking the sun and moon from view.

Joel 2:11 The Lord utters his voice
at the head of his army;
how vast is his host!
Numberless are those who obey his command.
Truly the day of the Lord is great;
terrible indeed—who can endure it?

There is much we must have done to offend the Lord while possessed by the devil. Attacking His Son is an outrage. Joel 2:12–17 is instruction to all and to respected authority requesting help to encourage morality and call all to repentance. This infers the terrorists were the unconscious instrument of God.

Joel 2:12 Yet even now, says the Lord, Return to me with all your heart, with fasting, with weeping, and with mourning; rend your hearts and not your clothing.

Weeping and mourning came easily on September 11, 2001. People cried on the streets and in their homes. We failed to recognize that this was the result of the antichrist's rejection of Jesus and all He taught us—to love one another and treat each other kindly and fairly. Instead of looking to the sky and saying "I am sorry, Jesus," we blamed someone else. Repentance—how hard can it be? Who is willing to accept blame before the Lord God of hosts? It is time-repent for sinfulness, apologizing to the Lord our God for wrongdoings and work to reverse the damage done.

Joel 2:13 Return to the Lord, your God,
for he is gracious and merciful,
slow to anger, and abounding in steadfast love,
and relents from punishing.

The Lord God and Jesus are not asking for you to give up your clothes or comforts. Jesus just wants your heart, your acknowledgment of Him as Lord, and your dedication to His teachings.

In days past, the Lord God had written messages for us. We all may have our own messages from God, if listening. This emergency 911 message was written for the entire world. America was the home of the *World* Trade Center, and the message was meant to address the "world." If Jesus wanted to deliver a letter to us, this was the logical place to have it delivered. America is best equipped for world broadcasting, and we can give everyone the opportunity to read the letter. We got His letter, no question. We were all shown and allowed to read the letter. They showed it on television. This time, The Lord your God wrote His letter in metal on stone. The letter was short. It was the letter *T*, as in the cross of Jesus Christ. Quite simply, this letter tells all about Jesus. You can look up the meaning of *T*; it's in the Bible under "New Testament." Some followers of His, called apostles, wrote down exactly what He said and what He wanted us to do. You should read the entire letter, called the Gospels, if you want to find out more.

This passage from the Gospel of John expresses exactly what our problem must be for us to deserve the admonition we received on September 11, 2001: "This is how you can know the Spirit of God: every spirit that acknowledges Jesus Christ come in the flesh belongs to God, and every spirit that does not acknowledge Jesus does not belong to God. This is the spirit of the antichrist that, as you heard, is to come, but in fact is already in the world" (John 4:2–6).

Most everyone around the world acknowledges Jesus or knows of Him at least. You may not believe He is the Son of God, but most do acknowledge Jesus. Those who deny Him and trouble Him are the antichrist.

This is still an emergency call, a letter, to warn of worse future admonishment if His word given through Joel goes unheeded. Bring your hearts and minds back to the ways of your Lord. The cross of Christ, standing in the midst of the destruction, is a reminder that Lord God is still waiting for acceptance of His Son, Jesus, by those who reject Him. At the least, the antichrist must stop attacking Him publically. Media holds most of the power to, and responsibility for trashing Him and His Church.

> Joel 2:14 Who knows whether he will not turn and relent,
> and leave a blessing behind him,
> a grain-offering and a drink-offering
> for the Lord, your God?

The Eucharist is the offering and blessing offered by the Lord to all.

> Joel 2:15 Blow the trumpet in Zion;
> sanctify a fast;
> call a solemn assembly; gather the people.

September 11, 2001, was the emergency trumpet blast spoken of here. Prepare yourselves in prayer and fasting so you may hear the wisdom and word of the Lord directly. Gather the great of the faithful, the priests and ministers, and discuss the acceptance of Jesus as the Lord God and how to fulfill the Will of everyone's Lord God united around the Eucharist. Repent! Say you are sorry to the Lord, and ask Him for forgiveness. He is calling us again to return to Him through His Son, Jesus Christ. If you do apologize to Jesus, according to this part of the message from Joel, Jesus will forgive you and may even give you and the nation blessings to help your problems!

Is there any harm going to come to anyone for saying "I'm sorry." For some, the apology is just not good enough. Sometimes it is difficult to accept because of the amount of hurt involved. With Jesus, the priests say, He will forgive you every time, but you do need to ask. This was a calling to everyone, an invitation. It was a time for sorrow but also an event to rejoice in.

Joel 2:16 Sanctify the congregation;
assemble the aged; gather the children,
even infants at the breast.
Let the bridegroom leave his room,
and the bride her canopy.

Your attention is requested! Bring everyone into the fold and to gain the protection of the Lord. This passage is intended for those most able to spread the message of His letter we received. This is urgent! We need to gather together and come to a common decision as a people to accept Jesus as Savior, whose cross was displayed in the aftermath of 9/11. We should come forward and decide on the future, now knowing the awesome power of the Lord God and His obvious command for us to stop harming His Son, His Church and return to His Love. One by one or as unified people, we need to accept His request and deny Him no longer.

For copyright reasons, a maximum of 36 verses of the New Revised Standard Edition Bible may be displayed. A further 45 verses have been omitted. Numbers were added to aid in comparing to other Bible translations.

Joel continues using the King James version of the Bible[12]

Joel 2:17 Let the priests, the ministers of the LORD, weep
between the porch and the altar, and let them say,
Spare thy people, O LORD, and give not thine heritage

12 *The Holy Bible of the Old and New Testaments, Translated out of The Original Tongues.* New York: American Bible Society, 1850.

> to reproach, that the heathen should rule over them: wherefore should they say among the people, Where [is] their God?

It is primarily the priests who are addressed in this passage, but written to be about the death of Jesus, including priests then and now. Having accepted Jesus as Lord, clergy know what needs to be done to regain God's love and protection. They can pray to know the answers, just as Joel prayed to receive this message he was to deliver. Without our apology to Jesus, He has no reason to protect and defend anyone, but He has pity and is merciful. When we come to know Jesus is the true Savior sent to us for our benefit, He will bless us with kindness. When we totally ignore His teaching and deliberately commit sin against Him, we probably should receive wrath; it is no different from a deliberately disobedient child whose behavior ends up harming someone. Be it physically, emotionally, or financially that we harm another, we deserve what we get if it is intentional—particularly when we have no remorse.

Blessings for God's People

Joel 2:12–17 Instruction to respected authority requesting help to encourage morality.

> Joel 2:18–19 Then will the LORD be jealous for his land, and pity his people. Yea, the LORD will answer and say unto his people, Behold, I will send you corn, and wine, and oil, and ye shall be satisfied therewith: and I will no more make you a reproach among the heathen:

The acceptance of Jesus in the sacraments will be the promised source of our protection. You will gain the benefits of Jesus in the Eucharist and the Holy Spirit with Sacrament of Confirmation, and thereby gain eternal life. One of the Catholic sacraments is reconciliation; it is an admission of guilt and repentance to return to grace with Jesus. These are available to everyone.

> Joel 2:20, But I will remove far off from you the northern [army], and will drive him into a land barren and desolate, with his face toward the east sea, and his hinder part toward the utmost sea, and his stink shall come up, and his ill savour shall come up, because he hath done great things. Be not afraid, ye beasts of the field: for the pastures of the wilderness do spring, for the tree beareth her fruit, the fig tree and the vine do yield their strength.

This passage may be intended to confirm to us that we will gain the protection of the Lord Jesus Christ through His sacraments and our worship of him. The northerner, equate with the spirit of the antichrist banished. He will drive them away, helping us when we act.

> Joel 2:21 Fear not, O land; be glad and rejoice: for the LORD will do great things.

The cross on the rubble and the image of the devil in the smoke were miracles. It was a great thing, making the existence of God easy to believe. These signs were a gift to us that could not have come without the destruction of the twin towers. In this way, 9/11 was a blessing as well as a warning. Accept it as such; take heed, believe and rejoice. Know that God will do great things for us and show us great signs for us to learn from. If we comply, we will be blessed, if not the signs may be great but come in the form of further catastrophe.

Joel 2:22 Be not afraid, ye beasts of the field: for the pastures of the wilderness do spring, for the tree beareth her fruit, the fig tree and the vine do yield their strength.

Even for the repentant guilty there is salvation and welcoming like that of the prodigal son.

Joel 2:23 Be glad then, ye children of Zion, and rejoice in the LORD your God: for he hath given you the former rain moderately, and he will cause to come down for you the rain, the former rain, and the latter rain in the first [month].

We will receive the miracle of proper rain and an abundance of harvest, not draught or flood waters. The waters of Baptism will also bring new life and the Holy Spirit. He promises a resurrection into heaven for you if you follow His teaching. To describe the truth about Jesus is to include the message of His resurrection. The early rain in this passage could mean baptism into the church; the late rain is perhaps the new life eternal granted after death for those have been baptized into the Church and follow His Word.

Joel 2:24 And the floors shall be full of wheat, and the fats shall overflow with wine and oil.

This is about the resurrection and the gift God sent in Jesus. The Teacher of Justice, the benefits provided by His body (the grain) and blood (the wine) in the Eucharist is distributed to those attending the Memorial Celebration of the Mass in a Catholic Church. It is what Jesus left behind at the Last Supper, the institution of the Eucharist. The oil, the chrism oils used in some sacraments of anointing of the sick and confirmation into the faith. The remark tells that there is plenty to go around for everyone. You are welcome to join the Holy Church and share in the blessings provided in the Eucharist.

Joel 2:25 And I will restore to you the years that the locust
hath eaten, the cankerworm, and the caterpillar, and the
palmerworm, my great army which I sent among you.

Jesus promises the benefits of Himself and the Holy Spirit for the loss incurred on 9/11. Having equated the aircraft being used to destroy the WTC twin towers, as having been done by locust, grasshoppers, and cutters—the message of Joel reports that it was God's great army delivering Divine Justice. An act of terror caused the catastrophe, this we know; but God left His signature with the Cross of Hope on the ruins and provided the message we received from it. His full role is for each to conclude and act upon.

Joel 2:26 And ye shall eat in plenty, and be satisfied, and
praise the name of the LORD your God, that hath dealt
wondrously with you: and my people shall never be
ashamed.

These miracles of 9/11 are a blessing assuring Christians to have no fear, He is with you. Christians should never feel ashamed of their faith.

Joel 2:27 And ye shall eat in plenty, and be satisfied, and
praise the name of the LORD your God, that hath dealt
wondrously with you: and my people shall never be
ashamed.
28 And it shall come to pass afterward, [that] I will pour out my
spirit upon all flesh; and your sons and your daughters
shall prophesy, your old men shall dream dreams, your
young men shall see visions:

Such is the power of the Holy Spirit.

29 And also upon the servants and upon the handmaids in those days will I pour out my spirit.

30 And I will show wonders in the heavens and in the earth, blood and fire, and pillars of smoke.

31 The sun shall be turned into darkness and the moon into blood, before the great and terrible day of the Lord come.

32 And it shall come to pass that whosoever shall call upon the name of the Lord shall be delivered: for in mount Zion and in Jerusalem shall be deliverance, as the Lord hath said, and in the remnant whom the Lord shall call.

Jesus is the Lord God, one in being with the Father and the Holy Spirit. This sounds as though there are more signs to follow 9/11. We have experienced many global catastrophes since 9/11. If we look there should be a message in each. We have work to be done to get back in the good graces of our Lord, learn the signs and find the reasons.

Chapter 3 of Joel[13]

Joel 3:1 For behold, in those days, and in that time, when I shall bring again the captivity of Judah and Jerusalem,

Everyone has an opinion about the events of 9/11. Many have looked for an explanation or for a prophecy that answers the mysteries of 9/11. It is a calling to those who reject Jesus as the Christ. The Book of Joel could be the prophecy fulfilled again in 9/11 that brings acceptance.

---

13 Ibid

Even a child can see the visions of the faces in the falling columns of smoke. Many have had dreams about it, though they may be frightful.

> Joel 3:2 I will also gather all nations, and will bring them down into the valley of Jehoshaphat, and will plead with them there for my people and [for] my heritage Israel, whom they have scattered among the nations, and parted my land.

Many nations have suffered catastrophe since 9/11. It is their message. Everyone is welcome to come to the feast of the Eucharist in the Catholic Church.

> Joel 3:3 And they have cast lots for my people; and have given a boy for an harlot, and sold a girl for wine, that they might drink.

The Lords flock is being mistreated. This is a reminder to all that do. A woman or girl was one image in the smoke. Was it anyone in particular?

> Joel 3:4 Yea, and what have ye to do with me, O Tyre, and Zidon, and all the coasts of Philistia? will ye render me a recompence? and if ye recompense me, swiftly [and] speedily will I return your recompence upon your own head;

As for Philistia, the recompence came back to them just as the Lord spoke. There is no winning going against the God and His Son Jesus Christ, He will chastise His people Himself if they need correction. It sounds again that Philistia was just the unconscious instrument of God in the attack, but war came in retaliation driving them away. Take no boast of your work says the Lord, it was His hand that delivered the blow. If 9/11 was our warning wake-up call at the hand of our Lord, the next time the Lord has to reveal Himself, the catastrophe will be much more serious. Pay attention to the future signs.

Joel 3:5 Because ye have taken my silver and my gold, and have carried into your temples my goodly pleasant things:

If you have yet to realize 9/11 was the calling to cease public broadcasting of the antichrist message, there was that pesky remnant left at the Trade Center after the disaster, a cross of Jesus Christ. Catholics all know that by calling on the Lord Jesus Christ we will be rescued. We waited and deliverance came. Those who act antichrist, in seeing the cross—were officially summoned to give religious liberty to the Jesus, Christ the King. At minimum, stop abusing Him and His Church. This calling goes out to everyone in the world as well. The antichrist, acting under the spell of the Devil; are also God's sheep, -- He loves us all—and wants you to love Him.

Those who bilk or pilfer from the Holy Church are equally as guilty of being antichrist.

Judgment upon the Nation[14]

Joel 3:6-7 The children also of Judah and the children of Jerusalem have ye sold unto the Grecians, that ye might remove them far from their border.

7 Behold, I will raise them out of the place whither ye have sold them, and will return your recompence upon your own head:

14 Ibid

The judgment imposed and consequences of your behavior are at the discretion of the Lord. The world, from long ago, we are all the children of Judah, any harm done to anyone is wrong.

Joel 3:8-9 And I will sell your sons and your daughters into the hand of the children of Judah, and they shall sell them to the Sabeans, to a people far off: for the LORD hath spoken [it].
9 Proclaim ye this among the Gentiles; Prepare war, wake up the mighty men, let all the men of war draw near; let them come up:

Consider this a warning to the antichrist. This is exactly what happened after 9/11. This is Gods calling everyone and He will help the cause.

Joel 3:10-14 Beat your plowshares into swords, and your pruninghooks into spears: let the weak say, I [am] strong.
11 Assemble yourselves, and come, all ye heathen, and gather yourselves together round about: thither cause thy mighty ones to come down, O LORD.
12 Let the heathen be wakened, and come up to the valley of Jehoshaphat: for there will I sit to judge all the heathen round about.
13 Put ye in the sickle, for the harvest is ripe: come, get you down; for the press is full, the fats overflow; for their wickedness [is] great.
14 Multitudes, multitudes in the valley of decision: for the day of the LORD [is] near in the valley of decision.

9/11 was God's judgment for His own people. *War* begins after 9/11. Men against Men, they fight to the death, punishing themselves with their own hands. The attack and the retaliation are also penalties for both sides. The root cause must be established to spare us all. The invitation from God is to celebrate the Eucharist, and the Church should welcome all who hear His call.

Joel 3:15–16 The sun and the moon shall be darkened, and the
stars shall withdraw their shining.
16 The LORD also shall roar out of Zion, and utter his voice
from Jerusalem; and the heavens and the earth shall
shake: but the LORD [will be] the hope of his people, and
the strength of the children of Israel.

All nations are called to be United Nations, to sit together, to listen to the message received and not pass judgment but rather establish in unity a purpose. The message in 9/11 is an unmistakable call to Jesus Christ. Expect resistance as the antichrist is alive and thriving, but keep faith steadfast in Jesus as it says on the Image of Divine Mercy-Jesus, I Trust in You.

Joel 3:17–21 So shall ye know that I [am] the LORD your God
dwelling in Zion, my holy mountain: then shall Jerusalem
be holy, and there shall no strangers pass through her
any more.
18 And it shall come to pass in that day, [that] the mountains
shall drop down new wine, and the hills shall flow with
milk, and all the rivers of Judah shall flow with waters,
and a fountain shall come forth of the house of the LORD,
and shall water the valley of Shittim.
19 Egypt shall be a desolation, and Edom shall be a desolate
wilderness, for the violence [against] the children of
Judah, because they have shed innocent blood in their
land.
20 But Judah shall dwell for ever, and Jerusalem from
generation to generation.

21 For I will cleanse their blood [that] I have not cleansed: for the LORD dwelleth in Zion.

And so it is written in scripture. The similarities to and imagery of 9/11 and the resulting wars and upheaval that followed are evident. It is all included in the book of Joel. The vocabulary is descriptive enough to indicate that 9/11 was at least one event this prophecy could have been intended to predict the same as it does for the Passion and Crucifixion of Christ. If the behavior of God's people warranted its manifestation, it had to occur. The Lord commands repentance from His people, better now than wait. He will clean the blood of sin, as He says. It is the very nature of divine prophecy to reach fulfillment, though for our sake, perhaps only if needed. The Lord would not give a prophet an empty threat. The Lord alone provides prophesy for us, and here in this reading from Isaiah, he defends the validity of His prophetic messages.

Exhortations to the Exiles

Isaiah 48: 3–5

3 Things of the past I foretold long ago, they went forth from my mouth, I let you hear of them; then suddenly I took action and they came to be.
4 Because I know that you are stubborn and that your neck is an iron sinew and your forehead bronze,
5 I foretold them to you of old; before they took place I let you hear of them, That you might not say, "My idol did them, my statue, my molten image commanded them."

For some reason, the devil in the smoke and the cross of Christ has not been discussed by mainstream media. In fact, they seem to have deliberately avoided it, even though they are obvious. What is there to fear that makes it off-limits to major media outlets? It is somewhat of an outrage that these signs and message that have sparked controversy in the public square, haven't been given air time or received any commentary. It is baffling. God is waiting on your answer. What is known however, is the lack of an invitation that could have been extended to Catholic priests, to say a few words at the ten year memorial ceremony and the complaints made known by those who lobbied unsuccessfully to exclude the cross itself from the 9/11 memorial. Rather than being invited, Catholic priests were actually uninvited. Some of the victims, including a priest were Catholic. Organizers simply deny there is any connection with Jesus in 9/11, while others have even blamed Jesus for not preventing it from happening. There is still an anti-Catholic bigotry at work, a growing epidemic in America that was begun long ago.

These old prophesies may not be concretely conjoined with 9/11, but they do hold a lesson to be learned about the risks involved with harming the reputation of Jesus, His Church and His followers. For Babylon it was straightforward; God can and will give foreknowledge of catastrophe when it serves his greater purpose and our best interest. God's wrath is also well documented in the Old Testament for other reasons. Whether the Lord God brought wrath on 9/11 and for what reason is up for each to decide. If however you do recognize Jesus as Lord in 9/11, you simply cannot undo the reality. Thus far, with verdict still out, opinions differ greatly. Generally people have been satisfied with whatever they need to conclude, bowing to peer pressure and forwarding their own religious mindset or lack thereof. We all have been given free will and religious liberty to worship as we personally decide. This *right* is God given and should not be restricted or any faith abused by another. That aside, there is new evidence to support that 9/11 was actually *all about Jesus*, it proving Jesus as the Christ and the truth of his resurrection from the dead that has been so fervently denied.

Chapter 5

Mother of Christ Crusade[15]

It may be very presumptuous to believe that these Old Testament prophecies were actually intended in part to help to decipher the message sent to the world on September 11, 2001. The interpretation of the abstract is always imaginative. We do know prophesy predicts something and that God was the author for both Joel and Isaiah. They might be ancient, but they originate from the source of all life. They may be a little more abstract than one might like when trying to conclude they actually could describe the events of 9/11 and the involvement of God, but two points are brought to our attention worth further consideration, one from an earlier chapter of Isaiah. In Isaiah 10, Assyria is the unconscious instrument of God. It has happened once, why not again in 9/11? Joel, read traditionally, describes the death of Jesus using imagery including, his Passion and death, and of His Body and Blood in the Sacrament of the Holy Eucharist consecrated during the Mass of the Catholic Church. It also has the imagery of 9/11. The practical application of these two points to 9/11 weigh heavy but they may not be near enough to prove 9/11 was an act of God specifically due to the antichrist actions of some, nor likely to convert an atheist to Catholicism on they're own.

15 de Marchi, John, with Sr. Maria Lucia of the Immaculate Heart. *Mother of Christ Crusade*, Billings, Montana: Mother of Christ Crusade, Inc., 1947.

The next prophetic messages are the direct prediction of the 9/11 catastrophe when fully revealed. The source of this 9/11 presage is Our Lady, who by accurately predicting 9/11, proves Her own divinity and as the Mother of God, again.

The authors of Mother of Christ Crusade, John de Marchi together with Sr. Maria Lucia of the Immaculate Heart of Mary, state this book contains Our Lady's peace plan. The predictions it contains originate from the time of the apparitions of Our Lady in Fatima, Portugal of 1917, are taken from the memoirs of Lucia de Jesus dos Santos, the eldest of the three children who witnessed the apparitions of Our Lady in Fatima first hand and recorded them. They are an extension of the miraculous predictions Our Lady gave for Fatima of the public sixth apparition. It was Lucia who actually brings up the topic of Joel in her memoirs, thus inferring the book of Joel must be examined as the one prophesy with the resulting consequence being 9/11. She validates this prophesy of Joel, as being related to 9/11. It is the reason for the Joel Prophesy being used to introduce her continued work with Our Lady after leaving Fatima and written about in the *Crusade*. Most Catholics have been under the impression the Fatima Miracles have come to an end with the assassination attempt on Blessed Pope John Paul II, that all presaged events from Fatima have taken place. That however, is not entirely the case. What has not been considered is that Our Lady continued to visit Lucia Santos after she left Fatima. It was during these later apparitions with Our Lady that she received additional predictions, perhaps completing the messages begun in Fatima, particularly those that came with the "Vision of Hell" of the third apparition. It is these extended predictions Lucia received from Our Lady that are thoroughly explored.

The real divinity of Jesus' Mother the Blessed Virgin Mary, has already been proven to tens of thousands, to those who witnessed the fruition of the prediction made by Our Lady, of the apparition all could see, that took place on October 13th, 1917, in Fatima, Portugal. It however wasn't enough for men to take heed of her warnings.

This little known book, *Mother of Christ Crusade,* innocently presents details of the daily lives of the three children who saw Our Lady in Fatima. The punctuation and capitalization of some words presented in this complete work reflect how they were presented in the Crusade. Most are not the way they would be written if the traditionally accepted guidelines way were followed. They are not publishers over sight. There are no copyright restrictions for using this book. The passages that are copied are quoted as presented. It has no page numbers entered, only chapters. The page numbers referenced in this presentation, begin with page one assigned to the first page of chapter I; "The Angel".

The Angel appeared first, three times; then Our Lady appeared to them in six apparitions and Lucia gives the exact happenings during each in the *Crusade*. She includes how and by whom they were mistreated when the news and message of these visitation miracles were made public while they refused to disclose the additional *secret messages* delivered by Our Lady in entirety. She tells how neighbors and friends hit, mocked and ridiculed them at first. They were even abducted by the authorities, the local magistrate in Portugal. Once abducted, they were imprisoned and threatened with death for refusing to divulge the secrets they withheld. The motivation of the authorities and the media at that time was an effort made only to effectually squash the renewed enthusiasm Catholics were gaining through the reports of the apparition miracles. Authorities and press tried every means to discredit the children and the Church, attempting to paint the whole affair as an elaborate hoax put on by the Church to advance their own agenda. The children, Our Lady as their companion, never divulged the secrets they learned. They were locked away in some archive. Eventually, the apparition miracles brought so much attention to the children it led them to escape any public appearances. Not long after the apparitions, after endless questioning by believers and non-believers alike, Lucia Santos left Fatima to enroll at a convent school and eventually became Sister Maria Lucia of the Immaculate Heart of Mary. The secrets she withheld from authorities and the location of her destination convent school, she had promised to never tell, and for good reason. The truth is she needed to work in secret, to hide, she had a mission to carry out—one that had been given to her directly by Our Lady. Her commitment was to spread a devotion to the Immaculate Heart of Mary at God's request, similar to the already established devotion to the Sacred Heart of Jesus. Our Lady also asked for the consecration and conversion of Russia to her Immaculate Heart.[16] Recent images photographed in the skies over Russia of the crucifix of Jesus are evidence of Her continued desire. The apparitions occurring in Fatima have since been authenticated by the Catholic Church as true Miracles, and the three children canonized as saints. Everything in the Mother of Christ Crusade revolves around the Catholic Church and these three Catholic children.

The Fatima Apparitions

The year was 1917 when an angel first appeared to the children of Fatima. Each time the Virgin Mary or an angel appeared in an apparition, a prayer message was given to the children. Some information was personal, meant only for them. However, the messages to be passed on were intended for the entire world to hear and see. Lucia's goal is to show what it takes to bring peace upon the world, how prevent further war, to stop social atrocities like abortion, pornography, and worldwide promotion of adulterous

16 De Marchi, *Mother of Christ Crusade*, Chapter V, p 66

sex.[17] These mandates from God were given along with instructions and reminders for men on how to conduct themselves to stay in God's grace. Lucia includes the requests the Virgin Mary wishes we would do for her in prayer. Our Lady gave the consequences for failure to comply with God's Holy Will.

At the time, 1917, World War I was coming to an end. In one apparition, Our Lady promised peace if people would heed her warnings to stop the sacrileges and indifference that so greatly offended and outraged Our Lord. If not, another great war would come and men would again be brought to war with all its suffering and miserable consequences. Does this mean World War II was an act of God, and we should have seen it coming for ignoring her warning and continuing our ways? By telling the children of another war in advance, Our Lady did presage World War II. Yes; World War II was another presaged consequence. There was no side to blame but our own. It is all due to our indifference towards God's law. We ignored God's Word, and for it we were drawn into war. Was there presented to us a message, when it was specifically "Pearl Harbor" being bombed that brought the US into WWII. Does a parable about finding a pearl come to mind? Interesting the Feast of the Immaculate Heart of Mary is the day following Pearl Harbor Day. Sure, in WWII there were many innocent people who lost their lives apparently because of the sins of others; it is just the nature of war. In total, about 48,000,000[18] were killed in WWII. More than one-half were civilians. Our need is the prevention of war and catastrophe

---

17 De Marchi, *Mother of Christ Crusade*, end of chapter XIV

18 Gregory Frumkin, *Population Changes in Europe Since 1939* (European estimates)
B. Urlanis, *Wars and Population* (Soviet Union and the Far East)
Singer and Small, *Wages of War* (the Americas and Ethiopia)
I.C.B. Dear, editor, *The Oxford Companion to World War II* (British Commonwealth)

by preventing those who have outraged our God, from continuing to do so.

Mother of Christ Crusade was approved for publication August 11, 1947, at the close of World War II. Strangely, the book doesn't address *man*, but rather *men*, speaking to the sins of men.[19] Indeed, most of the millions lost in World War II were men. World War II was one of the bigger Fatima prophecies. Our Lady had said an even greater war would break out if men did not mend their ways, and hence, World War II began, presaged by Our Lady.[20] Our Lady added to her prediction the reason as well, that war is just punishment for the sins of men. There is further evidence we were warned in advance. See for yourselves, the *Crusade* contains the exact words and messages Our Lady said to Lucia Santos, and Francisco and Jacinta Marto.

During Her final visitation, Our Lady put on a miraculous cosmic display, before an estimated audience of about seventy, to one hundred thousand amazed people. It was the Sixth Apparition, taking place on October 13, 1917, that got the world's attention and converted so many people to Catholicism. Numerous observers reported on the event, exclaiming it proved the divinity of Jesus' Immaculate Mother, the Virgin Mary. Its prediction and manifestation also proved to those in attendance something more empirical, the very existence of God.

These people didn't need prophecy to piece history together to arrive at the conclusion, *there is a God*. They heard the presage of Our Lady from Lucia Santos, the divine prediction from Our Lady that this miraculous cosmic event would take place on October 13, 1917. Then, as promised, they experienced the awesome power

19 de Marchi, *Mother of Christ Crusade*, Chapter I, p 10
20 de Marchi, *Mother of Christ Crusade*, 1947, Chapter V. Third Apparition, p 66

of God firsthand during the sixth apparition. We can read about these miracles and taking them on faith, accept the word of the near one hundred thousand who saw the miracles in the sky that day, but it was seeing it firsthand that made believers out of those there—even those with the hardest of hearts. "I'll believe it when I see it myself," the hardest heart remarks, then they did. Afterward, they were totally convinced of the divinity of the Virgin Mary and of Jesus as the Christ. You can't condemn anyone because they need to see a miracle in order to believe. St. Thomas needed to poke his fingers in the wounds of the Risen Jesus Christ before he would be convinced—and he was an apostle!

Oddly, I've never seen a publicly broadcast documentary from major media outlets about the apparitions or of the cosmic display taking place in the skies over Fatima on October 13, 1917 either. Today, it is as if the same efforts made to discredit Jesus Christ, the Virgin Mary and the Holy Church in Fatima when the apparitions first began, have not ceased. Thankfully, we can read the reports from those who saw the apparition in person, two were actually written by press agents on assignment sent to the scene. The *Mother of Christ Crusade* also includes some of the detailed reports from the public about the cosmic events taking place during the miraculous Sixth Apparition. It should be convincing enough for you to believe in Jesus Christ as the Son of God, and the divinity of His Immaculate Mother, the Virgin Mary, providing you are impressed enough by what they wrote and accept it as fact. Actually, the accurate prediction alone is miraculous enough to prove the same. The apparition took place just as Our Lady said it would, passed on to the public by Lucia Santos: the specific place, date, and time. In the skies over Fatima, the miracle of the sun did occur exactly as presaged.

Mother of Christ Crusade begins with the visitations of an angel. Then he appears to three related children in a little hamlet in

Portugal named Fatima. It is their story that is told to us. Soon after his visits, Our Lady appeared to them with messages, some of which the children kept secret. One was a vision of Hell, with details that remind one of 9/11.

Lucia Santos wrote everything she learned through these Fatima visits into the *Crusade* book, adding more information received from Our Lady and from Jesus, after ultimately becoming Sister Maria Lucia of the Immaculate Heart of Mary at a convent school. Her mission, she says, was to begin a global devotion to the Immaculate Heart of Mary and facilitate the conversion of Russia. This outcome was what Lucia reported Our Lady asked of her directly, not a presumptuous interpretation of the text.

Mother of Christ Crusade is dedicated to world peace and offers itself for this purpose. The cover of the book features Our Lady, Mary the Virgin Mother of God, with the three Fatima children kneeling before her. The text of *Mother of Christ Crusade* is a direct testimony of exactly what Our Lady said to Lucia de Jesus dos Santos and her two cousins, Jacinta and Francisco Marto, taken from her memoirs. The book seems to give the innocent story of the children, but there is a twist; it has hidden content and a parallel meaning of a completely different nature. The prefix page states the *Crusade* contains "the presage of what the Immaculate Heart, has prepared for the world", and it does!

The inside the back cover reports, it was written by Sr. Lucy together with Fr. John de Marchi. He spent three and a half years in her company gathering all the facts and she carefully verified all the facts in every detail personally.[21]

---

21 de Marchi, *Mother of Christ Crusade*,1947, Chapter XIV inside back cover page

The preface page of the book sets the tone.

Nihil Ostat:

[It means "no objection" by the Catholic Church to the description of the mysteries of Fatima presented.]

Francis J. Maloney, S.T.L., *Censor Librorum*

[It seems Sister Lucia was given clearance by the Holy Church's sensor of books to write this book, tell of her experience and make her point.]

Imprimatur:

James E. Cassidy, Bishop of Fall River

August 11, 1947

Fall River, Mass.

[The people responsible for censorship gave permission for Sister Lucia to publish this book, approved as presented in 1947.]

By

John De Marchi, I.M.C.

DECLARATION

In conformity with the decree of Pope Urban VIII, we do not wish to anticipate the judgment of the Church in our appraisal of the characters and occurrences spoken of herein. We submit wholeheartedly to the infallible wisdom and judgment of Holy Mother Church.

What has happened in Portugal proclaims the miracle. It is the presage of what the Immaculate Heart has prepared for the world.

His Eminence,

The Cardinal Patriarch of Lisbon

The following appears inside the back cover:

EXACT TRUTH

Our Lady's message is extremely important. She needs your help and support to spread it now!

The *Mother of Christ Crusade* was written using the diary collection of Lucia de Jesus dos Santos, and completed after she became Sister Maria Lucia of the Immaculate Heart of Mary]

Lucia's topic is divine presage: predictions of serious future events. The *Crusade* is dated 1947, yet Lucia reports in the text, that fifty years had passed since the apparitions in Fatima.[22] That would make the date of her statement actually 1967. Considering the discrepancy in the dates, there had to be something more to the *Mother of Christ Crusade* than meets the eye. You will see the book has its own peculiarities, such as capitalizing some words not traditionally capitalized. In the discussion of Lucia's statements, words have been

---

22 Ibid, Chapter XIII, p 190

capitalized just as she did. Learning the secrets this book contains is a real adventure!

The word *presage* is very important. A presage is a prediction of a future event. They are considered an omen. The presage of what the Immaculate Heart of Mary has prepared for the world is more than just a prediction. Since it is divine in nature—it will happen! *Mother of Christ Crusade* speaks not only of what happened in Fatima, Lucia has added future presages.

The Fatima miracles known about have come true as presaged. The story Lucia tells, sounds simple and straightforward but it also carries cautions about sin and advice on worship, becoming a helpful learning tool for us to understand God. Passed on to us through the children are the reasons for our worldly troubles: the sacrilegious acts Jesus finds outrageously offensive are spelled out, yet some we have chosen to continue. We have ignored His Word and have thus far resisted the repentance, the change mandated in the *Crusade* and the book of Joel. Each time Our Lady or the Angel appeared to the children, information and instructions were given. Some of this they could report to others, but other learned secrets, they were forbidden to tell. Jacinta reminded Lucia to keep the secrets, even if they kill you.[23] In time, these secrets would reach the world. For some they are good and for others, bad.

Seeing Our Lady, Immaculate Mary, and having the privilege of receiving a message from Her had to have been an ethereal experience. Know that praying the Rosary proved to be an important link to the miracles and visions Lucia, Jacinta, and Francisco experienced. It seems to have been a necessary element to have the privilege to witness—to truly *see*—Our Lady. Remember to use

23 IBID, chapter XII, p 177

it when needed. Imagine them—only seven, nine, and ten years of age—already praying the Rosary almost every day! This reflects an important part of Our Lady's message; it a permanent request repeated throughout the apparitions, to pray the Rosary every day. The Children of Fatima were already in the habit of saying prayers morning, noon, and night. The devotion they exhibited demonstrating their unwavering faith; it was extraordinary. Our Lady knew their steadfast faith would withstand the periods of trial and inquisition from those who would question their integrity and the truth of their story that would accompany the public disclosure of the apparitions. Our Lady was well aware few people would believe the children had even seen Her, much less that she would choose them, of all people, to reveal Herself. This secret may be in part because of where they live, in "Fatima". The name is significant. The power of the Rosary the children gained however is not reserved for the chosen few. Its benefits may astonish you. The site of the apparitions has become Portugal's national Shrine of Our Lady of Fatima. The Catholic Churches Feast day for Our Lady of Fatima is October 31st.

I expect the roots of atheism are grounded in the lack of experience with miracles by those following the creed "I'll believe it when I see it." This book should help anyone believe.

The secret message Lucia received was meant for the world to hear, yet she was sworn to secrecy, and promised never to tell. Without saying, she was assigned the task of somehow passing the message on. Her incredibly imaginative presentation is meticulously done, fully thorough, and utterly amazing.

The following is a review of the chapters in the *Crusade*, including the exact words the angel and Our Lady said to the children and the details of each apparition visit. Added is a possible underlying parallel interpretation gaining credibility as it progresses. Before going forward, it is best to have read the *Mother of Christ Crusade* cover to cover, though not entirely necessary. Try to imagine yourselves in their place.

I. THE ANGEL

Before Immaculate Mary came to the Children of Fatima, an angel appeared showing them how they should pray. Eventually he offered them the Eucharist, Holy Communion, or the Body and Blood of Jesus Christ, to strengthen them and make them Holy. The Angel came to help them prepare for the visits of Mary, the Mother of God.

An obscure event took place first, not one of the six apparitions of Our Lady. Lucia de Jesus dos Santos and three of her playmates, not her cousins, observed a cloud, slightly transparent, with a human outline. The white figure appeared twice more to the children. It was inexplicable to them. Lucia said the appearances were curious and left a "deep impression on their minds", but little else was said about it, and the incident was soon forgotten. The year then was believed to be 1916.

In 1917, when Lucia was with her two cousins Jacinta and Francisco Marto on their routine daily outing leading the sheep to pasture, the angel came to visit the three of them for the first time.

"It began to drizzle and seeking shelter, we climbled the slope, followed by our sheep. It was then that we entered the cave that was to become so sacred.[24] . . . The children were playing, when a strong wind shook the trees and made them raise their eyes to see what was happening, for the day was serene. There above the

24 Ibid, Chapter I, p 2

trees toward the east, we began to see a light whiter than snow. It was the form of a young man, transparent, more brilliant than a crystal pierced by the rays of the sun. [25]...The angel landed near them, knelt on the ground, bowed very low, and said: "Fear not, I am the Angel of Peace, Pray with me!" They imitated him while he recited this prayer:

My God, I believe, I adore, I hope, and I love You. I beg pardon of You for those who do not believe, do not adore, do not hope, and do not love You. He repeated this three times and then stood up and said, Pray this way, the Hearts of Jesus and Mary are attentive to your supplication. Having said this, he disappeared and the awareness of the supernatural was so intense that they remained there in the same position, unaware of their very existence ... the spell they were under eventually, wore off. They would not think of speaking of it. It imposed secrecy of itself. It was so "intimate" that it was not easy to utter a single word about it.[26]

On a day, when the children were tired and relaxing at the well, the angel suddenly appeared again and asked, "What are you doing? Pray! Pray a great deal! The Hearts of Jesus and Mary have designs for of mercy for you! Offer unceasingly to the Most High prayers and sacrifices!"

But how are we to sacrifice? Lucia asked him.

Offer up everything within your power as a sacrifice to the Lord in an act of reparation for the sin by which He is offended and of supplication for the conversion of sinners. Thus, invoke peace upon our country. I am Her Guardian Angel: the Angel of Portugal. Above

25 Ibid,
26 Ibid, p 5

all, accept and bear with submission the sufferings that the Lord may send you.[27] He then vanished into thin air.

In autumn, an angel appeared for the third time, this time with a Host and chalice in his hand. By some miraculous power, he was able to leave the Host and chalice suspended in midair to lay prostrate on the ground. Lucia reports He recited this prayer three times: "Most Holy Trinity, Father, Son, and Holy Ghost, I adore You profoundly, and I offer You the Most Precious Body Blood Soul and Divinity of Jesus Christ, present in all the tabernacles of the earth, in reparation for the outrages, sacrileges, and indifferences by which He Himself is offended. And by the infinite merits of His Most Sacred Heart and the Immaculate Heart of Mary, I beg of You, the conversion of all sinners."

He stood up took hold of the Host and chalice and said, "Take and drink the Body and Blood of Jesus Christ, horribly outraged by ungrateful men. Make reparation for their crimes and console your God."[28] He gave Lucia the Holy Eucharist. To Francisco and Jacinta, he gave a drink from the chalice containing the Blood of Christ, each a part of Holy Communion in the Catholic faith, with the grace and benefits the sacrament provides. They all prostrated themselves on the ground again, led by the angel, and began to recite the prayer, beginning with "Most Holy Trinity ..." Then he disappeared.

Lucia said "the full meaning of the vision unfolded slowly and astonishingly to their young minds. Their whole being became absorbed by a new strange but happy feeling of the inward presence of God. They kept silent for some time. Francisco was the first to break it" wanting to know what the angel said. He alone was unable to hear the angel speak. He was not allowed the full content of the visit, not even aware he had received the Blood of Christ from the chalice.

---

27 Ibid, p 7

28 De Marchi, *Mother of Christ Crusade*, Chapter I, p 10

The Body and Blood of Jesus, is the real presence of Jesus through transubstantiation. The Eucharist is more than symbolic; it contains the benefits of having Jesus with you. With Him, in a literal sense, He provides benefits. Important to note is the fact these children are Catholic, and the sacrament they received identifies Catholicism. Catholics know that the unconsecrated host tastes different than one blessed by the priest. The Eucharist *is* different than a plain host. When Our Lady chose these three young Catholic children of Fatima to appear to, it was not a random choice and it should have unified Christianity.

The Angel brought the message that Jesus and Mary had designs of mercy for them, something they would be told more about when Our Lady herself appeared to them.

There is underlying explanation for why only the girls could hear the angel. It is part of the parallel message. His words enlightened them, reminding them of their coming transition into womanhood and how marriage and having children was a worthy station in life, and by its very nature, held sacrifices and sufferings of its own. The drops of blood falling from the chalice could be symbolic of their own sufferings to come. Raising a family could be what the Lord may ask them to accept and bear with submission. Although the revelation mortified them, there was some comfort in finding they could feel the inward presence of God, that having children was especially pleasing to God. Knowing the gift of life lived within them made them feel this way. Intentional abortion and sexual assault is foreign and entirely contrary to this message.

Francisco knew afterward, the angel's message was intentionally kept from him. He didn't catch on to the reason for their fear. The girls were mortified by the message they heard, somehow he didn't fear the same message because it was not directed at him. This sheds light on the mystery to be solved.

Naturally, the whole revelation learned at such a young age mortified them, both the presence of the angel and the message. If the angel provided the whole picture of relationships, mortification wouldn't be surprising. It struck them so hard the girls could hardly speak when they thought of what the angel had said, while Francisco having been excluded from the Angel's message was dying to know more. Lucia told him he would have to wait. The next day, she did tell Francisco some of what the angel said. Francisco was not satisfied with her answers. He became insistent and missed no opportunity to ask more questions—so many questions, in fact, that it prompted Jacinta to say, "Take care! We must not speak much about these matters."[29] This explains Jacinta's fear: she gives the impression she was afraid if she told about what happened she would be harmed in some way. In later years, Lucia revealed that "the words of the angel were like a light that made her realize who God was and how He loved us and wanted to be loved, and they showed her the value of sacrifice, to what degree it pleased Him and how it was rewarded with the conversion of sinners." When the angel departed for the last time, from that moment on, they began to offer to the Lord everything that mortified them without trying to find any other ways of mortification or penance, passing hour after hour bowed to the ground, repeating the prayer the angel had taught them, in the position he took when in prayer. The subliminal message in this chapter of the *Crusade* can be thought to describe life's facts, love, marriage, and the most important sacrifice of all, and one most pleasing to God: children! Having an abortion at that time was out of the question. Naturally, the whole process of growing into adulthood mortified them. They didn't want to talk about it even with each other and kept it secret, not uttering a single word about the visit or the message to anyone else. They were too young to be talking about the angel's message, but they now knew the

---

29 Ibid, p 9

truth. They prayed about this over and over, maybe for strength and for further understanding.'Children being children, the "spell" they were under did wear off, and it was not long before they went back to their daily rounds of playing "singing and dancing."'[30] This parallel meaning may seem the product of imagination, but it is not. The foundation of it is actually spelled out.

"Singing and dancing" the children's innocent play, and the transparent human outline, are introduced with first appearance of the message carrying Angel.[31] "Singing and dancing" goes on to be mentioned repeatedly, becoming a theme. Initially their favorite form of play is accompanied by Francisco playing his flute. Later suddenly, the girls no longer enjoy it and abandon it altogether. The transparent man, the invisible man the children heard speaking, represents music. It is the change to a different kind music they dislike that causes them to stop, music that mortifies the girls but Francisco fails to notice.

II. The Children of Fatima

Lucia de Jesus dos Santos, the eldest of the three children, was born March 22, 1907, to Antonio dos Santos and his wife, Maria Rosa. Lucia "was always healthy and strong, attractive, with a flat nose, big dark eyes that glistened under heavy lids, making her most attractive."[32] She had a wonderful disposition and was very affectionate toward children, which made her the favorite babysitter of the area. She was singularly gifted at holding the children's attention. She enjoyed dressing up for festivals and was always in the most colorful clothes, and she loved dancing. Several different spellings of Lucia's name appear in *Mother of Christ Crusade*: Lucia de Jesus dos Santos or L'ucia, Lu'cia, Lucy, and Lucia.

---

30 Ibid, p 5
31 de Marchi, *Mother of Christ Crusade*, Chapter I, p 4-5
32 Ibid, Chapter II, p 14

Lucia's cousins Francisco and Jacinta Marto lived nearby and were Lucia's "companions and playmates."[33] Francisco was born June 11, 1908. He was curiously calm but condescending, with an air of superiority and a temper. "He carried a flute," and used it to accompany singing and dancing. The importance Lucia gave music and dancing in their lives is remarkable, in fact, a touch extraordinary.

Jacinta is described as whimsical and lighthearted. She was born March 11, 1910, a simply wonderful and delightful child. "A quiet, untroublesome infant, she grew to be a loveable child, though not without an early tendency to selfishness." She once had reduced the Rosary to a series of the first two words of the "Hail Mary", a practice which of course, they hastily abandoned in due time. She loved Lucia very much because Lucia was very wise and dance well, "and with her we could spend the whole day singing and dancing."[34] When the church bells rang, they stopped playing and dancing, had lunch, said the Angelus prayer, and went back to their singing and dancing. When going out to graze the sheep as was her daily routine, Lucia would choose the pastureland, at the end of the "Cab'eco"[35].—a favorite place of hers, footnoted in the Crusade as "The Head, a rocky elevation some 60 feet high." It had a grassy hill and offered shade trees: olive, pine, holmoak, as well as the "cave". Note the space Lucia leaves after the word feet and the different spelling of cave as "cahve".

Lucia says of Francisco that sometimes he would irritate her when they were playing; for this she would make him "sit still for a spell" and then, feeling sorry for him, bring him back in the game.

---

33 *Ibid*, Chapter I, p 2
34 Ibid Chapter II, p 23
35 Ibid, Chapter I,

There is mention of Lucia's father who after finishing his chores and performing his religious duties would spend his free time among his friends at the tavern. Francisco in Lucia's opinion, was much like his father. This mention of the tavern could explain why Francisco's behavior was described as "fearless and condescending, wilder, quick to lose his patience, and at times fusses like a young calf." Assuming Francisco's father, "Senhor" Manual Marto, was one of Antonio Santos' friends who visited the tavern after chores and religious duties, and if he had displayed the effects alcohol can have on behavior at times, it could just be that Francisco's fearless outspoken behavior was meant to be explained as learned behavior from his father, while under the influence. Whatever the reason, drinking alcohol is introduced in Lucia's story when it has nothing to do with the visitations of the angel or Our Lady. Given the Marto family was poor it is unreasonable to think Senhor Santos really regularly went to a tavern. The inference is drinking in excess negatively influences children and is considered one of the sins of men, those referred to by the Angel. There is a hint that this is a parallel meaning when it is remarked of Jacinta's refusal to reveal the secrets Our Lady gave them that were not to be told, "It was a secret that could not be extracted even with a corkscrew."[36] There is something else to investigate, the facial features Lucia is assigned sound suspiciously like she was the subject of child abuse. Later the issue of parents hitting children is made directly. ". . . But it was too late for Lucia; she had already received her thrashing. Some neighbors were as bad in their unbelief. They were very mean to the little ten-year-old girl, calling her names and, at times, even striking the child. No one dared to strike the Marto children, however; Ti Marto watched them too closely. Little Jacinta, in her eagerness to suffer for poor sinners, one day said to Lucia, I wish my parents were like yours so they would hit me. Then I would have more sacrifices to offer to Our Lord."[37]

36 De Marchi, *Mother of Christ Crusade*, Chapter VI, p 73
37 Ibid, chapter VI Sacrifices and Sufferings, p 77

It is a statement she makes, that Lucia's parents hit her for punishment. Neither is really reasonably true, and saying such only raises suspicions about the true nature of the *Crusade.* This is just a part of Lucia's method, her way of including the hidden messages she has entered in the *Crusade,* these pointing out two of the sins of men; excessive use of alcohol and child abuse as a result. The mistreatment of women will become a dominant theme in the *Crusade* book. It tells some of the sins and sinners as told to Lucia by Our Lady during the apparitions at Fatima. The back pages of the *Crusade* states outright that with, the mass slaughtering of babies from abortion, worldwide promotion of adulterous sex, wars, and terrorism, and turmoil now worldwide, and getting worse daily, and pornography flaunted publically everywhere, that we cannot wait. Spread this Emergency Message. This Life and Death message of Our Lady must be spread fast now. After all, the angels visit was in part to say that it is specifically the sacrileges and indifferences of men that are the reason Our Lord is so terribly outraged. Lucia outlines them in the final pages. Our Lady repeatedly asked the children to "pray the Rosary every day" to help the poor sinners.

III. First Apparition May 13, 1917

"May, the month of flowers, follows the long April rains that wash the face of mother earth after her long winter sleep. Then God covers the world with flowers. What can be more beautiful than the dainty, many-colored flowers of May?

On Sunday the thirteenth of May, in the year 1917, in the midst of the First World War, God sent to earth the loveliest flower of the ages, His own beautiful Mother, Mary, whom we address as Queen of the May".[38]

38 Ibid, Chapter III, p 24

In making this statement, God and Jesus, are one in the same. The Christian Blessed Trinity consists of the Father, the Son and the Holy Spirit as one God. Together and unified they are One God and each God. When Lucia says Our Lady is the loveliest flower of the ages she infers, the other dainty many-colored flowers are other people, members of the human race. It is Lucia's way of telling us --- God is the creator of all life, and we have the duty to present this fact to our children in schools.

Each chapter of an apparition is informative and includes daily activities, particularly what the children were doing when the apparitions began. The thirteenth of May, 1917 was a Sunday, and Mass was the first priority. "Heaven forbid" they would miss Mass on Sunday, no matter what the weather or situation at home. Even if their mothers were nursing babies, they would have to make arrangements; the parents would go to different Masses, each taking their turn watching the babies. By saying this Lucia is giving an example for us to follow and how to not miss Mass. We have to remember that before she wrote her memoirs she was actually speaking with the Virgin Mary, the Mother of God. Try to believe she wrote throughout the *Crusade* exactly what she intended, what was told her, so Heaven actually does forbid missing Mass on Sunday.

Our Lady's first visit began this way in chapter III: "The children were playing, building castles out of rocks. Francisco was the mason and architect, while Lucia and Jacinta gathered the stones. "While they were thus busily intent upon their building projects, a sudden bright shaft of light pierced the air. In their efforts to describe it they called it a flash of lightening. Frightened, they dropped their stones, looked first at each other, then at the sky which was clear and bright without the least spot of a cloud. No breeze stirred the air, the sun was shining strong. Such perfect weather belied this flash of lightening, the forerunner of a storm. The children decided that they had better start for home before it rained. Quickly they gathered the sheep and started down the hill. Halfway down, just as they were passing a tall oak tree, another shaft of light split the air. Suddenly there was a bright shaft of light, like lightning piercing the air. At that moment, the sun shone brightly; there was not a cloud in the sky. The flash belied the perfect weather. Believing a storm might be coming, they decided to head home, when a second flash of light split the air. Panicky with fear, and as if led by some unknown power, they took a few steps, turned towards the right and there, standing over the foliage of a small holmoak they saw a most beautiful lady. It was a lady all dressed in white. Lucia records, more brilliant than the sun, shedding rays of light, clear and stronger than a crystal glass filled with the most sparking water pierced by the burning rays of the sun".[39]

"Fear not, I will not harm you," the lady said.

"Where are you from?" Lucia made bold to ask.

"I am from Heaven."

"What do you want of me?"

"I came to ask you to come here for six consecutive months, on the thirteenth day, at this same hour. I will tell you later who I am and what I want. And I shall return here a seventh time," she said.

"And I, am I, too, going to go to Heaven?" Lucia asked.

"Yes, you shall" she replied.

"And Jacinta?"

39 De Marchi, *Mother of Christ Crusade*, Chapter III, p 27

"Yes."

"And Francisco?"

"Yes, he shall go too, but he must say many Rosaries."

Francisco, like Lucia and Jacinta, "was immersed in the glorious light that shown from the Lady, but he was not seeing the Lady. Neither could he hear the Lady's voice, though he could hear Lucia talking". Francisco suggested throwing a stone at Her to see if She was real.

"Throw a stone at the Lady? Never!" Lucia said. "So you are Our Lady, and Francisco can't see you?"

"Let him say the Rosary, the Lady answered, and in that way he too will see me."

"Lucia passed on the command. Francisco quickly took his Rosary from his pocket to do as Our Lady said. Before he finished the first decade, the Lady became visible to him with almost blinding splendor."

Lucia inquired about two girls who had recently died who used to come to the house to learn sewing from her sisters. "Maria do Rosario, daughter of José das Neves, is she in heaven?"

"Yes," Our Lady replied.

"And Amelia?"

"She is still in purgatory."

...Then the Lady said to the children: "Do you want to offer yourselves to God, to endure all the sufferings that He may choose to send you, as an act of reparation for the sins by which He is offended and as a supplication for the conversion of sinners?"

"Yes," Lucia replied.

"Then you are going to suffer a great deal, but the grace of God will be your comfort."

"As she pronounced these words, the Lady opened Her hands and shed upon the children—a highly intense light that was as a reflex glancing from them. "This light penetrated us to the heart, Lucia reported, and its very recesses, and allowed us to see ourselves in God, Who was that light, more clearly than we see ourselves in a mirror. Then we were moved by an inward impulse, also communicated to us, to fall to our knees, while, we repeated to ourselves: Most Holy Trinity, I adore You! My God, My God, I love You in the Most Blessed Sacrament."[40]

Our Lady spoke to them one more time. "Say the Rosary every day to earn peace for the world and the end to the war. She began then to elevate Herself serenely, going in the direction of the East until She disappeared in the immensity of space, still surrounded by a most brilliant light that seemed to open a path for Her through the myriad galaxies of stars."

The children knew the Lady was unhappy about something, and they tried recalling exactly what she said, trying to understand the meaning of every word. "They felt the same joy now as when the Angel visited them, only when the Angel came, they felt a sort of annihilation before his presence, whereas with Our Lady, they received strength and courage. Instead of bodily exhaustion, they

40 De Marchi, *Mother of Christ Crusade*, Chapter III

felt a certain physical strength. In place of annihilation before the Divine Presence, we felt exultation and joy; in place of difficulty in speaking we felt a sort of communicative enthusiasm." [41] Why the word annihilation was used could allude to future presage, those not spoken of directly. It could also refer to a personal threat made against them.

Lucia thought it best to keep the vision a secret, for fear of ridicule remembering the bitter experience she had had after the angel appeared to her with the other playmates a year before his more recent visit with Francisco and Jacinta along. Playmates, is a hint at pornography in print and now on the internet from chapter I. The news of that previous encounter had soon spread throughout the neighborhood. What rumor was actually spread around is never said, it is left open for the reader. It is one of the subliminal messages to look deeper for other meaning. This time, having little Jacinta with her when Our Lady visited, and seeing the joy that shown on her face, Lucia had little doubt Jacinta would be unable to keep the secret to herself, even though they had all agreed to do so. Lucia said they tried to recall every word Our Lady said to not miss any meaning. When reading the *Crusade* we to must recall every word and determine Lucia's intended meaning.

Seeing Our Lady was simply too great an experience for Jacinta to keep quiet. The youngest, exhilarated and trusting as she was, could not keep the secret. She told her parents the whole story. Jacinta said, "It was a lady so beautiful, so pretty...dressed in white with a gold chain around Her neck extending down to her breast, her head was covered with a white mantle, yes, very white... I don't know but it was whiter even than milk... which covered her to her feet... all embroidered with gold... how beautiful!"[42]

41 Ibid
42 Ibid, Chapter III, p 35

Francisco confirmed the words of Jacinta. ... Antonio Silva tried to offer his explanation, "If the children saw a lady all dressed in white... who could it be but Our Lady?" Manual Marto, now referred to as Ti Marto, "meanwhile, was mulling it over in his mind, trying to fit together the religious principles involved. Finally he said, since the beginning of time, Our Lady has appeared many times and in many ways. This is what has been helping us. If the world is in bad shape today, it would be worse, had there not been cases of this sort. The power of God is great! We do not yet know what it is, but it will be something... Gods will be done."[43] The what, will be shown to refer to the future.

Ti Marto said he believed what the children had said almost at once, knowing the children had received no formal education. "Were it not for Providence they would never have thought of it." Thought of what exactly is not answered. He praised the power of God and said, "God's Will be done. ...Sometime later, when Bishop of Leiria published his official decision on the apparitions, he said more or less what Ti Marto said."

Jacinta and Francisco's mother refused to believe and ridiculed the children. Most didn't believe Jacinta, which made her very sad—particularly her mother's unbelieving attitude. Many neighbors ridiculed and teased the children, calling them liars. Jacinta and Francisco's father's words before retiring for the night may have been the best advice anyone could give, that they should "leave it in God's hands."

Lucia's father didn't react the same, he ignored the report calling it women's gossip, and remained indifferent to the affair. It was different with her mother; she had punishment on her mind. In

43 Ibid, p 37

efforts to force Lucia to confess it was a lie, "she tried caresses, threats, then resorted to the broomstick."[44] What she did to Lucia with the broomstick isn't said but having punishment on her mind, a beating isn't out of the realm of possibility. We know she received a thrashing. Further, the children "playing jacks" before the angel arrived the first time in chapter one, may be more telling of Lucia's parallel topic of verbally abusing children or women.

Those were long days for the children, for there was no song or peace of mind to help speed the hours away. Their greatest trial came from their families. When Lucia was questioned further by her family, her answer was either silence or continued confirmation of what she had already told. The children realized that what Our Lady had said was proving true; they were going to suffer a great deal. They counted on Our Lady's promise, "the grace of God would be their comfort."

There were multiple miracles describe during this First Apparition: Our Lady came within a flash of intense light, like lightening on a cloudless sky. When she leaves, though it was midday, the sky opened to receive Her through "the myriad galaxies and stars." It was a vision of the night sky seen at midday. During the apparition the sheep they were tending had wandered into the neighbors garden that had chickpeas and the children feared they would cause damage, Our Lady kept the sheep from eating chickpeas—a small miracle to any sheepherder. By preventing damage to other's property, She protected the children from punishment. She is capable of doing the same for us. She also shed a highly intense light that allowed them to see themselves more clearly than in a mirror. What She showed them was their future, what they were to be reminded of during the Third Visit of Our Lady in chapter V, to instill in them greater fervor and devotion in their future vocation.

---

44 Ibid, Chapter III, p 40

Earlier, praying the Rosary was shown to be very desirable. In this apparition, Mary was holding a Rosary of Her own. Jacinta told her parents how Our Lady had such a beautiful Rosary and how she held her hands in prayer. Lucia makes a specific point, now the Rosary itself becomes sacred, and therefore it must be treated with respect. Disrespecting it disrespects Our Lady herself. Many Catholics carry one at all times, to be prayed whenever they can. Lucia pointed out that every word of the Our Father and Hail Mary must be said when praying the Rosary.

The fine print in this chapter III holds a message all its own. It is intentionally indirect, so as to hide it. The message is oblique but condemns a particular sexual orientation in its choice of words. This message is addressed in two ways. If one examines the letters of words for the physical positions they demonstrate, they define the orientation. Specific, but as yet unknown words to back up this interpretation will be shown later. Just know the Word of God is involved. The opinion conveyed is not that of Lucia, but that of the Lord through Our Lady, Her word as good as God.

This brings up another point. Marriage is the mutual relation of a husband and wife who are joined in a kind of social and legal dependence for the purpose of having and maintaining a family. A wedding ceremony is traditionally performed in a Church, where it is asked that God sanctions the union and others promise not to disrupt it. Marriage is sacred—a blessed union—and its institution reserved for the Church. During the ceremony, the minister or priest invokes God's blessing on the newlyweds, a blessing that cannot be granted a couple by a civil servant. There is no "marriage" without God involved. Civil officials cannot and should not presume they can invoke God's blessing on a marriage. "By the power vested in me, I now pronounce you man and wife." This power comes from God, reserved for those who have been ordained by the Church.

Civil servants are presuming they have the power to bestow God's blessing. They are not afforded this right, nor change the definition of marriage any more than they can legislate to change God's natural law. If this interpretation of the fine print in this chapter was intended to deliver this parallel meaning and was also included in the details of what the children told their parents, when they were explaining how they saw Our Lady, it would have been foreign to the children, and Ti Marto was doubly correct in saying that without Divine Providence they never would have thought of it. It would have created such a stir in Fatima repeating it. Jacinta told Francisco not to talk about the angel's message, it wasn't right for them to be discussing such things. Meanwhile, ridicule and disbelief followed them everywhere.

Legislating against Gods natural Law in itself might be reason enough for Our Lady and Our Lord to come again and reveal Themselves in 9/11. This would be a warning. It is unconstitutional to legislate against the Sacraments of the Church, by virtue of the law separating Church and state. No matter how states rule on gay "marriage," Our Lady and Our Lord condemn it. It is not a blessed union, it is not a *marriage*.

IV. Second Apparition June 13, 1917

The news of the first apparition had spread through the countryside. Along with the children now both sets of parents were also being ridiculed by neighbors. Not everyone was disbelieving in the apparition and the seriousness with which some people were accepting the truth from the children made the parents even more distraught. Senhora Maria Rosa Santos decided she would go and get the advice of the Pastor. She met Ti Marto on the way home and told him of the Pastors advice to allow the children to go to the Cova on the thirteenth and then to bring them back to him. He planned to interrogate them individually. Ti Marto felt it a good idea to visit the Pastor himself. He remarked to Ti Marto: "What a mess this is, sometimes it is white, sometimes it is black."[45] He left it up to Ti Marto to decide if he should bring the children back after the second apparition. This conversation took place the day before the second apparition. The expression goes, not always black and white, not white and black. Entering this quote Lucia is leaving another clue.

Not everyone disbelieved, before this second visit, some people who had heard about the first apparition anticipated the next and would arrive at the site of the first apparition ahead of the children. Maria Carreira, later known as Maria da Capelinha, was one of them. She had been sick, and "and for seven years before the apparitions the doctors gave me up completely." Now she was cured, attributing her recovery to Our Lady.

Jacinta's mother was still intent on keeping her children from going to the Cova da Iria. It was the day before the thirteenth and tomorrow was a feast day of the Church. In their effort to keep the children from going to the Cova, both mothers tried to entice them to attend the feast day celebration of St. Anthony instead of going to the Cova. Jacinta's mother asked her "don't you want to go and get your roll? Besides, there is the band, and rockets and a special sermon."[46]

[Here the band, rockets and rolls elude Lucia's alternate message and, identifies Rock and Roll Bands and rock music. This is also when the girls abruptly lose interest in singing and dancing. Lucia makes her point that the reason the girls give up their once favorite form of play is because Rock and Roll has become offensive to them personally.]

45 Ibid, Chapter IV, p 43
46 Ibid, Chapter IV, p 46

Fully intent on going to the Cova to see Our Lady the children made plans for the next day. Lucia was going the feast first, but only to meet up with some girls who made their First Communion with her, planning to take them to the Cova with her. Altogether there were fourteen. She would meet up with Jacinta and Francisco at the Cova. Along the way, Lucia's brother Antonio tried to keep them from going to the Cova, as he was going to the feast day celebration. He even "offered a bribe of a few pennies". A penny will take on great significance in the future to aid in revealing Lucia's intended message. Along the way, "where the gate to the shrine is now situated, they were met by a small group of women, among them Maria da Capelinha and her crippled seventeen year old son. Her two daughters had decided to go to the feast instead. They all arrived at the Cova, at the three foot tall holmoak tree. About noon they all began the Rosary. Soon Lucia called, "Jacinta, Quiet, Our Lady is coming."

Lucia said, "You told me to come here. What do you want me to do?"

Our Lady replied, "I want you to come here on the thirteenth of next month. Say the Rosary, inserting between the mysteries the following ejaculation: 'O My Jesus, forgive us. Save us from the fire of Hell. Bring all souls to heaven, especially those in most need." This prayer is now a regular part of the Rosary, known as the Fatima prayer. "I want you to learn to read and write and later I will tell you what else I want," Our Lady said.

Then Lucia asked Our Lady "if She would cure a sick person who was recommended to her." Our Lady answered.

"If he is converted, he will be cured within a year."

Then Lucia asks, "I would like to ask you also to take us to Heaven."

'Yes, Our Lady answered, "I will take Jacinta and Francisco very soon. You, however, must stay here a longer time. Jesus wants to use you to make me "know" and loved. He wants to establish the Devotion to My Immaculate Heart in the World. I promise salvation to those who embrace it, and their souls will be loved by God as flowers placed by myself to adorn His throne.' [Here people are flowers again. Mary is one of Gods flowers. All of us equally, we are His work Lucia tells, not to be selectively aborted, one atrocity forbidden in the closing pages of the *Crusade*.]

Lucia asks, "am I going to stay here alone".

"No, my daughter" Our Lady replies. "Does this cause you to suffer a great deal? I will never leave you. My Immaculate Heart will be your refuge and the way that will lead you to God."

Lucia reported that as she said these last words, "The Blessed Virgin opened her hands and communicated for the second time the reflex of immense light that enveloped her. We saw ourselves in it as if immersed in God. Jacinta and Francisco seemed to be on the side that was ascending to Heaven, and I was on the side that was spreading over the earth. There was a Heart before the palm of the right hand of Our Lady with thorns piercing it. We understood this was the Immaculate Heart of Mary, so offended by the sins of mankind, desiring reparation." [47] Instead of just men, the sins of all mankind are included.

Maria da Capelinha, having been cured, was why she was on hand for this next scheduled visit of Our Lady and was able to offer these observations: "When Our Lady left the tree, it was like the hissing of a rocket. After Our Lady left the tree people were surprised to

---

47 Ibid, p 53

see the highest branches, which before were standing upright, now inclined toward the East, as if it had been tread upon." Some people broke the branches and leaves of the tree while others placed carnations around the holmoak tree, and they still do even to this day. Lucia cleared the area around the holmoak. "I gave the place the shape of a round thrashing floor. I also tied a silk ribbon on the branches of the holmoak and I was the first one to place flowers on it."

"The little ones told what they were allowed to tell, but kept the rest secret. About four o'clock they left for home." Lucia said they tried to recall every word Our Lady said to not miss any meaning. It is inferred that when reading the *Crusade* we too must recall every word Lucia gives and determine Lucia's intended meaning. Jacinta had told others that Our Lady had told them a secret. Their refusal to reveal it brought them torment, enduring bribes, and ridicule. The pastor suggested it could be the work of the devil, yet he was ambivalent. The children became the center of attention, finding peace and reassurance only from one another.

V. Thrid Apparition July 13, 1917

The chapter heading of "Thrid Apparition" includes the misspelling of the word third. It is a clue Lucia gives to understand her secret message, not a typographical error. She may be telling us we need to get rid of something.

The pastor said the entire affair was the invention of the devil, though he may have been testing Lucia's resolve and that of the believers. His expressions of doubt and that the apparitions were the work of the devil, left Lucia in despair, So much so, she began to fear that the Lady they saw was the devil. Lucia's mother said to her, after finding she had been hiding from the people gathering for the thirteenth of July, the next scheduled apparition: "what a little wooden saint you are, eaten up with termites."[48] It should be taken as another hint at extended meaning. How would Lucia ever be able to persuade the people to believe what had happened is true?

Lucia was leading the Rosary... when the Rosary was over Lucia stood up, looked toward the East and cried out. "Close the umbrellas close the umbrellas. Our Lady is coming!"

Ti Marto said, "looking closely, I saw something like a small grayish cloud hovering over the holmoak. The sun turned hazy and a refreshing breeze began to blow. It did not seem that we were at the height of summer. The silence of the crowd was impressive. Then I began to hear a hum as of a gadfly within an empty jug, but did not hear a word."

Our Lady said, "I want you to return here on the thirteenth of next month. Continue to say the Rosary every day in honor of Our Lady of the Rosary to obtain peace for the world and an end to the war; for she alone can save it. Continue to come here every month. In October, I will say who I am, and what I desire and I will perform a miracle all shall see so that they believe."

"Lucia then spoke of the petitions of the people. Our Lady answered, Some I will cure and others not. As to the crippled boy, I will not cure him or take him out of his poverty, but he must say the Rosary every day with his family."

Lucia asked about the case of a sick person who wished to be taken soon to Heaven.

"He should not try to hurry things. I know well when I shall come for him."

---

48 Ibid, Chapter V, p 61

Lucia asked for the conversion of people. The answer of the Lady was, as with the crippled boy, the recitation of the Rosary. Then to remind the children of their special vocation and to inspire them to greater fervor and give them courage for the future the Lady said.

"Sacrifice yourselves for sinners and say, often, especially when you make some sacrifice: My Jesus, it is for love of You, for the conversion of sinners, and in reparation for the sins committed against the Immaculate Heart of Mary."

Lucia said, Our Lady "opened Her hands, as she had done the two previous months. The light reflecting from them seemed to penetrate into the earth, and we saw as if into a sea of fire; immersed in the fire were devils and souls in human form, as if they were transparent black or bronze embers floating in the fire and swayed by the flames that issued from them, along with clouds of smoke, falling upon every side just like the falling of sparks in great fires, without weight or equilibrium, amidst wailing and cries of pain and despair that horrified and shook us with terror. We could tell the devils by their horrible and nauseous figures of baleful and unknown animals, but transparent as the black coals in fire."[49] Frightened the children raised their eyes to Our Lady for help as Lucia cried out, Oh ... Our Lady!"

Our lady explained "You have seen Hell, where the souls of poor sinners go. To save them, God wants to establish throughout the world the devotion to my Immaculate Heart. If people will do what I will tell you, many souls will be saved and there will be peace. The war is going to end. But if they do not stop offending God, another and worse war will break out in the reign of Pius XI. When you see a night illuminated by an unknown light, know that this is a great sign that God gives you, that he is going to punish the

---

49 Ibid, p 65- 66

world for its crimes by means of war, hunger, and persecution of the church and of the Holy Father. To forestall this, I shall come to ask the consecration of Russia to my Immaculate Heart, and the Communion of Reparation on the First Saturdays. If they heed My request, Russia will be converted, and there will be peace. If not, she shall spread her errors throughout the world, promoting wars and persecutions of the Church; the good will be martyred, the Holy Father will have much to suffer, various nations will be annihilated; in the end my Immaculate Heart shall triumph. The Holy Father will consecrate Russia to me, which will be converted, and some time of peace will be given to the world. In Portugal, the dogma of the faith will be kept always. Do not tell this to anyone. To Francisco, yes, you may tell it."[50]

Lucia said, "Don't you want anything else from me?

[This apparition will be shown in part to be describing the hell of 9/11. It stands as a part of the divine prediction of 9/11, thereby proving the divinity of Our Lady for presaging it and of Jesus Christ as the Lord Son of God, as evidenced by the I-beam iron cross of Christ left standing on the rubble of the fallen WTC towers. Consider the possibility the "I beam" could be God's reference to Jesus as "Light of the World". The description of the devil in the smoke and other unknown animals seen in the smoke of 9/11 should be noted. The floating embers could well be of burning sheets of paper that slowly drifted down from the fire.]

With her heart aching and wanting to do something heroic, Lucia asked, "Don't you want anything else from me?"

"No. Today I desire nothing else from you."

---

50 Ibid, Chapter V, p 67

"At this, something like thunder was heard, and a little arch that had been set up to hold vigil lanterns shook as if there had been an earthquake."[51] This mention of an earthquake could be more presages to come, something to be attentive to, particularly if signs make it relevant to this message from Fatima when any take place.

Crowds had grown for this apparition, gathering at the spot of the apparitions over the holy holmoak tree, hoping to see Our Lady. Most said they could hear only Lucia. One woman reported seeing a small gray cloud in the spot where the apparition took place. The people were becoming ruthless in their efforts to find out the secret of what exactly Our Lady had said. The children insisted to them it was "a secret."

Lucia did say this, "For some it is good; for others, it is evil."[52] She then courageously refused to divulge any information. Right after the apparition, the crowd pressed in. The two mothers feared their children would be killed. They were relieved when they saw Francisco being carried by one of his relatives and Jacinta on the shoulders of her father. Lucia was being carried by a very tall man, so tall, in fact, that Lucia's mother was distracted from her worry. "Oh, what a big man,"[53] she blurted out. It is a clue. The "big man" will be explained later, even seen if one wishes.

Lucia was told of an additional secret; the one she referred to when she commented that "for some it would be good, for others evil." She never said what it was in her lifetime. They were told secret predictions of the highest order and told to withhold them until their revelation would serve as testament to themselves. The inclusion by Our Lady of "various nations will be annihilated" is worthy of

---

51 Ibid, p 67
52 Ibid
53 Ibid, p 68

serious consideration, not as a description of WWII, rather of the consequences for ignoring the changes needing to be made signaled by the warning message of 9/11.

This is a suggestion that more presages are included in *Mother of Christ Crusade*, present but hidden. They come to light later but are kept secret for now. Behavioral modification to avoid the sins, to which Lucia has eluded, becomes a mandate if you take stock in believing there was a secret presage given the children, especially considering the mention of the annihilation of nations. The change Lucia is going to present has not happened yet. WWII could be what she was referring to, but not necessarily and options against the will of God come with significant risk.

VI. Sacrifices and Sufferings

The children spent their time contemplating the visions of Hell and why so many people were there and what they had done to get there:

Jacinta asks, Lucia, what have these people done to go to Hell?

Lucia says, Maybe they said ugly words, stole, swore. . . .

And do they go to Hell just for one word?

If it is a big sin..." Lucia replies.[54]

The F word has gotten to be one of favorites of filmmakers and producers. Its purpose in any work for entertainment purposes is unfathomable. To most it is vulgar and repulsive, and must be considered as one word that is a big sin to use or call another.

54 De Marchi, *Mother of Christ Crusade*, chapter VI, p 71

Why did Our Lady "hold in Her hand a Heart spreading upon the world that great light that is God?" It was a revealing question. They hoped to have Our Lady show everyone the image of Hell so they too could understand it, thinking that would keep them from sinning. The people they saw in their vision were alive, burning as wood in a fire. Jacinta had visions of the pope. "I saw the Holy Father in a very big house. He was kneeling before a table, holding his face in his hands and he was crying. Outside, there were many people; some were throwing stones at him, others were swearing at him and saying ugly words to him. How pitiful it was! We must pray a lot for him."[55] If this was presaged, it came true.

Jacinta it reports in this chapter "I want to suffer for sinners." She refuses to take water from Lucia. "Jacinta however became very weak and was almost fainting. The rhythmic noises of crickets, frogs and insects began to pound in her ears like thunder. Holding her head in her hands, she cried out in utter desperation, My head aches so. Tell the crickets and frogs to stop."[56] [The unusual capitalization of "My" is one of Lucia's markers. This identifies Rock and Roll as the music that turned the girls away from singing and dancing. It is true some is repulsive, abusive and demeans the dignity of all women. It has also developed to include antichrist messages, particularly ones that are anti-Catholic. Jacinta gives the directive, tell them to stop. Concluding this topic in the chapter on sufferings and sacrifices emphasizes its importance in terms of cause and effect. Flashback to the antennae towers disappearing into the dust of the WTC crumbling beneath them.]

The activity of visitors to the children's homes was continuous. There was no longer even time for chores. Lucia's family was of little means. Their garden had been trampled, and everything was ruined.

55 Ibid, p 72
56 Ibid, chapter VI, p 71

It became such a hardship that the family had to sell their sheep. “Go to the Cova da Iria. Ask that Lady for something to eat,” Lucia’s sisters would say. This type of ridicule made Lucia “fearful of even picking up a slice of bread.”

The children prayed continually, expressing their love for the Lord and the Immaculate Heart of Mary. The newspaper media got involved. The children were portrayed as victims of an elaborate hoax. The papers accused the clergy of producing a factory of miracles. The unbelievers invented false details of the apparitions to discredit the children and explain away the fact of the apparitions, calling them epileptics or the victims of fraud, greed, or collective suggestions. The ridicule and accusations of the newspapers served only to divide the people, stirring up enemies of the Church on the one hand, yet also serving to stir up and increase the faith of the believers. The sacrifices they made to defend their faith became intense. There was much to suffer. For the children, it was a sacrifice of themselves, to Our Lady.

The children were reminded at home that many people were visiting the Cova da Iria only because of them. They were being cautioned, but their confidence was complete. They faced fear and temptation with bribes. People were consumed by the mysterious prediction. Everyone wanted to know the secret.

VII. Fourth Apparition

Fatima is in the county of Ou’rem. The administrator was the chief magistrate, Artur Oliveira Santos, a civil officer with the power to enforce the law. He was baptized a Catholic but later abandoned the faith, bowing to peer pressure to join the Masonic Lodge of Leiria. The Magistrate, also the publisher of a local newspaper, held immense power and tried to undermine the faith of the people in the Church and the priests. He was intent on preventing the Church from gaining strength and tried stifling any renewed enthusiasm, counting on the cringing spirits of the people who feared him to quiet them.

To this end, he summoned the children to court, determined to know the secret. He confronted Lucia's father. "Do the people of Fatima believe in these things?" Lucia's father said no, that it was just woman's talk, remaining indifferent. Ti Marto, on the other hand, defended his children. The magistrate dismissed Lucia, "warning her that if he did not learn her secret, he would take her life."

The Thirteenth of August

The day of the next apparition, a surprise visit by the magistrate to the Marto house demonstrated the seriousness of his intentions to know the secret and prevent any further interest of the people in things supernatural—something he had no control over. At home, Ti Marto was called out of the garden. The magistrate was waiting. He said he, too, wanted to see the miracle, and offered to take the children to Cova da Iria himself. He told to the families to go ahead to Fatima then stopped at the rectory; he had some questions he needed to ask the children. At the rectory, the pastor was waiting, having already decided the apparitions were not the work of the devil but rather plain inventions of the children. When the families arrived, the children were sent up to the pastor, who merely told them that lying would send them to Hell. He then asked, "Who taught you these things you are going about saying?" Lucia replied, "Our Lady." She said she would not tell the secret, but that she would ask Our Lady today if she could tell him. With that, the magistrate interrupted and told the children they would ride together to the Cova. He had his carriage parked at the bottom of the steps of the rectory. The children were then tricked into the carriage. It headed in the direction of the Cova, but it quickly turned about and bolted toward Ou'rem. He had abducted them. It happens regularly to this day, with sometimes fatal outcomes.

The magistrate tried to convince the children he was taking them to the pastor in Ou'rem first, but he proceeded to his own house instead. He locked them in a room and told them they would not come out until they told the secret. The magistrate had lied about the innocent nature of his desire to take them to the Cova.

The <<HOAX>> August 13, 1917

On the August 13, the day slated for the next apparition, a crowd even larger than that of July 13 had travelled to the Holy spot. Maria de Chaplinha's eyewitness account said many people were praying. Her personal constant prayer as she walked along was, "May Our Lady guide me according to God's Holly Will."[57]At about eleven o'clock in the morning, people gathered around the holmoak, praying and singing religious hymns. The children's families continued on to the Cova, but they soon realized the magistrate had kidnapped the children. As anger set in, it thundered—a sudden crack of thunder so powerful, some "began to cry, fearful they were going to be killed." This was followed by a flash. "Immediately, we all noticed a cloud, very white, beautiful and bright, that came and stayed over the holmoak."[58] The time of the apparition for those gathered had arrived.

During the apparition, people's faces glowed rose, red, blue, and all the colors of the rainbow. The ground appeared to be in little squares, all different colors of the rainbow. The vigil lanterns above the tree appeared to be made of gold. It looked like the tree had no branches or leaves, yet it was covered with flowers. Later, Ti Marto would say he had foreseen this event happening, and that he knew he would see it again. When the signs disappeared, the people realized that Our Lady had come and, not finding the children, left. This question arose, how was Ti Marto so sure he would see it again, and where?

---

57 Ibid, Chapter VII, The Hoax, p 87
58 Ibid, Chapter VII, p 69

The angry crowd was ready to march to the Our'em, having already decided the magistrate and pastor were guilty of kidnapping the children. Ti Marto stepped in to calm them, reasoning it had all been allowed to happen through the power of God, "to preserve for His Mother the name of Fatima, forever gracious and unstained, as is evidenced by the letter the Pastor wrote the following day for the newspapers." He believed no harm should come to anyone.

Rumors spread that the pastor was an accomplice of the magistrate. He called it an "unjust insidious calumny", and he said "...if he had been involved, the parish would be mourning her Pastor today." The Virgin Mother must have intervened to prevent this snare of the devil from striking him dead.

Thousands of witnesses concluded the presence of the pastor or the children was not necessary for Our Lady to manifest Her power.[59] They had experienced enough to confirm for themselves the truth of the apparitions. The faithful put Our Lady first, before their children, even though they were abducted by the magistrate. After the apparition however, they began a search to find them.

THE ORDEAL

Meanwhile, the children had been taken to the magistrate's house where his wife proved to be very kind. The following morning however, they were "taken to the County House, where they were subjected to relentless questioning", bribed with gold coins, threatened with being thrown into a tank of boiling oil—all in an effort to learn the secret. They were put through the same inhuman "third degree"[60] all afternoon. The children continued to refuse to tell it. At the end of this test, they were sent to jail. They offered their suffering up for the reparation of sins, and to the Immaculate

59 Ibid., Chapter VII, p 89
60 Ibid., Chapter VII, The Ordeal, p 90

Heart of Mary. In jail, the inmates consoled the children, but even they tried to learn the secret. The magistrate called for the children again, and reiterated his threat to throw them in the boiling oil; they proudly resisted. The tables were turned. The magistrate, not having accomplished his goal, now feared the people would retaliate. He himself returned the children to Fatima, unaware that it was the celebration of the Feast of the Assumption.

You get the idea of Lucia's pattern. She is directing attention to the mistreatment of specifically Catholics, especially these young Catholic children in particular. Important to note is the ultimatum they were given; succumb to my wishes or you will be killed. This imposition on the children, the threat of death instills fear, mortification. This will become the central topic of the *Crusade*. This threat of death is still imposed on young Catholic children to this day.

THE SECRET

The next morning after Sunday Mass, having heard that the children were seen on the rectory balcony, the crowd marched over to the pastor's house. The children were there and had been returned to their families. The dangerous crowd outside now turned on the magistrate. Ti Marto was able to calm the angry crowd, but their lack of faith made it impossible for them to recognize that no one was to blame and that the "whole affair was allowed by the One above." This point may have been made in reference to 9/11. Our Lady had made Her presence known to the faithful August 13, those who had gathered before at the site of the earlier apparitions.

The magistrate, who had gone to a nearby inn after dropping off the children, returned to the rectory. The pastor, having the respect of the community with Ti Marto, together they managed to have him enter the rectory safely. The three talked over the whole affair. The magistrate told Ti Marto the children had told him the secret. Ti

Marto disputed that idea, dismissed the possibility, and escorted the magistrate out to his carriage to ensure the safety of his departure. It is noted that the abduction, interrogation, and jailing of the children served one purpose that was providential. "Since everything became a matter of official record, the magistrate unwittingly had made the existence of a secret revelation undeniable."[61]

THE NINETEENTH OF AUGUST

The children missed their appointment with Our Lady on the thirteenth, since they were being held hostage by the magistrate at the time. He interfered with the children's appointment for their visit with Our Lady. Obstructing and disrupting the sanctity of another's faith isn't new but it seems lately Christians have been receiving the bulk of religious abuse in public society, as their right to practice their faith freely is being challenged.

On Sunday August 19, Lucia and the children went to the Cova da Iria after Mass and said the Rosary.

> After lunch Lucia, together with Francisco and his elder brother John, left for a place called Valinhos . . . . about four o'clock, Lucia became aware of the signs that always immediately preceded the apparitions of Our Lady: the sudden cooling of the air, the paling of the sun, and the typical flash. The children had already been having a wonderful premonition that they were to experience the supernatural again.[62]
>
> Now Our Lady was coming and Jacinta was not there. Lucia called out to John, go quickly and get Jacinta, Our Lady is coming!

61 Ibid, The Secret, p 97
62 Ibid., p 97

The boy did not want to go. He too wanted to see Our Lady. Go fast, Lucia insisted and I will give you four pennies, if you bring Jacinta back with you. Here's two now and I'll keep the other two for you when you return. Begging Jacinta's mother he said, "Let her come, little mother, they want her there now. ...God be with you: Jacinta is at her godmother's house. ...Just as John and Jacinta reached the field, a second flash rent the air. A few moments, later, the brilliant Lady appeared over a holmoak, a slightly taller one than that at the Cova da Iria."[63]

When Our Lady arrived, Lucia asked, "What do you want of me?

Our Lady answered, "I want you to continue to come to the Cova da Iria on the thirteenth and to continue to say the Rosary every day."

"She asked Our Lady if She was willing to perform a miracle that all might see and believe."

"Yes, Our Lady answered. In the last month I will perform a miracle so that all may believe in my apparitions. If they had not taken you to the village, the miracle would have been greater. Saint Joseph will come with the Baby Jesus to give peace to the world. Our Lord will also come to bless the people. Besides, Our Lady of the Rosary and Our Lady Sorrows will come."[64]

Lucia asked, "... What should we do with the money and the offerings that the people leave at Cova da Iria?"

---

63 Ibid., p 99

64 Ibid, Chapter VII, The Nineteenth of August, p 97

> "Two litters should be made; you and Jacinta are to carry on with two other girls dressed in white; Francisco is to carry the other with three boys, also dressed in white robes. The money placed on the litters is for the Feast of Our Lady of the Rosary."
>
> Lucia asked about some of the sick who had been recommended to her.
>
> "Yes, I shall cure some within the year." She went on teaching them to pray rather for health of souls rather than of bodies. "Pray! Pray a great deal and make sacrifices for sinners, for many souls go to Hell for not having someone to pray and make sacrifices for them."
>
> When Our Lady departed, and began to rise towards the East as before, John was disappointed. He tried hard to see Our Lady but had seen nothing. However he heard something like the hissing of a rocket, when Lucia said, Jacinta, see Our Lady is going away.

"John and Lucia stayed behind at the Valinhos with the sheep while Francisco and Jacinta rushed home with the precious branch to tell their parents of the unexpected visit of Our Lady." This branch was actually from the Cova da Iria, one that had been broken off when "the older people stripped the holmoak of its foliage." Valinhos and the Cova da Iria must be close to one another. Jacinta must have picked it up in the morning at the Cova or found it on the way to Valinhos. It was a branch that the "resplendent robe of Our Lady had touched." Taking home this special branch, Jacinta first encountered Lucia's mother and sister. She gave it to her aunt whose "face showed great surprise as she put the branch to her nose."

"What does it smell of! she said continuing to smell it. It is not perfume, it's not incense or perfumed soap; it's not the smell of roses or anything I know but it is a good smell. The whole family gathered and each wanted to hold the branch and smell the beautiful odor. Leave it here, Jacinta. Someone will come along and tell us what kind of odor it is."[65]

"From that moment, Lucia's mother and whole family began to modify their opinion of the apparitions."

Jacinta then leaves for home with the branch. When she arrived she said, "Look father, Our lady appeared to us again at Valinhos!'

As she came in I sensed a magnificent fragrance which I could not explain. I stretched out my hands towards the branch saying, "What are you bringing in Jacinta?'

"It is the little branch on which Our Lady placed her feet.'

"I smelled it but the odor was gone," he said.

"Our lady did not have to perform a miracle to prove her case to him."

Here Ti Marto implies it is we that need a miracle for Our Lady to prove Her case to us. That needed miracle came during 9/11. This chapter ends with fine print explaining that when Lucia's sister and her husband had come to town: "They noticed the cooling of the air, the paling of the sun and the pattern of different colors over everything. . . . This was the very hour of the apparition at Valinhos."[66] The point can be made this is entered to be the defense

65 Ibid, Chapter VII, Nineteenth of August, p 102
66 Ibid., p 103, Fine print

of proper marriage and children as the natural result made favored by God.

The smell given off from the branch is that of a baby, a newborn. When Jacinta entered the room to show her father, he could smell the odor but not on the branch, making Jacinta herself his miracle, as all children are one of the multi-colored dainty flowers Our Lord blooms on earth. Lucia implies each one of us in truth, are created, given life only by the grace of God. The point Lucia makes is a case against abortion of unborn babies, supporting the need declared on the final pages, that this little book is about "an emergency plan", in part to stop abortions, a demand that is now put in motion by Our Lady herself. The association of the word *emergency* with 911, the number to call in such cases, does not look to be just a coincidence.

Notice the date, the nineteenth of August, when an apparition took place. It was not on the thirteenth like all the others, since the children were incarcerated on the thirteenth. Significantly, the apparition on the nineteenth took place at 4:00 p.m., and not at noon, the hour of the sun, like the other apparitions had. The variation is a curious change.

Several questions are raised in this section. The question of why Our Lady appeared taller at Valinhos than at the Cova da Iria is one. This remark is actually a tangible clue given to help discover one of Lucia's secrets, and the divine presages Lucia conveys.

This hissing sound John heard at Valinhos is commonly used to describe the sound a snake makes. He needed to be bribed to retrieve Jacinta for Lucia. It is also a clue. Combined with rocket, considering the comment about the rockets, rolls and band of the feast of St. Anthony in the second apparition, this expression associates a snake or evil with some rock and roll music lyrics.

The two pennies, given to John; does it represent the suggestion that Lucia is asking a different question, such as, does this make sense to you yet? Sense, being a homonym with cents makes it possible. It may seem suspicious to think so, for the time being at least, until the message of the *Crusade* is revealed. There is a specific reason for mentioning a penny.

VIII. Fifth Apparition: September 13, 1917

"The words that most deeply embedded themselves on the minds of the children were the last words spoken by Our Lady at Valinhos, Pray! Pray a great deal and make sacrifices for sinners, for many souls go to Hell for not having someone to pray and make sacrifices for them." These words the words the Angel also spoke "awakened in the children an even stronger desire for mortification, prayer, and suffering. Their one longing was to close that terrifying furnace of Hell so that no more souls could go there."[67]

While the children sought every means of pleasing Our Lady, praying as much as they could the Angel's prayer and the Rosary, in addition to refusing water and even "a few bunches of grapes" as a way of sacrificing, there were men determined to discredit the children and make a fiasco of the apparitions, just like the magistrate using his newspaper and his friends had planned from the beginning. The magistrate had help in "Jose do Vale, the editor of a leftist newspaper. His idea was to put an end to the Fatima affair with a public meeting, distributing pamphlets in the towns and villages telling the 'truth' about Fatima and the Church. Jose do Vale thought that the best time to get the people together would be after the last Mass at the Church of Fatima."[68] This act was an obvious violation of Catholic religious liberty. These people saw it as an opportunity to destroy the Church in Portugal. Trying to rouse the faithful after Mass, the

67 Ibid, Chapter VIII, p 104
68 Ibid., p 107

“one of the evil ones” began speaking against the Church. Some people prepared for them and had brought donkeys and tied them to the holmoak with hay to keep them there. The people likened the evil ones, those speaking against the Church, to animals, while the men-folk began to call intruders mule-heads and clodhoppers and hillbillies.[69] [Lucia has just described the evil one of 9/11. They are those who speak against the Church. They called back at the especially wicked remarks: Viva Jesus e Maria or Hail Jesus and Mary, the cross of Jesus Christ in the rubble of 9/11].[70] Their guards they brought with them tried to chase the hecklers to no avail. You could say the news media of the day was antichrist.

The time of the next apparition of September was approaching: September 13, 1917. Many thousands had come to believe in the visions of Our Lady by this time, but many refused to believe and caused the children great suffering with their repetitive abuse and questions.

So many now gathered to see the apparitions that they could barely move when they neared the holmoak tree. There was no human respect in the crowd. Many wanted favors of Our Lady and asked the children to put their petitions to Our Lady. To some Lucia said “Yes”.

The hour had arrived. As usual the children began with the Rosary, with the people responding. “They had seen the flash. Our Lady would be coming soon. “A globe of light” appeared before the crowd, and the All Holy Queen of Angels was standing over the holmoak.”

“What do you want of me? Lucia spoke very humbly.”

69 Ibid., p 109
70 Ibid., p 108

Our Lady said "Let the people continue to say the Rosary every day to bring an end to the war. In the last month, in October, I will perform a miracle so that all may believe in my apparitions. If they would not have taken you to the village, the miracle would have been greater. Saint Joseph will come with the Baby Jesus to bring peace to the world. Our Lord will also come to bless the people. Besides, Our Lady of the Rosary and Our Lady of Sorrows will come. God is pleased with your sacrifices but does not wish for you to sleep with the rope. Wear it only during the day."[71]

Lucia said, "They have requested me to ask You many things. This girl is a deaf mute. Don't you want to cure her?"

"In the course of a year she will be improved," answered Our Lady.

"Will you help these other people?"

"Some I will cure but the others, no. Our Lord does not have confidence in them."

"The people would like to have a chapel built here," Lucia suggested.

"Use half of the money received so far for the litters. One of them, place the statue of Our Lady of the Rosary. The other half of the money should be set aside to help with the building of the chapel," Our Lady instructed.

"Many people say I am a swindler and should be hanged or burned. Please perform a Miracle for all to believe," Lucia asked.

"Yes, in October, I will perform a miracle so that all may believe."

---

71 Ibid., p111

"Some people gave me these two letters for you and a bottle of cologne."

"None of that is necessary for Heaven."

When Our Lady began to leave, "Lucia pointed to the East and shouted to the people, "if you want to see Our Lady, look that way. They looked eagerly towards the East and many saw the luminous globe now ascending toward Heaven." Many were converted that day."

There is an account of this miracle by two priests who observed this apparition. One remarked that he saw "the globe with the extraordinary light." The children "had seen the Mother of God herself; to us had been shown the chariot that had bourne her from Heaven to the barren inhospitable hills of Aire."

This was what the children wanted and needed, an apparition that all could see to relieve them of the burden they carried having to withstand the relentless questioning of the unbelievers, and the destruction of their families property by those who sought them out.

There were, "other signs reported on this day. There was a sudden cooling of the air; and the sun was dimmed, so much so that thousands of people could see the stars even though it was mid-day. Also there was a rain of iridescent pedals that vanished upon reaching the ground."

Many individual words are important, just as in previous chapters. They give more clues to Lucia's hidden message. The "luscious looking grapes" the word bourne, Aire and the globe have particular importance. Lucia keeps capitalizing the word "East", Our Lady always departed to the East. The chariot mentioned by the priest, is also found in the book of Isaiah and the book of Joel, serving to the support the supposition they are somehow related to this mysterious little book. The elements of imagery in these previous passages can easily be thought descriptive of 9/11.

IX. Sixth Apparition: October 13, 1917

"During the last three apparitions, Our Lady promised the children that the last time she would appear (to them), in October, she would effect a miracle that everyone could see and thereby believe."[72] Our Lady allowed everyone to experience this apparition. People wanting to see the apparition arrived from all over the country. News of the apparition spread throughout the country like wildfire. Think of it, being warned ahead of time of a great miracle! Doubters ridiculed the believers, intent on proving it all a hoax and discredit the Church. They even threatened to throw bombs. The parents were afraid their children might be killed, and they offered them a final chance to deny their story, threatening that something drastic could occur. Unshaken, the children remained calm and steadfast, confident Our Lady would do what she promised.

People arrived days ahead—the peasants and the wealthy—in oxcarts, luxurious carriages, and on foot. On the day before the miracle, religious songs filled the air while thousands upon thousands prayed, some weeping.

October 13 began as a miserable day: pouring rain, cold and windy. At noon, Lucia said, "Our Lady is coming. I saw the flash." The doubters were silenced. The miracle that was promised had begun to take place. Lucia saw the flash again, and Our Lady came, Her snow-white feet resting on the holmoak tree that had been adorned with flowers and ribbons.

---

72 Ibid., Chapter IX, p 115

X. Sixth Apparition (Continued)

"Silence silence, Our Lady is coming, Lucia cried out as she saw the flash."

"... What do you want of me," Lucia inquired of the Queen of Heaven.

"I want to tell you that they must build a chapel here in my honor; that I am the Lady of the Rosary; that they continue to pray the Rosary every day. The war will end and the solders will return to their homes soon."

Lucia said she had many favors to ask. "Do you wish to grant them or not?"

"Some I will, others I will not. They must mend their lives and ask forgiveness for their sins. Offend not Our Lord any more, for He is already very much offended." This is the same message included in the book of Joel.

"Do you want anything else from me," the girl asked.

The reply, "I desire nothing else."

Our Lady opened her hands, which emitted a flood of light. While rising, she pointed toward the sun and the light gleaming from her hands brightened the sun itself. Lucia said, "There she goes!" At that moment, an immense cry of wonder and astonishment came from the multitude. The sun had become as pale as the moon. To the left of the sun, St. Joseph was holding the child Jesus. St. Joseph emerged from the clouds only to his chest, sufficient for him to raise his right hand together with Jesus, making the sign of the cross three times over the world. As St. Joseph did this, Our Lady stood, in all Her brilliance, to the right of the sun, dressed in the blue and white robes of Our Lady of the Rosary.

Meanwhile, Jacinta and Francisco were bathed in marvelous colors and signs of the sun. Lucia was privileged to see "Our Lord dressed in red as the divine redeemer", blessing the world as Our Lady had foretold. Like St. Joseph, He was seen only from His chest up. Beside Him stood Our Lady, now dressed in the purple robes of Our Lady of Sorrows but without the sword. Finally the Blessed Virgin appeared again to Lucia in all Her ethereal brightness, clothed in the simple brown robes of Mount Carmel.[73]

As the children stared enraptured by these most beautiful heavenly visions, the countless thousands were amazed and overpowered by the miracles in the skies. The sun took on extraordinary colors. Eyewitnesses said they could look at the sun with ease. Ti Marto said it didn't bother his eyes at all. The sun seemed to be continually fading and glowing in one fashion or another. It threw shafts of light one way and another, painting everything in different colors. Ti Marto thought being able to look at the sun without hurting the eyes was proof of the miracles. The sun continued its play of light and then started dancing. At one point it stopped, but then began dancing again and then seemed to loosen itself from the skies and appeared as if it were going to fall upon the people; there was terrible suspense. Maria Capelinha gave her impressions of the miracle. The sun cast different

73 Ibid., Chapter X, p 131

colors: yellow, blue, and white. It trembled constantly. It looked like a revolving ball of fire falling upon the people. As the sun hurled itself toward the earth in a mighty zigzag motion, the multitude cried out in terror."[74] 'Ai Jesus, we are all going to die here. After this, the sun swerved back to its orbit and rested in the sky. Some begged for mercy, Our Lady save us; many others made acts of contrition. One lady was even confessing her sins aloud.

The Lord could easily have destroyed the world that day. He saved the world through the blessing of St. Joseph over the world and the love of the Immaculate Heart of Mary. The Lord is so much offended by the sins of mankind, and particularly by the mistreatment of children—especially at the hands of officials . . . .[75]

[Our Lady said the miracles would have been much greater if the children had not been so mistreated. Mary considers the children Her own, and reminds us of this important warning; what you do to the least of my brethren, you do unto me.

Many thousands had witnessed the tremendous signs in the sky, and all agreed it was the most tremendous and awe inspiring sight they had ever witnessed.]

At one o'clock, the hour of the sun,[76] the rain stopped *O Dia* reported. "The sky had a certain grayish tint of pearl and a strange clearness filled the gloomy landscape. The sun seemed to be veiled with transparent gauze to enable

74 Ibid., p 132
75 Ibid.
76 Ibid., p 133

us to look at it without difficulty. The grayish tint of mother of pearl began changing as if into a shining silver disc that was growing slowly until it broke through the clouds, and the silvery sun, still shrouded in the same grayish lightness of gauze, was seen to rotate and wandered within the circle of the receded clouds. The people cried out with one voice, the thousands of creatures of God whom faith raised up to Heaven, fell to their knees upon the muddy ground. Then as if it were shining through the stained glass of a great cathedral, the light became a rare blue, spreading its rays upon the gigantic nave... Slowly the blue faded away and now the light seemed to be filtered through yellow stained glass. Yellow spots were falling now upon the white kerchiefs and the dark poor skirts of course wool. They were spots which repeated themselves indefinitely over the "lowly"[77] holmoaks, the rocks and hills. All the people were weeping and praying bareheaded, weighed down by the greatness of the miracle expected. These were seconds, moments that seemed like hours; they were so fully lived.

O Seculo, another newspaper of Lisbon, carried a more detailed account of the extraordinary events. From the height of the road where people parked their carriages and where many hundreds stood, afraid to brave the muddy soil, we saw the immense multitude turn towards the sun at its highest, free of all clouds. The sun called to mind a plate of dull silver. It could be stared at without the least effort. It did not burn or blind. It seemed that an eclipse was taking place. All of the sudden a tremendous shout burst forth, Miracle, miracle! Marvel, marvel! Before the astonished eyes of the people, whose attitude carried us back to biblical

---

77 Ibid., p 134

times, and who, white with terror, heads uncovered gazed at the blue sky, the sun trembled and made brusque unheard-of movements beyond all cosmic laws; the sun danced, "int" the typical expression of the peasants.

On the running board of the bus from Torres Noves, an old man whose stature and gentle manly features recall those of Paul Deroulede, turned toward the sun recited the Credo in a loud voice... I saw him latter addressing those about him who still kept their hats on, begging them vehemently to take them off before this overwhelming demonstration of the existence of God. Similar scenes were repeated at other places. A lady, bathed in tears and almost choking with grief, sobbed, How pitiful. There are men who still do not bear their heads before such a stupendous miracle."

Immediately afterward, the people asked each other if they had seen anything and what they had seen. The greatest number avowed that they saw the sun trembling and dancing; others declared that they saw the smiling face of the Blessed Virgin herself. They swore the sun turned around on itself as if it were a wheel of fireworks, and that it had fallen to the point of almost burning the earth with its rays. Some say they saw it change colors successively."

...Dr. Almeida Garret, professor at the University of Coimbra, is most informative and corroborates the others." As he was waiting with serene expectation looking upon the site of the past apparitions, his curiosity faded because the hour of the anticipated apparition—noon—had come and gone with nothing to draw his attention. He began to hear people rustling, and turning to the look the same direction, all their eyes fixed on the skies. The sun had broken jubilantly through the thick layer of clouds just a few moments before. It was shining clearly and intensely. "I turned to this magnet that was drawing all eyes." It looked to me as a luminous and brilliant disc, with a bright, well-defined rim. It did not hurt the eyes. The comparison (which he heard while still at Fatima) with "a disc of dull silver" did not seem right to him. The color was brighter, far more active and richer than dull silver, with the tinted luster of orient of Pearl. It did not resemble the moon on a clear night. Everyone saw and felt that it was a body with life. It was not spherical like the moon, neither did it have an equal tonality of color, it looked like a small, brightly polished wheel of iridescent mother-of-pearl. It could not be taken for the sun as though seen through fog. There was no fog at that time. (The rain and the fog had stopped.) The sun was not opaque, veiled, or diffused. It gave off light and heat, brightly outlined by a beveled rim. The sky was banked with light clouds, patched with blue here and there. Sometimes the sun stood out alone in rifts of clear sky. The clouds scuttled along from west to east without dimming the sun. They gave the impression of passing behind it, while white puffs gliding sometimes in front of the sun seemed to take on the color of rose or a delicate blue.

It was a wonder that all this time you could look at the sun, a blaze of light and burning heat, without any pain or damage to the retina. This phenomenon must have lasted ten minutes except for two interruptions when the sun darted forth its more refulgent, lightning-like rays that forced them to turn away.

The sun had an eccentricity of movement. It was not the scintillation of a celestial body at its highest power. It was rotating upon itself with exceedingly great speed. Suddenly, the people broke out with a cry of extreme anguish. The sun, still rotating, had unloosened itself from the sky and was hurling toward the earth. This huge, fiery millstone threatened to crush us with its weight. It was a dreadful sensation.

During this solar occurrence, the air took on successively different colors. While looking at the sun, he noticed everything around him darkened. He looked at what was nearby and cast his eyes toward the horizon. Everything had the color of amethyst: the sky, the air—everything and everybody, a little oak nearby was casting a heavy purple shadow on the ground.

Fearing impairment of the retina, which was improbable, because then I could not have seen everything in purple, he turned about, closed his eyes, cupping his hands over them to cut off all light. With his back turned, he opened his eyes and realized that the landscape and the air retained the purple hue.

It did not give the impression of being an eclipse...While still looking at the sun, he noticed the air had cleared and heard a peasant nearby say, "This lady looks yellow!" As a matter of fact, everything far and near had changed now. People seemed to have jaundice. I smiled when I saw everyone looking disfigured and ugly. His hand had the same color ...

The testimony of this learned man demonstrated how difficult it was to describe adequately the marvelous signs that occurred in the skies on that day. October 13, 1917, was "a day to remember" for all the people who witnessed the events. The reporter for the Ordem, a newspaper of Oporto, wrote about it in these words. The sun was sometimes surrounded by blood red flames, at other times it was aureole with yellow and soft purple; again it seemed to be a processor of the swiftest rotation and then seemed to detach itself from the heavens, come near the earth, and give forth a tremendous heat.

Another witness, the Reverend Manuel da Silva, wrote a letter to a friend the evening of the thirteenth in which he tried to describe the events of the day. He spoke about the morning's rain and then "immediately the sun came out with a well-defined rim and seemed to come down to the height of the clouds. It started to rotate intermittently around itself like a wheel of fireworks, for about eight minutes. Everything became almost dark and the people's features became yellow. All were kneeling in the mud."

"In'acio Lourenco was a boy nine years old at the time, living in the village of Aljustrel, ten miles away from Fatima. He is a priest, and he remembers this day vividly. He was in school.

About noon, we were startled by the cries and exclamations of the people going by the school. The teacher was the first to run outside to the street with all the children following her. The people cried and wept on the street; they were all pointing toward the sun. It was 'the miracle' promised by Our Lady. I feel unable to describe it as I saw it and felt it at the time. I was gazing and the sun; it looked so pale to me, it did not blind. It was like a ball of snow rotating upon itself. All of the sudden, it seemed to be falling, zigzag, threatening the earth. Seized with fear, I hid myself amidst the people. Everyone was crying, waiting for the end of the world.

> Nearby, there was a godless man who had spent the morning making fun of the simpletons who had gone to Fatima just to see a girl. I looked at him and he was numbed, his eyes riveted on the sun. I saw him tremble from head to foot. Then he raised his eyes toward heaven, as he was kneeling in the mud, and cried out "Our Lady, Our Lady." Everyone was crying and weeping, asking God to forgive their sins. After this was over, we ran to the chapels, some to one, others to the other one in our village. They were soon filled.
>
> During the minutes that the miracle lasted everything around us reflected all the colors of the rainbow. We looked at each other and one seemed blue, another yellow, red, and so on. "It increased the terror of the people". After ten minutes the sun resumed its place, as pale and without splendor. When everyone realized the danger was over, there was an outburst of joy. Everyone broke out in a hymn of praise for Our Lady.
>
> As the miracle came to its end and the people arose from the muddy ground, another surprise awaited them. A few minutes before, they were standing in the pouring rain soaked to the skin. Now they noticed their clothes were perfectly dry. How kind was Our Lady to Her friends who braved rain and mud, and put on their very best clothes for Her visit.

The Bishop of Leira wrote a pastoral letter stating that those who witnessed the events of this day were fortunate indeed. The children long before said the day the hour and the place," he said. "The news spread quickly over the whole of Portugal, and although the day was chilly and pouring rain, many thousands of people gathered. They saw the different manifestations of the sun paying homage to the Queen of Heaven and Earth, who is more radiant than the sun in all of its splendor. This phenomenon, which no astronomical observatory registered, was not natural. It was seen by people of all classes, members of the Church and non-Catholics. It was seen by reporters of the principal newspapers and by people miles away." These are his official words, spoken after long study and careful interrogations of many witnesses of the apparition. There is no possibility of error when close to a hundred thousand people concur in the testimony. God in Heaven had called the people of the world to join with the heavens in praising the Lord Jesus and praying in honor of His Blessed Mother, the Virgin Mary.

This Sixth Apparition is the "what happened in Portugal, proclaims the miracle," mentioned in the preface. "It is the presage of what the Immaculate Heart of Mary has prepared for the world." The Sixth Apparition has dual significance and could be intended as part of the presage of September 11, 2001.

Early on, Our Lady said our future would include the promotion of wars and the persecution of the church, that the good will be martyred and the pope will have much to suffer, and that several nations will be annihilated. This last presage, "several nations will be annihilated" mentioned earlier is extremely serious—especially if your nation is on the list. There is something serious going on when God has to come down here Himself. The good news is that if we stop offending God and instead please Him by establishing devotion to the Immaculate Heart of Mary and practice a Communion of Reparation on the First Saturdays of the month, we can prevent future problems. It's been done before, repenting in order for God to spare us.

How would you react if a prophecy seemed written specifically for September 11, 2001—one that included the date and time of the catastrophe, even indicating New York City was the place it would occur could be found? What if you were given images recorded long ago, representing the actual disaster? Would you conclude only God could know all of the specifics in advance? Would you believe in God more than before and be more flexible, living in a way more pleasing to Him? If He told you what He liked about our behavior and the things He will not accept, would you agree to refrain from the evil? There is Good News, Babylon! There is such a book, and the contents should be convincing enough for you to believe.

The *Crusade* is that book and has already pointed out the most offensive sins of our time. Like the prophet Jonah who spread the news to Nineveh, Lucia Santos was told by the Blessed Virgin Mary to announce publically, that Our Lady would bless the world with a miraculous apparition. She confidently added the time and place, saying that it could be seen by everyone at noon on October 13, 1917, in Fatima, Portugal. Over a hundred thousand people were on hand to witness the event. The presage of Our Lady spoken to the children became fact; the burden of disbelief and ridicule was lifted from their shoulders. There was no question the events they witnessed were supernatural, an act of God. The words spoken by Our Lady may just as well have come from the mouth of God, but they were received from Our lady, and were the start of establishing a devotion to the Immaculate Heart of Mary. Lucia's work had begun. Those privileged to see Our Lady and the miracles in person could not deny what they had seen proved the very existence of God. Though we were not present, the testimony of by some estimates near a hundred thousand witnesses should be enough for our generation to at least consider a belief in God. She has also given us the *Crusade* with its instructions to seek reparation for our sins, as an aid in continuing her mission.

This cosmic display was Our Lady's sixth visit. The report Lucia gave in the first apparition states Our Lady said she would come six times then: "Also I shall come here again a seventh time." So where is the message of the seventh time? That visit may have been during 9/11, Her part in it yet to be concretely established.

The sins that most outrage God are listed on the second last page of *Crusade*, under the heading of "An Emergency Plan." They include the mass slaughtering of unborn babies, worldwide promotion of adulterous sex, making war, terrorizing people, and pornography. To satisfy the request Our Lady is asking of us, these are the most important issues we need to address.

The village of Fatima had been buzzing about the belief and disbelief in the existence of the apparitions but now they sought after *secrets* the children still held. Lucia never "says" but still reveals the seventh visit and the secret presage. What the children kept from everyone was a part of the message received with the vision of Hell, during the "Thrid Apparition", the secret prediction of September 11, 2001. If only through presage, Our Lady has established Herself as having a role. The cross of Jesus Christ left standing on the rubble is the sign, Jesus is being taken down by those who act antichrist. 9/11 is part of and the beginning of Our Lady's "Peace Plan". Yes, she truly wants peace not war, belief in Her Resurrected Son Jesus as Lord and the conversion of non-believers. The children are Catholic, and currently only the Catholic Church venerates Our Lady and members do make reparation to Her Immaculate Heart.

XI. Francisco Leads the Way

In *Crusade,* Lucia says, "What is often overlooked by those who read about Fatima now is the fact that for years nothing was revealed of the content of the revelations as given in the foregoing pages. Only the urgency to pray and do penance, and the promise of a miracle, were mentioned by the children."[78] This chapter adds a different

78 Ibid., Chapter XI, p 144

spin to the secret words. It is the content of the revelations as given in the foregoing pages that is important in determining the true message of the *Crusade*.

> After the first apparition of Our Lady, the children pledged one another to secrecy for fear of being ridiculed. But since the message of Fatima was intended by Our Lady not merely for the children but for the whole world, God used Jacinta's enthusiasm to make know the fact of the apparition to the world."[79]

> After the second apparition on June 13, however, their secrecy was of a different order. What does she mean? Lucia reported The Blessed Virgin opened Her hands and communicated to them for the second time the reflex of immense light that enveloped Her, and in it they could see themselves in God, just as in the first apparition. The secrecy Lucia said was now, "of a different order." This "order" could be for the "Holy Orders" to the Sisterhood for the girls and the priesthood for Francisco. Some don't believe Holy Orders applies to the Sisterhood, perhaps it could. Surely they receive a calling of their own with a different purpose. As Lucia said in her memoirs, "When we said [before the apparition of July the 13] that Our Lady had revealed a secret to us, we referred to this [reparation to the Immaculate Heart]. Our Lady did not tell us at this time to keep (this revelation) secret, but we felt that God moved us to it. (*Memoirs*, Dec. 8, 1941). This inclination of the children to silence was confirmed by Our Lady when, on July 13, she told them what Lucia calls, and what is know as, the Secret proper. It was only after many years that any of

79 Ibid., p 145

> the substance of this secret revelation was made know by Lucia; and even to this date there are important words of Our Lady yet undisclosed.[80]

Lucia misspells "known" as know twice in the last passage telling us a clue of exactly what to look for and that finding these undisclosed words is one key to know the message. Her repeated use of the word revelation is not to be overlooked either; she is trying to say something. "After the last apparition on October 13th, 1917, the children tried to return to their ordinary routine life; Francisco and Jacinta to await the day when Mary would come take them to Heaven: Lucia hoping soon to begin her work of spreading devotion and love for the Immaculate Heart of Mary. Henceforth, however they were marked children, marked by men as well as by God."[81]

[This raises two issues. First, they are marked children and have reason to fear for their safety because they know but have not revealed the secret, and that God wants them. Secondly, the Mary that is coming for them may not necessarily mean the Virgin Mary. By using Mary she may infer the homonym Marry and meaning into the Church in vocation. Each had seen themselves in the reflex of light. It would be a reflex response to become a priest or nun after a personal visit from the Mother of God.]

"Mary helped them in their dilemma. She sent them a priest named Reverend Faustino Ferreira, pastor of the neighboring village and dean of the district. They loved him and followed his councils faithfully. He realized that it was not his words influencing the children rather it was the Mother of God. ...She was the artist, gently though firmly molding their souls to the model of Her first born, the

80 Ibid., p 146
81 Ibid

Child Jesus."[82] This gives another clue to their having been given a calling for a vocation in the Church and Reverend Faustino could be offering them one.

"Francisco testified that he saw Our Lady, and Her radiant beauty was blinding to the eyes, but he never heard her speak." He could not tell what She said. "Jacinta could tell more, but she candidly admitted that sometimes she had not heard Our Lady very well but had forgotten many things. If people wanted to know more, they should ask Lucia. Lucia would repeat the story word for word every time; but sometimes and in fact very often people would try to make her reveal the secrets of the revelations. Then Jacinta and Lucia kept silence sometimes to the point of being impolite."[83] Even priests came to try to pry the secret out of them, and though they didn't want to be rude, they did not reveal the secret."

"Our Lady had instructed Francisco through Lucia, that she would take him to heaven[84] soon, that he must say many Rosaries." For one time, [heaven] is not capitalized. With all other Heaven's capitalized, this heaven where they are going may not be the Heaven we all led to assume. "He never forgot these *words* and like St. Dominic became a real apostle of the Rosary." It is a wonder how a little boy was expected to become a real apostle of the Rosary if he were only to live a short time longer. Francisco hasn't enough time left to actually evangelize and at this time he is too young to enter typical formation.

"After the last apparition on October 13, the children tried to return to their normal lives. Francisco and Jacinta waited for Mary to take them to Heaven. Lucia was ready to get started trying to begin

82 Ibid., p 147
83 Ibid., p 146
84 Ibid. p 147

a devotion to the Immaculate Heart. When people came to see them to ask questions, the children's innocence, seriousness, and simplicity was enough to convince the learned and unlearned of their utter truthfulness."

People would come to ask Francisco what he wanted to be when he grew up: a carpenter, a soldier, a doctor, a priest. He only replied that all he wanted to do was die and go to heaven. Although the public apparitions ended October 12th, the pastor said Our Lady appeared to Jacinta three more times.[85] This is a deliberate typographical error Lucia entered as the last public apparition was actually October 13th that does more than draw attention to the lower cased "heaven".

Lucia's story continues, and Francisco became gravely ill. Our Lady had said She would be taking him to Heaven soon, but he maintained his selfsame spirit of love and sacrifice. He was a very sick boy, and some medicines he had to take were not particularly agreeable. "Yet he would take any medicine we gave him," his mother said. "He never fussed. I could never find out what he liked. If I gave him a glass of milk, he took it; and when I gave him an egg, he sucked it. He took any bitter medicine without making a face. He gave us hope that he would recover, but he always repeated that it was useless since Our Lady was going to come for him soon."

Francisco's godmother once said, "If Our Lady will cure you, I promise to offer your weight in wheat."

"That is useless. Our Lady will not do you this favor," he said.

"Francisco was right. As the days went on, he lost the strength to get up from his bed. He was sinking very fast under the weight of

---

85 ibid, p 149

his persistently high fever. However, his ready smile and continual cheerfulness misled everyone as to his true condition."[86]

"The influenza epidemic did not by-pass Lucia's family. Most of them were taken sick, though Lucia was spared. She helped nurse the sick in her family, and every chance she had she ran over to the Marto house to see if she could help them. She especially wanted to be with Francisco and Jacinta. She knew they would leave her soon. She divided her time between their two rooms. During these visits, they exchanged the confidences of their hearts."

"Have you made a lot of sacrifices today?" Lucia asked Jacinta.

"I have made a lot. My mother went out, and many times I wanted to get out of bed and go to Francisco's room but I didn't."

"Lucia told Jacinta what she herself was able to do to prove her love for Our Lady. She told about her little prayers and sacrifices."

"I did that too," Jacinta said. "I love the Lord and Our Lady, and I never get tired of telling Them that I love Them. When I tell that to Them, it seems sometimes I have a fire burning in my breast, a fire that does not consume ... Oh how I would like to be able to go again to the hills to say the Rosary in the Cova. But I can't anymore. When you go to the Cova da Iria, pray for me, Lucia." [87]

Francisco knew well he would not recover. "Look, Lucia I am going soon to Heaven."

"Jacinta seemed to be interested only in the conversion of sinners; she wanted to save people from Hell." . . . "Francisco's only desire

86 Ibid., p 153
87 Ibid., Chapter XI, p 153

was to console Our Lord and Our Lady, who seemed to him so sorrowful." "I feel sick, Francisco confided to Lucia. But I'll be in Heaven soon." Leaving home would make one sick at such a young age, but arriving up in heaven he was anxious to do.

In his last days, Francisco was not able to recite his prayers. "Mother I can't say the Rosary, I can't even say the Hail Mary without being distracted." He wanted to go to confession before he died and receive Holy Communion. He confessed his sins by himself, but the priest did arrive in time for Communion ringing a bell when he arrived with the Eucharist.

Francisco had kept his rope of penance under his pillow. He given it to Lucia but said he wanted it back if he ever got up. Before Francisco died, the children all prayed for the conversion of sinners and to make reparation for the sins of men committed against the Immaculate Heart of Mary. He had given his life for it. The rope might be identified as the rope seen around the waist of some priests and nuns.

"Friday morning, the fourth day of April, in the year 1919, Our Lady came to claim him for her own."

XII. Jacinta's Death

Jacinta offers many suggestions about and sheds light on sins, sacrileges, and indifferences by which Our Lord Jesus is terribly offended: cussing, swearing, immodest dress, and abortion to name a few. She was worried about the war to come—about how many would die and go to Hell. Jacinta repeats to Lucia the serious words of Our Lady in the Third apparition told Lucia, "But when you see that night lightened by that strange light, you also run away to Heaven."

"Don't you know you cannot run away to Heaven?"[88] Lucia replies.

Jacinta answers, "Yes, you can't do that. But don't be afraid. I'll pray a lot for you in Heaven, and for the Holy Father also, and for Portugal, for the war will not come here and for all priests." Jacinta has brought up and important question; what is meant by "that night lightened by that strange light"? She also says that she is going to "run away to Heaven." Lucia's reply is confusing as well, begging the question of what Jacinta is talking about, it is as if they are all running away to heaven.

Jacinta presents another important request of Lucia's work in this passage: "Pray a great deal for governments. Pity those governments that persecute the religion of Our Lord. If governments left the Church in peace and gave liberty to the Holy Religion, they would be blessed by God." Yes it is true; to leave the Church in peace and no longer persecute its members is the right and fair thing to do to please God. From the government's perspective, obtaining God's blessing should be sought after. Here in America, "In God We Trust" is declared as a responsibility. When God speaks we must trust Him. Written declarations and documents cannot abide by this, though they record the law of the land, only the structure and rules. It is the elected representatives in government who must vote to keep it so. Lucia substantiates this, having made known her opinion of the current nature of media characterized by its broadcast of some Rock and Roll music detrimental to the Church. This message Jacinta presents is made again by Lucia, having recording it in the Crusade. It is meant to address the world, all nations. She is not speaking for herself. In the words of Ti Marto, were it not for the help of providence, they would never even have thought of it.[89] If it is confirmed she entered divine presage in the *Crusade*, it would follow everything she writes is of similar origin and given credibility and what she passes on to us

88 Ibid., Chapter XII, p 161
89 Ibid., Chapter III, the First Apparition, p 31

is God's message. If representatives do trust God as the US Chamber wall declares, they should vote accordingly especially when He makes His desire known as He has in 9/11.

Equal freedom for the faith established by the Church, has been given major emphasis in the *Crusade*, the inferences for it and the reinforcement of it are repeated over and over. An example of this is referred to on the last page of the book, where it says "We need YOUR dime." In this case the authors are referring to the Liberty dime—and it doesn't say *want*, it says *need*, as in necessary. Religious liberty is the inferred topic, particularly for the Catholic Church by virtue of the children being Catholic and Our Lady choosing them to appear too. This will be shown to be true, and is part of Our Lady's "peace plan".

To some the idea of assuring the Church its freedom from oppression brings fear. But think of the words, "Jesus, I Trust in You," and try to believe the blessings promised to those who release the Church from persecution will follow. There is nothing to fear. Ridiculing or trying to squelch other faiths has historically only brought trouble, not the peace and harmony humanity craves. It has been proven time and time again illustrated by the ramifications of abusing any other faith or in some cases, the country in which they live. Tolerance and acceptance is called for, since every religion has to be in favor of being blessed by God.

As the Church goes, so goes the country. It was interesting, that when the earthquake hit Washington DC recently, two specific monuments were damaged, the National Cathedral of the Immaculate Conception and the Washington Monument. Maybe it's a sign!

Jacinta suggests, women are told not to wear too revealing of clothing. Jacinta emphasized the Angel's Prayer given them during his visits, as he instructed the children it was repeated three times:

> My God, I believe, I adore, I hope, and I love You. I beg pardon of You for those who do not believe, do not adore, do not hope, and do not love You.
>
> My God, I believe, I adore, I hope, and I love You. I beg pardon of You for those who do not believe, do not adore, do not hope, and do not love You.
>
> My God, I believe, I adore, I hope, and I love You. I beg pardon of You for those who do not believe, do not adore, do not hope, and do not love You.

This prayer is quoted here as written in the Crusade. The reason for the unconventional use of capitalization of the same words Lucia does when she discusses her intended meaning, is to express due respect for God. Maybe Lucia is telling us capitalization should be used when making reference to God and the Holy Ones. She may have used them to indicate the involvement of a capital city in presage. Lucia's use of word capitalization may have been used to help her tie the Crusade to the events taking place on 9/11, and the involvement of the capital city of some other country, well before that day. The technique she uses could be understood only after 9/11, but Lucia's method in the *Crusade* does hint at presage, retrospectively.

Jacinta's mother would bring her milk or broth, but she did not drink it. Then Lucia asked, "How is it that you disobey your mother?" Her mother brought the milk back, and she did drink it. Her mother came with luscious grapes one time, but Jacinta offered them up, not eating them as an act of suffering. The milk and grapes were each discovered to be clues, helping to solve a mystery Lucia dangled at the conclusion of the *Crusade*.

Jacinta said she kissed the picture of Our Lord and His Sacred Heart, but she wanted Lucia to find her a picture of Mary and Her Immaculate Heart too. Lucia did look but there were none to be found, she told Jacinta. A devotion to the Immaculate Heart was one of Lucia's goals, adding that Jesus asks that people worship His Sacred Heart and venerate the Immaculate Heart at the same time. Lucia, not finding any pictures of the Immaculate Heart, and her reminder to venerate the Sacred Heart of Jesus, both gain significance.

She wanted to go to the Cova everyday like Lucia did. When winter came, her parents would not hear of her going to the Cova, but she did prevail upon them to allow her to go to Mass.[90]

Jacinta urged Lucia "never to tell the secret even if they kill you." Here is another indication Jacinta did not die. Though Jacinta may not remember what Our Lady said word for word like Lucia does, she does know "the secret", what Lucia referred to as "the Secret proper".

"If people amend their ways, Our Lord will come to the aid of the world. If they do not amend their ways, punishment shall come. A terrible social cataclysm will come."[91] This could reasonably bring with it the very image of Hell they had seen in the third apparition, a part of which has yet to be disclosed. Divine justice shall inflict such a horrible punishment, everyone who can, should flee from the city. This calamity, now foreboding, must be disclosed little by little and with discretion. [92] If people would mend their lives, Our Lord would forgive the world; if not, punishment, would come—a punishment such as never has been seen, which was to take place around 1940.

90 Ibid., Chapter XII, p 164
91 Ibid.,, p 175
92 Ibid, p 175

Jacinta thought of these terrible misfortunes that people were bringing upon themselves through their hatred and disobedience to Our Lord and Our Lady filled the child with inconsolable sadness. It pained her more than her illness to realize the wicked way men were treating Jesus and Mary. [93] She referred to these as the evil men in the fifth apparition. When she says pity those governments that persecute the religion of Our Lord and if governments left the Church in peace and gave liberty to the Holy Religion, they would be blessed by God,[94] She delivers a huge promise from Our Lord. There are the other hints of the need to regain Catholic religious liberty in the *Crusade* mentioned previously, but Jacinta makes obvious here, helping to dispel any reservations.

Jacinta continues; Confession is a sacrament of mercy, and people should approach it with confidence and joy. "The Mother of God wants a larger number of virgin souls to bind themselves to her by a vow of chastity."[95] This statement passed on by Our Lady signals to men, that interfering with a commitment to chastity and offending Our Lady is rather unwise. "To be religious, one has to be pure in soul and in body. Preserve chastity, dress modestly, avoid sin, do not steal, and never lie—always tell the truth, even when it is hard. Whoever does not fulfill promises made to Our Lady will not be blessed in life", are Jacinta's words. I expect this last sentence applies to Jesus as well, not just promises with Our Lady: if you make promises to Her or God it is expected and rewarded if you follow through.

"If only they knew what eternity is," Jacinta discussed the faults of a certain priest who had been forbidden to say Mass. . . . People should not talk about the priests, rather they should pray for them."

---

93 Ibid, p 176
94 Ibid, p 177
95 Ibid, p 177

Doctors do not know how to treat their patients with success, because they have no love for God."[96] From Jacinta's point of view, they discount the miraculous influence God, the source of life, might have on the condition of the patient.

Jacinta's doctors wanted to do surgery on her, and although she said it would not help, they went ahead. Jacinta's surgery to control her purulent pleurisy was unique, done under local anesthetic doctors removed a couple of ribs. The wound remaining is the size of a fist. It was very painful. Our Lady graciously came and took away all her pain; her doctor testified to this and her one example of what God can do. The doctors were hopeful of success. The bed Jacinta is assigned to is, X38. X38 has coincidental significance.

Regardless of the measures made to save her life, following Francisco, it is written his sister Jacinta dies, leaving for heaven just as she desired, but there is a contradiction made needing an explanation. The undertaker seemed a bit perplexed about the condition of Jacinta's body in a casket. He had never before or since, had a case like Jacinta's, he said. "It seems to me that I can still today see the little angel. Laid in a casket, she seemed to be still alive, in her full body with rosy cheeks and lips. I have seen many bodies in my business, young and old. Never did a thing of this sort happen to me before or since. The pleasant aroma that exhaled from her body cannot be explained. The worst unbeliever could not question it. Though the child had been dead for three days the aroma was like a bouquet of flowers." He says these facts could not be explained. It may be that they were not inexplicable; instead he was simply forbidden to do it because it was the children's road to safety. This variation of meaning raises the question: did she actually die or was she just faking her death publically, with the assistance of the

96 Ibid, p 178-179

authorities and friends, so she could secretly "run away to heaven"? Without question the authorities must have been very cooperative after the outcome of the predicted sixth apparition. When they saw it take place, they would be likely to go along with this simple wish of the child, her family and Our Lady, and allow her go off into hiding to avoid the public attention she desired to escape. After all, she exhaled a pleasant aroma from her body, she was breathing. This would explain why she and Lucia spoke with one another about running away to heaven, and Lucia's odd response; Yes, you can't do that.[97]

XIII. The Chapel at the Cova da Iria

The repetition of certain issues in the *Crusade* book is planned, to make the elusive intent of the message unmistakable. It is validation that it was truly written with the direction of Our Lady, the Virgin Mary, to help prove Her divinity.

This chapter is about the resistance the faithful encountered when trying to establish a devotional cove and chapel dedicated to Our Lady. To those opposed, they believed it served as a threat somehow. People began leaving money and even produce at the little holmoak tree. Maria da Capelinha tried to pass it off to Ti Marto, then the Pastor, but both refused the offer, the pastor telling her to keep it until things clear up. She increased the treasury with the goal of building a little chapel at the Cova. The people were waiting anxiously for construction to begin. On the other hand, "the civil authorities were absolutely opposed to the chapel and the Church authorities were prudently indifferent." Hostile government officials and protesters tried to stop the display of the statue that went up to complete the shrine in Fatima. Some people said they would destroy the Cova. In one case, the roof of the original chapel was blown off

97 Ibid, p 151

by a bomb, while another bomb planted in the Cova failed to go off. It isn't a rare case when sacred statues and art are destroyed or desecrated. This antichrist activity is carried out to this very day by those who demean, mistreat, and act in some way against the Catholic Church. The bomb caused the destruction of Church property. The same has happened recently at a Catholic Shrine. Somehow they believe it is inconsequential to denounce the Holy Church and encourage others to do the same.

In Fatima, groups of protesters came to disrupt the building of the shrine intent on disrupting any efforts that might bolster the Church. This chapter is just another expression regarding interference with Catholic religious liberty. The magistrate and his friends were at it again, working to disrupt the development of a devotion to the Immaculate Heart. What Lucia knows about the magistrate's friends remains an unknown. Jacinta had already told of her mission in her dying statements made while in Portugal: they concerned the restoration of "religious liberty," her own, and for the Catholic Church. She shared her concerns that some in government were using their position to oppresses the Catholic Church, and protect others who did. This remark is intended not just for Portugal in her day, or America now, but a blanket statement for the entire world, today and in the future. In many countries, Christians are killed; they are persecuted in even more. No one comes to *their* defense.

If 9/11 had something to do with Our Lady's seventh visit, it could actually be at ground zero where Our Lady wishes to have a chapel built in Her honor, dedicated to the Immaculate Heart of Mary. It seems reasonable to assume then, the cross would mark the spot where the "chapel" is to be built if it were decidedly true.

XIV. Lucia's Mission

After Francisco and Jacinta's death Lucia felt all alone and longed to be with her two cousins. "Besides, thousands upon thousands flocked to Fatima to visit the site of the apparitions and all wanted to speak with Lucia. They came to her home every hour of the day." They asked every sort of question; how she missed her cousin's, with whom having all these strangers to face would have been easier. "She wanted to just go and be alone with Our Lord and Our Lady. And the one thing that hurt Lucia perhaps more than everything else was that the constant stream of visitors disturbed and upset the peace of her home."

"Meanwhile, in January, 1918, only three months after the last apparition the Holy See, after a lapse of sixty years, reestablished the Diocese of Leiria, Portugal of which the village of Fatima is a part. The reverend Joseph Correia da Silva was named Bishop and took possession of the See on August the fifth, 1920. Bishop Silva considered it his most important duty to obtain the complete facts on the Fatima apparitions so that he might safeguard and foster true devotion to God and His Mother.[98] The Bishop moved slowly and prudently, refusing to make any decisions or to take any action except after long and prayerful deliberation. He investigated every source of information and had his first interview with Lucia on the thirteenth of June, 1921. Having heard of the frequent intrusions upon Lucia and her family...he informed (Lucia and her mother) of his plan to send Lucia to a convent school, where she would not be known and where no one would bother her."

"You must not tell anyone when or where you are going, the bishop said to Lucia, informing her that she had to leave within five days."

Yes, Bishop Lucia respectfully replied.

---

98 Ibid, Chapter XIV, p 195

"You must not tell a soul at school who you are.

Yes, Bishop.

"And you must not utter a word about Fatima.

Yes, Bishop. Lucia would do whatever he commanded.

Before leaving, Lucia took a tour around the area where the angel had appeared, then to Valinhos where Our Lady appeared, past the bog and little pond on her way finally to the Cova. Not noticing the passing of time, the sun was setting as she went to the parish church and knelt at the altar rail thanking Our Lord for the wonderful privileges of her faith. . . She stopped a moment before each statue to bid goodbye to the saints and ask their help on her journey. These sites were all landmarks to her. "In the convent, Our Lady did not leave Lucia alone. She came to visit her many times. At the Cova da Iria, Our Lady had already told Lucia of the bitter sorrow of her heart over the ingratitude and sinfulness of mankind."[99] This is the first time mankind is brought into focus rather than men exclusively. She asked that the first Saturday of every month be set aside by all as a day of reparation to her Immaculate Heart. Our Lady again appeared to Lucia on December 10, 1925, while she was in her room at the convent. The Child Jesus was at Our Lady's side, elevated upon a cloud of light. Our Lady, resting one hand upon Lucia's shoulder, held in her other hand a heart surrounded with sharp thorns.[100] The Child Jesus spoke first to Lucia:

"Have pity on the Heart of your Most Holy Mother. It is covered with the thorns with which ungrateful men pierce it at every moment, and there is no one to remove them with an act of reparation."

---

99 Ibid, p 201
100 Ibid., p 201-203

Then Our Lady said to Lucia: "My Daughter, look at my heart encircled with the thorns with which ungrateful men pierce it at every moment by their blasphemies and ingratitude. Do you at least try to console me and announce in my name that I promise to assist at the hour of death with the graces necessary for salvation all those who, on the first Saturday of five consecutive months, go to Confession and receive Holy Communion, recite the Rosary and keep me company for quarter of an hour while meditating on the mysteries of the Rosary with intention of making reparation to me."[101]

...A year passed, and on the fifteenth of December, 1926, the Child Jesus again appeared to Lucia, inquiring if she had spread this devotion of reparation to the Immaculate Heart of His Mother. She pointed out to Our Lord how her confessor had pointed out to her so many difficulties, and though the Mother Superior ardently desired to propagate the devotion, her confessor also warned her that she could do nothing by herself.

It is true that your superior alone can do nothing, but with My grace she can do all", Our Lord answered.[102]

Lucia reports Our Lady deserves and desires several things. Our Lady had asked long ago for the conversion of Russia. Lucia was given the task of asking for this to occur. It appears Our Lady continues to call for the conversion of Russia. Evidence of this can be found in the recent video of a fantastic, miraculous, and breathtaking display, where Jesus Christ calls out to the Russian people Himself, using an image of a Crucifix in the sky formed by the sun and clouds over Sharya, Russia.[103] Another video, called "Jesus apparition? or Hoax," provides more miraculous

101 Ibid., p 203

102 Ibid

103 Sign of the crucified Christ above Russia www.youtube.com /watch?V=m17_RKgq9+U March 8,2009

evidence of the event.[104] Jesus must be continuing to ask Russia to worship Him and consecrate Russia to the Immaculate Heart of Mary. It is a request that Lucia presented to Russian authorities herself at one stage of her journey after Fatima, to help spread the devotion to the Immaculate Heart of Mary as Our Lady requested of her.

Our Lady would like everyone to say one Rosary each day. She also asked a shrine be built at the location after the sixth apparition.

Lucia wrote her mother, asking her to start up a new devotion with others and practice it as an apostle in the crusade of reparation. She said that this devotion: . . . it consists only in what is written on the back of the enclosed little stamp.[105] Being virtually impossible to put everything on a little stamp, this remark has hidden content and is a hint to the presage of what the Immaculate Heart has in store for the world. The revelation and its true intended meaning must be found on a stamp somewhere.

It was Lucia's intention to spread a devotion to the Immaculate Heart of Mary in reparation for sinners around the world, but that was not all she had planned. She reported having further apparitions of Our Lady. What predictions she learned from them, she does not write about in the *Crusade*, but we do know there are some unfound words that have not yet been disclosed according to those statements she made in chapter 11, Francisco Leads the Way. Lucia wrote to the Bishop, adding the words of Our Lord: as long as the king of France did not listen to my request (when He asked St. Margaret Mary to obtain the consecration of France to the Sacred Heart by the king) the Holy Father will consecrate Russia to me, but it will be too late.[106] When the

---

104 You Tube, "Jesus apparition ? or Hoax" www.youtube.com /watch?V=m17_RKgq9+U March 8, 2009
105 de Marchi, *Mother of Christ Crusade*, Chapter XIV, p 204
106 Ibid, p 211

pope could not get the consecration of France to the Sacred Heart by the king, in 1938, Germany invaded Austria and prepared for WWII. World War II broke out in September 1939, six months after Pius XI died. The Great Northern Lights of 1938. . . This was the sign, Lucia said, that God used to make me understand that His Justice was ready to deal the blow upon the guilty nations.[107] WWII presents a strong argument in favor of consecration to the Immaculate Heart of Mary. Prevention is the best medicine. Know from this that God does give signs, thus establishing the devil in the smoke and the cross in the rubble of 9/11 are assuredly signs from God. Also, notice here in the *Crusade* text, the month "September" is cleverly or coincidentally set over Pius XI, creating the date September, 11.[108] It comes just prior to Lucia's discussion of the signs signaling WWII.

Lucia's other mission, with the divine aid of Our Lady, was to get another message to us other than those about WWII. The Marto children were taken to heaven. Most of Marto family came down with influenza also. What happened to them is a mystery.

So many people came to speak with Lucia, left alone down below, that she needed to get away too. Our Lady had already shown her in the Second and Third Apparitions that she wanted her to become a nun or Sister. To this end, and with the help of the Bishop of Leiria, she left for a convent school to continue her mission as she promised—and to spread a global devotion of the Immaculate Heart of Mary.

". . . On the last day of October of the same year (1942), the Bishops gathered at the Cathedral of Lisbon to join with the Holy Father in fulfilling the request of Our Lady. The pope at that time consecrated the Church and the world to her Immaculate Heart, including the people of Russia by these words: Give peace to the peoples

107 Ibid, p 212
108 Ibid, paragraph 2, p 211

separated from us by error or by schism and especially to the one who professes such singular devotion to thee and in whose homes an honored place was ever accorded thy venerable icon (today perhaps often hidden to await better days); bring them back into *one fold* of Christ under the one true Shepherd. Six weeks later, on the feast of the Immaculate Conception, in the presence of 40,000 people, the Holy Father repeated this consecration at St. Peters in Rome. This consecration was a decisive event in the history of the world; it marks the beginning of a new era, the Age of Mary." [109]

Lucia's report to the Holy Father that prompted this consecration of the world included, ". . . thy venerable icon. . . bring them back into one fold. . ." There is one holy icon in particular that appears to have been folded only in one place, vertically; the original image of Our Lady of Guadeloupe, chapter 21. Along this fold see if you notice the sequential numbers 911, presented vertically. The 9 is black, the 1's are white.

It is now requested we all consecrate ourselves personally, respecting the requests Our Lady confided to Lucia. The four essential elements to do this are grace, penance, the Rosary, and reparation. Saying the Rosary every day draws God's grace. Communions of Reparation personally are performed by praying as outlined by Our Lady, to Her Immaculate Heart on the First Saturday of each month, and to the Sacred Heart on the First Fridays of the month as brought forward by St. Margaret Mary. Lucia said the Lord desires this devotion be spread throughout the world.

Our Lord also said to Lucia, "The sacrifice required of every person is the fulfillment of his duties in life and the observance of My law. This is the penance I now seek and require."[110] The Lord has spoken.

---

109 Ibid., Chapter XIV, p 214
110 Ibid, p 215

There remains an important unanswered question in this statement. "Lucia informed her confessors, Her Mother Provincial, the Bishop of Leiria and the Reverend Joseph Galamba of this. The third part of the secret revealed to the three children at the Cova da Iria on July 13, 1917, has not yet been revealed. According to instructions from above, Lucia has written it down. It was sealed and by order of the Bishop of Leiria placed in his diocesan archives."[111] He may not have actually seen it before it was sealed. Learned at the same time, it could also be related to the vision of Hell and since still unknown, could be the presage and describe 9/11.

111 Ibid, p 209

Chapter 6

Punctuation and Misspellings Reveal Divine Inspiration

Mother of Christ Crusade contains multiple misspellings in the text, even after taking three and a half years to write it and Lucia checking it for accuracy having carefully verified every detail personally and labeling it as the Exact Truth.[112] There also remain the many important words of Our Lady as yet undisclosed, needing to be found. Lucia's misspellings may represent these unfound words. Many are listed and discussed later. There were things Our Lady predicted that have come true, such as World War II and the suffering of the pope, but these were written about in the passages. Lucia used curious punctuation and an extraordinary number of bullet points. The bullet points have significance for the Church, as they relate to the shooting of Blessed Pope John Paul the Great. Her use of them seems to be another question to be contemplated and answered.

The Presage of Pope John Paul II

It was mentioned by Our Lady that the pope would have to suffer a great deal for the sins of men. Pope John Paul II being shot was one of the presages told to the children at Fatima and was written about in *Mother of Christ Crusade*. The Holy Father was going to suffer greatly. Lucia knew this through the knowledge given her from Our Lady.

112 Ibid, inside the back cover

Everyone knows that Blessed Pope John Paul the Great survived the bullet wound. Having known he would be harmed with the knowledge provided by Lucia after the apparitions in Fatima, his decision afterward was to forgive the man who pulled the trigger—who may not have been entirely responsible for his action given as this was a divine presage—then to deal with the bullet he placed it in the crown of the Virgin Mary at the Shrine of Our Lady of the Rosary in Fatima. In doing so, he accomplished two things: acknowledging the presage of his suffering and drawing attention to "the point" he might be trying to convey—maybe meaning a "bullet point," to be exact, like those consistently used for punctuation in Sr. Maria Lucia's book *Mother of Christ Crusade.* It seems he was sending a message to look for "bullet points", hoping they be recognized in *Mother of Christ Crusade* in order for the discovery of the hidden message it holds yet to be found. He offered up painful sacrifice for the conversion of sinners. It seems that Our Lady had known Lucia would need to provide a directing clue to have someone discover her book, maybe even suggesting bullet points be used. If so, it would make the shooter another unconscious instrument of God, or in this case, of Our Lady.

Lucia's "bullet points" of punctuation have other interpretations suggested. They aren't the proper type of punctuation for her book, so they may well have an ulterior interpretation. She seems to be repeatedly saying, Do you get the point? Since "bullets" are kept in "clips" and "magazines" and "pill boxes", they could be a reference to sinful film clips and magazines that have to go, unwanted just because they are an embarrassment as well as sinful. Some are especially demeaning to the dignity of women, the predominant victims of sexual exploitation. Such material has the sociological impact, reducing the status of women to third-class citizens unworthy of being more than the object of lust. Such pornography promotes the rights of men to use women however they please.

It is certainly not the global norm, but its promotion by media is disturbing. It must be included as one of the sins of men. All of the harmful consequences pornography causes may be unknown, but it is easy to conclude that all forms are damaging to women and disruptive of marriage. The loss of women's social dignity results in their concluding that men are interested in nothing more than their own physical pleasure and are incapable of true love, thus contributing to a decline in a desire for marriage. More importantly, the law of free expression confirmed by the US Supreme Court is still an outrage to Our Lord no matter how the High Court rules. We are then being asked by God to refrain from participation individually.

The *Crusade* book is hard to make sense of at times. The desire to decipher it began because of one of the pictures with the large hand on Lucia's breast.[113] The *Crusade* was written *exactly* as Sister Lucia approved according to her memoirs. Our Lady said this mission of Lucia's was to be kept secret; she could not tell it to anyone. For this reason, it could only be passed on some other way if she planned to do it.

The Important Words Unknown Are the Misspelled Words in *Mother of Christ Crusade*

Why would there be so many misspelled words? In the opening paragraphs of chapter 11, Francisco Leads the Way, is where Lucia mentioned there were many important words that have not yet been found, but doing so would provide revelation. She also stated there is urgency in finding them, they have purpose. The assumptions and accusations presented after the definitions may sound preposterous and leading initially, but given here knowing there is profound evidence to defend them. Naturally, one can be moved to other conclusions making it necessary to keep an open mind.

113 Ibid., Chapter II, p 15

Some of these unfound words are those she deliberately misspelled. She used them to establish the theme and support a premise. It is the beginning of her leading us to what she wants us to learn and find. These unfound words are hidden from the reader, passed over as typos or publishing error. They are neither. The cumulative content of them is indeed revelation.

Taken individually the words have some meaning, but taken in sequence they tell a story and illuminate a portion of her message. Anyone who has had a Sister as a teacher in school would know they would not wish to misspell a word, so these must have been written deliberately. Recall that Our Lady told Lucia she must learn how to read and write. I am sure she did—including spelling properly.

Misspelled words naturally lead to a dictionary. To help understand more of what Lucia was talking about, each word was looked up, examining the variety of definitions provided. A publisher would make corrections for spelling errors therefore must have remained at her insistence. As spelled, these words do not exist; in these cases, the words adjacent to where their alphabetical position would be found were reviewed. These too could be important words, checked not knowing Lucia's method of disclosure. Since English was Lucia's second language, she could not be expected to include words in her seemingly simple story that are used rarely when speaking English or are not routinely used in print. She deliberately found some relatively rare words and included them in her innocent text to draw attention not to the words themselves, but rather to include those next to or near where the words are found in the dictionary.

Throughout the book, words are misspelled. The misspellings are not errors, and they will be shown to serve as continuing and supporting evidence of the book's intention to condemn the song "Only the Good Die Young" and legally stop its abuse of young Catholic virgins and Catholicism by public broadcast media groups who promote the song. It will be determined to be part of Our Lady's peace plan for everyone.

The three children of Fatima were virgins. During an apparition, Our Lady requested that more young women remain chaste and become nuns. Obviously, a predator pedophile being encouraged to rape specifically Catholic virgin minors while threatening death interferes with Our Lady's plan for the victim's future as a priest or nun. The section below has the more important "found" words to show their importance and to allow readers to speculate on her meaning. They confirm the interpretation and alternative narrative content regarding adulterous sex, war, rape, abortion, virgins, drinking, and drug abuse as sins outrageous to Our Lord. They even tend to criticize rock and roll music specifically for its part. The sins Lucia addressed on the second to last page, found under "An Emergency Plan," all need serious and immediate attention and correction. Lucia points out the language and intent of some rock and roll music—and the message in the lyrics of some songs that encourage sexual abuse of women, especially virgins.

In the case of "Only the Good Die Young," everything sacred to Catholics is abused, mocked, and demeaned, including the Rosary of Our Lady, the Virgin Mary, Virgin of virgins. The song is the benchmark of the antichrist at work in America. It is widely promoted by public broadcast media groups around the world, and purposefully denies Jesus and discredits his Church, bringing the images and signs from 9/11 to mind. This particular song broadcasted stands as a violation of the religious rights of Catholics safeguarded in the US Constitution and First Amendment. Abortion is also included as a target needing correction; it must be stopped now. The Supreme Court decision of Roe v. Wade is urged to be overturned—not at Lucia's request, but by that of Our Lady the Virgin Mary. We can not afford another 9/11.

These observations are mentioned now so that you may be aware to see the pattern Lucia creates using her misspellings. They merely suggest a deeper interpretation but the total number of relevant associations becomes more convincing of her purpose. She is sending a message and leading us to a conclusion, what ultimately that is exactly needs to be decided by everyone. Since some misspelled words are duplicated by Lucia, not knowing why, they are listed more than once.

List of Misspelled Words

The following are some of the misspellings found in the text of *Mother of Christ* Crusade and the definitions found for them along with the words adjacent.[114] Examine the definitions as they relate to 9/11.

Hopefully you too shall believe in Our Lady and Jesus Christ through Lucia's work.

In this example, "Later Ti Marto said to his wife, it is a feast day because of the Apparition." He discouraged her to go to the "Couva da Iria"[115]—not spelled *Cova*, as usual. The closest word found for Couva is *Couvades.* It is the practice of the husband of a woman in labor taking to his own bed as if he too were in labor. Pointing this out shows that both parents have a shared responsibility for the children and perhaps that divorce is condemned as against God's Will, due to the harm it causes to the family unit and it being against the proper raising of children. God is saying it is good, right, proper,

---

114 *Tormont Publications Inc., Webster's illustrated Encyclopedic Dictionary,* Tormont Publications Inc. 1990 edition. 338 St. Antoine St. East, Montreal, Canada, H2Y 1A3. 514-954-1441. ISBN 2-921171-32-5. *Webster's Seventh New Collegiate Dictionary,* G. and C. Merriam Company, Publishers, 1972 Edition

115 Ibid., Chapter IV, p 45

and best for husband and wife to remain together, for the sake of the children. They are in it together. Perhaps a little respect for women going through labor and delivery is in order. It makes sense. The central theme of chapter 2 is babies. Abortion is a non-issue, it's out of the question.

On page 17, chapter II of the *Crusade*, "Mrs. Marto, could read and in the evenings she would read and instruct not only her children in catechism, but the neighbor's children also. The book reads, she would read to them from the bible or other pious books and sedulously reminded them of their prayers." The closest word to *sedulously* in a dictionary is *seduce*! The paragraph ends with, "not a surprise Lucia could receive Communion at age 6 instead of 10 as the custom distated."[116] This has two meanings. First, Mrs. Marto was teaching catechism, but it was not just of a religious nature. She was also giving instructions in other subjects of this chapter, in this case, the facts of life, men, drinking, and seduction. This was purposeful in two ways; these topics prove that Catholic parents do give quite enough information about the ways of men to their children. See if you agree she is leading up to the song "Only the Good Die Young" ("OTGDY"), which claims the teachings of the Church don't give quite enough information to their young and about pedophiles and safety concerns about adults targeting children with threats if seduction is ineffective.

Maria Rosa, Mrs. Santos also wanted to be there at the Cova before the second apparition in case anyone tried to harm the children. She was not going to let anyone harm her Lucia or let her fall into the bad habit of lying.[117] All worried and excited, she decided to go to church first. Along the way, she met some "strangers", [Whether coincidentally or deliberately said *The Stranger* happens to be the

116 Ibid., Chapter II, p 17
117 De Marchi, *Mother of Christ Crusade*, Chapter IV, p 48

name of the CD by Billy Joel that "OTGDY" was released on in 1978], who she thought were going to the feast at the church. She told them they were going the wrong way. "That is not the way to Fatima." They said they just came from Fatima and were going to see the children who had seen Our Lady. "Where are you from?" she inquired. "From Carrascos," she answered. Does this refer to being harassed in a car by a man, as could be the situation that is in progress in the lyrics of "OTGDY"? You will see for yourselves later, referring to "OTGDY" is exactly what she means. "Where are the children?" they ask. "They are in Aljustrel but will soon be coming to the feast." In using the word *Aljustrel*, she infers everything presented in the *Crusade* is "all just relative"—a clue to seek an intended parallel meaning.

On page 23, Lucia would choose the pastureland she called the Cabe'co as a favorite place. The word *Cabe,co*, as she writes and spells it, including the comma, leads one to the word *cabby*—a taxi driver, possibly hinting at New York famous for its number of cabs. It had a "Gras-sy hill," and offered shade trees of "Olive, Pine and Holmoak," as well as "the Cave." *Gras-* and the *O,P,H,T*s of olive, pine and holmoak trees, translate as drawing attention to the use of marijuana and opiates, perhaps heroin, something Lucia couldn't know and not uncommon in New York City. Did the parallel events at the Cova have anything to do with the possibility she implies that drugs, sex, and rape are related? Since date rape has been linked to the unknown tricking with a dosage of drugs, taken together it could refer to sex, drugs, and rock and roll—all glamorized by media. Lucia could well be saying drug abuse is a sin and a major concern of Our Lord and Our Lady.

When Lucia, already at the feast at the church was asking her friends to come to the Cova da Iria with her there is this example. "Usually whenever Lu'cia (a spelling variation) suggested something to her friends, they concurred and went along with her. Altogether fourteen girls went with her." It sounds not unlike the current situation today, where girls have a fear of traveling alone, especially on foot, for reasons of safety. The threat of death is instilled in the minds of young listeners by broadcasting the song "OTGDY", giving more evidence broadcast music is what they heard when speaking with the transparent, invisible man of chapter I. Along the way to the Cova, Lucia's brother tried to stop them, and he offered a few pennies for them to not go, apparently to keep their companionship in some way. Does it beg this question to us, does this make any sense, her use of cents for its homonym to drive one to accept the Crusade has more than its innocent story? Do you understand the message, as Lucia hopes? Persuading a person to skip Mass or interfering with their religious duty is also a sin. For whatever the reason, Lucia did not directly say what needed to be said. What Our Lady told her to write was intended to be found, hidden not given.

In another example, a man asked his crippled son if he wished to go to the feast at church or to the Cova, and he chose the church. A woman came up with her crippled son and sat "dow." Is this in reference to the fall of the Dow Jones Industrial Average after 9/11 and a presage clue, one that could only be understood after 9/11?

"Others came from the church even though teased for wanting to go to the Cova to see if the events were true. Around eleven the children arrived. People asked if this was where Our Lady appeared. Yes, they said, she stood over the small holmoak tree, about three feet tall. Holmoaks are evergreen trees with prickly leaves like Christmas Holly." *Hollywood* and *Buddy Holly and the Crickets* could be the subject of this passage, but that is based on circumstantial evidence thus far.

If this interpretation is correct the presages and messages written into this little book must come directly from Our Lady because Lucia could not know these things herself ahead of time. They are all deemed part of an "Exact Truth." Lucia does use the misspelled words to prompt the use of a dictionary. The dictionary definitions of each word spelled properly, and the misspelled word supply clues and further details of her intended topic, that being presage as declared on the prefix page. The words looked up in a dictionary as misspelled seem to have additional significance since they do not fit. The following are more of the misspelled words, they're definition when spelled correctly and the words near where the "misspell" would be found along with their own definitions.[118] You may decide if these could be some unfound words to convey Our Lady's message.

I. The Angel

Suprised: surprised, means to attack unexpectedly, to capture by an unexpected attack, to take unawares, to strike with wonder and amazement because it was unexpected. By surprise is very much how the attacks on September 11, 2001, took place.

Supremely, or above all others or of the highest order. This may be a reference to Jesus, who reigns over both heaven and earth, or something else.

Supreme, suggests that Our Lady desires help from the Supreme Council of the Knights of Columbus. Further evidence indicates the Knights might somehow be involved in Our Lady's plan.

Supremo, a chief or leader having overall authority.

---

118 *Tormont Publications Inc., Webster's illustrated Encyclopedic Dictionary,* Tormont Publications Inc. 1990 edition. 338 St. Antoine St. East, Montreal, Canada, H2Y 1A3. 514-954-1441. ISBN 2-921171-32-5. *Webster's Seventh New Collegiate Dictionary,* G. and C. Merriam Company, Publishers, 1972 Edition

Climbled: climbed, to go upward with gradual progress, to slope upward, to raise oneself upward by grasping or clutching with the hands, to go upward upon or along a path to the top or over something.

Ascend, is a word routinely used to describe the ascent of aircraft. It is a clue to add *airliner* to a list of key words contributing to a conclusion 9/11 was one of Our Lady's secret presages hidden in the *Crusade*.

Climb-led, Lucia is trying to lead us somewhere. Lucia is providing a hint to help us find her new location, a place that may have a climb involved.

Climbed and bled, together as one word, suggests trauma, maybe from a sexual assault. Jacinta said to Francisco, when speaking about the events at the Cova, when the transparent man showed up, she and Lucia were mortified with fear at the possible outcome of the encounter. Jacinta said to Francisco, "We must not speak of these things," or tell about what happened at the Cova. An assault of course did not really happen at the Cova in Fatima but the fear factor instilled was real, real enough to stay silent about it, the same response one might expect from a victim of assault. This may seem to be reading into the texts meaning too far but supporting evidence will show it to be an intended inference of Lucia's when she included the message sent by the transparent man, in broadcast music.

II. The Children of Fatima

Sedulously: sedulously, means with diligence. Lucia, being a young Portuguese girl using English as a second language, could not have been expected to use a word so uncommon as compared to all other similar words available or those not used in common expression. She chose it carefully and deliberately, knowing closest to where sedulously would be found in the dictionary, is the words seduce, and seduction, it being one hidden message she intended to convey relating to OTGDY.

Of Mrs. Marto, she would read to them from the bible or other pious books and sedulously reminded them of their prayers.[119]

Seduce, is to persuade to disobedience or disloyalty; to lead astray; to entice into abandoning chastity. This is a reference to the lyrics of "OTGDY" that demean and dismiss the teachings of the Catholic Church and the dignity of women.

Sedition, is to go, or cause the incitement of resistance or insurrection against lawful authority. This easily relates to Jacinta's demand from Our Lady that governments must stop persecuting the Catholic Church. The children are only the messenger, not the source. Persecution of a particular religion is constitutionally unlawful in America. This defends the idea that the public broadcasting of the lyrics of "OTGDY" is illegal, while broadcasting it for 33years unchallenged, and indication of the power media has over justice to ignore it. We need not think she means to cause any more than a fair trial and the proper administration of law to protect the Catholic Church and all Christian's rights and sovereignty. She does seem to be encouraging the antichrist-like, to become Christians, perhaps even the entire nation, as Our Lady requested a chapel.

Distated: for Misstated**,** a lie, untruth; to mislead; to misunderstand the meaning or intention. This song lyric that "Catholic girls start much too late" having sex is a lie. Girls of other faiths don't necessarily start having sex at a young an age as the age of readiness for Confirmation as "OTGDY" claims only Catholic girls start much too late.

119 De Marchi, *Mother of Christ Crusade*, Chapter II, p 17

Lucia infers there is something not related to the religious Catechism being taught to the children by Mrs. Marto; her discussion with the children involved the ways of men in seducing women, especially when under the influence.

Distaste, dislike or aversion, distasted, is to feel repugnance , possibly for the song "OTGDY."

To offend, displease, harm emotionally.

Contemlpate: contemplate, to consider thoughtfully and thoroughly. This draws undivided attention to give the sentence special intention and attention. It suggests we contemplate the significance of every irregularity in the *Crusade*.

Conte, a short story of adventure.

Contemn, to view with contempt or despise.

Contemptuous, to act in spite of or advice to the opposite of what is generally considered right. A deliberate act against reason, the law, the common good, or the Catholic Church.

Olimpia: The letter "Y" is missing from the traditional spelling of the word Olympia when spoken. It raises the question of *why*? Why did 9/11 occur? Why is Mrs. Marto instructing the children in the ways of men, and why include it in the *Crusade*?

Chapter III. First Apparition

Clary: for clearly, fully understood or explained.

A clary, is a dirty sticky mess, their condition or a general remark about related topics. This is regarding the intended meaning of the fine print on pages 26 and 27 of chapter III. It is a different subject that Lucia includes as an outrage to God.

Whilly: drop the h and this could intend Willy or the common name Bill; and dropping the w, hilly, for sloping terrain.

Handes: this word's spelling draws attention to the shape of the Children's hands and fingers folded in prayer with Rosaries. The photo of the children with interlocking fingers is near the page that contained Mrs. Marto's catechism instruction in chapter II, not of religion catechism but of the ways of men that offend Our Lord: seduction, rape, and drinking. The hand on Lucia's breast also comes to mind.

Theis: belief in the existence of one God viewed as the creative source of man and the world, Who transcends all others yet is present in the world.

IV. Second Apparition

Easilly: easily, with ease, not difficult.

Easel, a frame for supporting an artist's painting. Lucia is painting a picture.

Ea-silly, he's silly. "OTGDY" is no laughing matter.

V. "Thrid" Apparition

Thrid: In the *Crusade* book itself, this chapter heading was deliberately misspelled, written as Thrid instead of Third. The r and i of "third" are transposed. third, of three, as thrice, a threefold quantity or degree. Trinity, as in the Holy Trinity of the Father, the Son and the Holy Spirit.

Thrift, wise economic management, as opposed to its opposite.

Thriftless, is lacking value or usefulness.

Bud: the early stages of a flower to be, such as a rose bud, is a misspelling placed instead of *but*.

Greate: the Great Divide, the US Continental Divide is used in the *Crusade* and refers to location;

Grate, is important later in the story, helping to pinpoint a location where a wooden grate is found.

Kiling: killing something is suggested, maybe Christians or Catholic virgin children, as are threatened in the song "OTGDY."

Kill-deer, a plaintive, penetrating cry. A scream for example.

VI. Sacrifices and Sufferings

Wend: is to proceed along one's way in travel.

Stifling: stifle, to kill by preventing respiration.

Stiff, is difficult to bend, hard, rigid. It is the condition of Rigor Mortis or stiffness after death; a dead body. Also, meaning to cheat, to suffocate or extinguish a flame, a life, or belief.

Plaqued: plaque, is to patch or repair by an MD; an ornamental brooch. A commemorative or identifying inscribed tablet.

Plague, an illness or death that becomes an epidemic or a widespread or significant amount; scourge of trouble.

Play Cued, like film strips or audio tape, referring to film and music.

Stirp: a lineage of a common ancestor, a large group of animals all from the same family.

Stirrup, like for riding a horse or the positioning legs for examination.

Stir-up, a commotion.

Strip-, A reasonable assumption, she means to admonish or find guilt in the practice of stripping oneself of clothing for the pleasure of others, or stripping someone in the act of rape.

VII. Fourth Apparition

Meagre: "me agree"; or meager education, unwise; little, sometimes made as a reference to children; or a small amount.

Permonition: a premonition, is a feeling or prediction, an omen. Drawing attention to the word *presage* on the title page of *Mother of Christ Crusade* that says the book contains presage of what the Immaculate Heart has prepared for the world; or otherwise, divine predictions. This is very important because it brings forward wonder and the need to discover what presages Our Lady has for the world contained in the *Mother of Christ Crusade*—what they might be and when they will occur. The first question is where are they to be found? They are not written in the text of the book other than the predictions of World War II, harm to the pope and a vision of Hell.

Permanent, fixed and changed indefinitely.

The Hoax

Travelled: when divided: travel-led, means going somewhere, leading along a path, or pointing in a direction to a given destination. The suggestion is that somehow within *Mother of Christ Crusade* there is a trail to be found. One might suspect it leads to Jesus Christ and the Immaculate Heart of Mary. That much is true, but she has another destination to point out, one she repeatedly hints about.

Holly Will: is for Holy Will of God, could refer to Buddy Holly or the prickly leaves of Holly combined with the names Will or Bill. Hollywood comes to mind. Sounds like *Holy Hill*, a place.

Know: know, to understand facts having learned truth. Used in place of the word "known," it is a statement that Lucia is telling us that she knows the truth relative to the magistrate kidnapping the three children and the secret yet to be known, thus far undisclosed and undiscovered.

Diferent: different, not the same as another, contrary, meaning another, or to be different or dissimilar in nature, contrary to norm.

Missing an *f,* could be some other *F,* or the F word.

Diethylstilbestrol, a teratogenic morning sickness drug that when taken in early pregnancy leads to severe birth defects.

Regedor: in Portugal, 1836–1976, a position similar to mayor; a public servant representing the central government from each parish. The county administrator, below them is the parish level, together guaranteeing the proper application of the laws and administrative regulations and exercising of police authority. This could be offered as a model to follow, administrating law in harmony with religious authority. Administering law so as to defend and respect in civil law, and the Law of God. Obedience to His law was a direct message from Jesus to Lucia.

Regardless, acting heedlessly and unmindfully, in spite of the consequences. Not accepting the advice of wisdom. Abortion continues, in spite of the Church's insistence it is against the Will of God. Shines light on the current administration of law disrespecting God's law when it comes to legalized abortion and pornography or affronts to conscious religious liberty. The song "OTGDY" was written and broadcast in spite of knowing it is unlawful to abuse and attempt to extinguish another religion or threaten with death the children of another specific religion. Lucia is specifically speaking of endangering Catholic virgins for the purpose of having sex with a minor.

Regent, one who rules or reigns and is of the ruling party, those in control; authority or principle of a governmental body, civil or private. The protection of the religious liberty of religious institutions to maintain one faith, they're own, without interference.

Regicide, is killing a king or assisting in his death. A plausible reference to the antichrist whose actions attempt to kill the history of and members of those following Christ the King.

Regime, is a regular pattern of occurrence or action, a mode of rule or management, a form of government or administration, often associated with dictatorships.

Furtively: furtive, is done by stealth, and means sly or stolen, covert. Lucia could be alluding to the description of the events leading up to and taking place on September 11, 2001. It is a reminder of the children's abduction by the powerful magistrate.

Fury, intense anger, an outburst of uncontrolled violent rage, one prone to fits of rage. The terrorist act of 9/11 created fury. The act of murdering is fury.

Secretly, done in private. Some secrets are kept because they are best left unsaid or its disclosure would endanger something or someone. Other secrets are kept because they are deceitful, illegal, or intentionally and purposefully harmful to others. Acts carried out with a secret ulterior motive or agenda.

Covertly, is done in secret, such as a covert attack like 9/11. It is, at times, the framework of corruption when done only in self-interest. It is also what Our Lady told the children to do with the new information they received during the apparitions in Fatima and how Lucia treated the secrets she learned at her convent, the knowledge imparted to her by Our Lady and Jesus Christ. This could be an identifying hint of the events that occurred on 9/11.

Prower: power, is force of current or impact. Strength, legal or physical, is generally comparative—one greater than another. To overpower the weaker is to be more powerful; to move by force; act from a position of control, the influence or authority over others, such as a sovereign state; the ability to act or produce an effect by force, using legal, official authority. Used to describe intensity of magnification, scope, or comprehensiveness, these are increases of power. The examination of each detail Lucia presents is critical to understanding her directives when reading *Mother of Christ Crusade*. In this instance, the inclusion of *magnification* is a magnificent tie in. When recognizing the importance of the coroner examining Jacinta's exhumed body, and his use of a magnifying glass for close inspection. It is not shown in some copies of *Mother of Christ Crusade*. Together they imply taking a careful and much closer look at her book using magnification.

Prow, is to project a part of anything forward, such as a body part or ski.

Prowl, is to roam through stealthily or stalk prey with predatory intent. Such is often the technique of pedophiles.

Prowle, regarded especially as a man who prowls at night, intent on theft or sexual gratification.

The Ordeal

Boilng: boiling, to bring to a boiling point; to generate bubbles of vapor when heated; to become agitated; to be moved, excited, or stirred up; to burst forth. Boiling was used in the case of the three children abducted by the magistrate. They were threatened with death by being boiled in oil if they did not reveal their secret. It was the magistrate who was boiling over, losing his temper and reason in threatening the children with death. The song lyrics of "Only the Good Die Young" makes a similar threat, young virgin Catholic children are threatened with death if they refuse the sexual advance of the one that follows the lyrics of the song.

A boil, is a painful swelling of the skin and subcutaneous tissue, with a hard pus-filled center, caused by bacterial infection. Often thought of as a sore spot or persistent irritation, it is definitely applicable to "OTGDY" and its plague on Catholic minds and the bodies of children.

To boil-over, is to be greatly excited with rage or passion, to seethe with intent. Catholics and Our Lord and Our Lady are seething according to Lucia. It also applies to Americans after 9/11.

Parentes: parents, of children.

Perenteral, is located outside the alimentary canal, when taken into the body other than through the digestive tract. Medically administered, it is by intravenous or intramuscular injection.

Parents, most often the violators when children are molested, fairly often it is at the hand of someone they know, even a parent.

Acept: accept, to receive with consent, to be able or designed to take or hold, to give admittance or approval to, to endure without protest, to receive as true, to take the responsibility of, to assume an obligation to pay, to receive officially (a legislative report). This is reference to the parents above who must accept children as not only a precious gift but also accept the responsibility to care for them. Lucia's instructions to marry and raise a family as responsible adults would, accepting children and not having an abortion.

Acephalous, is headless or lacking a clearly defined head. Sometimes it is meant to mean having no leader, thoughtless or reckless action. Lucia references this for purposes of location, given the caption on page 2, "The Head."

Acerate, having the form of or a tip like that of a needle. Lucia means to say, "Do you get the point?" A pointed tip. This refers to the picture on page 185 of the tip on the tower in the picture of Jacinta's exhumation.

Sunday the Nineteenth of August

old: instead of "told," foretold or predicted; to tell or explain. Lucia explained Our Lady as she appeared at a different holmoak, a little larger than the one in the Cova da Iria. Why? The reason is she is referencing different statues.

Old, aged, outdated, foretold or predicted, or already in existence for a long time.

VIII. Fifth Apparition

Sugested: suggest, to offer for consideration or action with purpose. To make evident indirectly, intimate, imply.

To serve as, or provide a motive for, or to prompt others to serve.

Insinuate, refers to a covert expression of something, usually unpleasant in a manner that suggests underhandedness.

To impart thoughts, or ideas indirectly to another person. In this context, it usually refers to a process whereby something is called to mind by a listener or viewer as a result of association of ideas or train of thought. Deduced as a logical consequence of, or implied secondary. The thoughts imparted to fear death by the song "OTGDY."

Cudgel: not misspelled, but a relatively uncommon word for a short, heavy club.

To cudgel, is to beat as with a cudgel. Dual intent for Lucia could be, to "cudgel one's brains," beat your brains out or thinking very hard to solve a problem, or to beat someone or something literally or figuratively.

Cuddy or Cuddie, is a donkey or blockhead. Stubborn.

Cuddle, is to hold close for warmth and affection.

Antecipating: anticipating, to give advanced thought or discussion, to foresee and deal with in advance, to speak or write in knowledge or expectation of a later matter. This is nearly the definition of prophesy itself.

Anthemion, a luminous white halo-like area occasionally seen in the sky opposite the sun, maybe a rainbow.

Procceded: proceed, to come forth from a source; to continue after pause or interruption; to go on in an ordered regulated way; to begin and carry on an action, process, or movement; to be in the process of a task being accomplished.

Procambium, is a layer of meristematic tissue from which vascular tissue is formed.

Pro-carp, is a specialized female reproductive organ in certain algae.

IX. Sixth Apparition

Some misspells are repeated.

Withchraft: with a craft or vehicle, in a car or transportation; to withdraw, to take back or away; to recall and retract; to retreat or retire. To remove the center of one's concern away from external activity and become detached.

Witchcraft, the magic of witches, and spells; intercourse with the devil.

Witch Hazel, an alcoholic solution of distillate of the bark of Witch hazel (H. virginiana).

Travelled: to travel, to move from a current location to a new destination.

Travel-led, leading to a different destination. This is a hint that Lucia is leading us to her new destination. In *Mother of Christ Crusade* it states that Lucia moved to a convent school in Tuy, Spain; however, she also states that her new destination was to be kept secret, on orders of the bishop. She said she would never tell, thereby eliminating Tuy, Spain, as the destination she promised not to tell. She must have had the apparitions in a different location.

Higways: highway, a public roadway with limited access for exit and entry.

In combination with the above, it is traveling far away in a car. The sequence above creates thoughts of abduction, such as what occurred to the children in Fatima when they were tricked into a carriage by the magistrate.

Highjack, as in an aircraft, a hint at the presage of 9/11.

Suplication: supplication, to make humble, to make an earnest and humble request of God through prayer, perhaps asking for help with a matter. A plea for help or mercy.

Supine, position is lying on the back or having the face upward, or having the palm upward. Indisposed to act or object, lethargic, passive, over powered. Considering the children's mortification after the angels visit when the message scared them.

Striped Cotton: describing the dresses of Lucia and Jacinta that have vertical or horizontal stripes in chapter I, p 15, created by an alternating pattern of light and dark or variance of color.

Stripe, a strike or blow with a rod or lash. The dress of Jacinta in the photo on page 15, was ripped through her and her dress is very enlightening and suggestive. If this was to be associated with playing jacks in chapter I, Jack the ripper could be her point.

Stripling, an adolescent boy.

Stripper, one who strips.

Hyms: hymns, religious songs of praise to God or the Lord Jesus. A homonym with *him*, for *men* is implied. This identifies both music and men, matching the above, suggesting his acts are a concern.

Maezina: no such word.

Maecenas, is a patron of art and literature.

Maestro, is a master in any art, especially a composer, conductor, or a teacher of music. A musician or one trained in music, as the leader of a band or orchestra or the director of a band or orchestra. This identifies a musician.

Mad-wart, the "gold of pleasure."

Mae, means *more* and sounds like the month of May.

X. Sixth Apparition (Continued)

Impelled: impel, to urge into action through moral pressure or necessity, compel; constrain; to drive forward against resistance, like stabbing. Abduction and rape. How many Catholic virgins have met this death at the hands of a pedophile? Providing the motivation or the release of conscious restraint of homicidal pedophiles, leads them to believe there is no consequence for their action, inferring the victims are unworthy of life if they resist sexual advancement. Media broadcasting this type of song publically to the world encourages all pedophiles. It might be thought a crime against humanity.

Impel-led, Lucia is impelling the reader to take action by exerting moral pressure, using what she presents in *Mother of Christ Crusade* to accomplish a goal.

Marvelled: to marvel, at something that creates intense surprise, or astonishing causing wonder.

Andrew Marvell, an English metaphysical poet. His frequently satirical work includes "To His Coy Mistress" and "The Definition of Love."

Marvel-led, Lucia suggests that where she is leading us is a marvelous and astonishing place. She led people to Fatima for the sixth apparition and possibly another place with the *Crusade.*

Martyr, one who sacrifices their life for their faith and convictions. Those who defend Christ at the cost of their lives are often made Saints. Young virgins who are killed resisting wrongful sexual advance by virtue of faith might be thought of as martyrs. They would also fall under the category of Holy Innocence.

Mira: mirage, is an optical phenomenon produced by heated air, an illusion unattainable under normal circumstances. Lucia describes what we might encounter, leading us to miraculous imagery of some nature like a mirage.

Miracle, an event that appears unexplainable by the laws of nature so is held to be supernatural in origin or an act of God.

UT: Utah, UT, Universal Time; indicating time or a timeline. The Catholic Church is said to be the Universal Church. The hour of the sun is now one o'clock instead of twelve noon in this chapter, an indication of daylight savings time.

int: intact, uncastrated, or physically virginal

"Demon"-stration: descriptive of the devil in the smoke at the WTC on September 11, 2001. In this case it could mean a repulsive demonic behavior.

Demonstration of a demon, as was seen in the smoke of 9/11.

Smilling: Smiling, is the act of creating an opening between the lips, in a position often revealing the teeth, appearing pleasant or agreeable.

Smirch, to soil stain or dirty with grime. To dishonor or defame.

Smirk, to smile in a self-conscious, knowing, self-satisfied manner.

XI. Francisco Leads the Way

Anoter: a note.

Anorthrosite, a plutonic rock, supporting that rock and roll was a part of the accurate interpretation of the text.

Another, distinctly different from the first.

Eucarist: for Eucharist, the Body and Blood, Soul and Divinity of Jesus Christ. The Sacrament of Holy Communion in the Catholic Church.

Euchre, a card game in which each player is dealt five cards and the player making trump is required to take at least three tricks.

Helpel: help, to provide a service or aid that is of use to someone. It rhymes with *scalpel.*

Helpless, the young, the weak, lacking power or strength, unable to manage by oneself.

Excanged: exchanged, *switched.* This becomes very important in discovering where Lucia went after leaving Portugal.

Excalibur, King Arthur's sword he removed from the stone. *Mother of Christ Crusade* will be the Excalibur sword.

Excavate, to make a cavity or hole in, to dig up, to remove by digging or scraping out.

Wearring: wearing, draws attention to the children's clothing. It is also customary that when getting married or becoming a priest or nun, you wear a ring and "marry" into the Church. This is also found where the woman named Mary is mentioned, the Mary that took the children to non-capitalized "heaven".

Wear- ring, wear a wedding ring. The traditional gesture or prelude to marriage and beginning a family is to give and receive a ring. A warring down.

Strenght: strength, the power to overcome. ht., the transposed letters *h and t,* are the abbreviation for height or altitude.

Streetwalker, is a prostitute who solicits sex on the street. The song implies Catholic virgins are nothing but prostitutes.

XII. Jacinta's Death

Abscess: infection, Jacinta had *purulent pleurisy* and a hole in her chest the size of a fist.

Strenght: repeated for its importance, the power to resist a force or attack, on legal or moral grounds, or the ability to prevent being overcome by another. It is the ht. she means to repeat over and over in the *Crusade*.

Streetwalker, a prostitute who solicits in the street.

Remonstrated: demonstrated, to explain and prove giving multiple points of evidence, to show evidence by popular support. It is another reference to demon that is applied to 9/11.

Remonstrance, is a speech or gesture of protest, opposition, reproof; especially a formal statement of public grievances.

Demonstration, disputing fairness thereof, or a call to fight. This suggests "OTGDY" be challenged as illegal as an affront to Catholicism, its religious liberty and for encouraging the endangerment of Catholic children.

Revolsion: revulsion, repulsive, offensive, distasteful.

Revoke, to void or annul by recalling, withdrawing, or reversing; cancel.

To revoke a decree,

Revelation, the Book of Revelation, new realization, striking evidence of proof. The *Crusade* will be shown to hold the proof necessary to enact Our Lady's peace plan.

Revolution, to overcome resistance. Legally forbidding the song to be played or sung in public would protect religious liberty from the abuse of free speech. It is a measure that would prevent the abuse of all faiths by antichrist media and violent Muslim extremists and lead to a more peaceful world. One might consider abuse of faith a hate crime.

Lenght: length, a specific measurement of distance or time, at last, finally.

Ht, the end letters *ht* again, is the abbreviation for *height*, and relates to Lucia's mention of "The Head"[120] at an altitude of sixty feet and a clue to the travel-led the direction she is leading us; length, a measurement of distance.

Great lengths, or going to extreme measures to accomplish a goal.

120 Ibid., Chapter I, p 2

L'Enfant, Pierre Charles: a US architect chosen by George Washington to survey and plan Washington, DC. He proposed radial boulevards and a system of parks that, because of their high cost and his imprudence, were not completed at that time. In the 1890s his plan was reconsidered and recommended for the cities central region. Draws attention to everything in Washington, DC, including the Pentagon, the city itself, the Supreme Court, the Congress, and the White House.

This reflects on the need for the Supreme Court to be involved in overturning Roe v. Wade and the call for the defense of religious liberty when religion is abused by free speech as is the case in the song "OTGDY."

ATT: American Telephone and Telegraph Company, modern day communications include wireless and the Internet. Lucia was able to talk to her parent's long distance after she left Portugal, though she said that in 1917 she had not yet used a phone. Perhaps this is a reference to media especially considering the latest internet capabilities of phones currently in use.

Generou-hearted man: Generous, a noble forbearing effort to give liberally of a great enough proportion to satisfy a need.

generic, not protected by trademark or copyright.

Calling, Probably meaning a calling for the religious.

XIII. The Chapel at the Cova da Iria

Anthorities: authorities, the law or its official representatives. The implication is to bring the *Crusade* information to the attention of the authorities. Men and the powers of law in justice. Draws attention to the authorities disrupting the procession and the activity of the church in Fatima.

Anther, a male part of a flower holding pollen, usually borne on a stalk. Lucia uses it to say the procession for the completion of the shrine was disrupted by the government officials, an act violating Catholic religious liberty.

Founds: for found, to find something. You must search to find something. Things to find somewhere; things found, like the important words, these misspellings, and the closer definitions and associations in a dictionary. We are looking for something like Lucia's true intention in writing *Mother of Christ Crusade*. Here Lucia insists there is something to find or find out.

Praved: prayed, to worship God in prayer or recitation of the Rosary.

Paved, to level the ground and resurface. A road, probably not a paved road in Portugal in 1917, but referring to somewhere else at a later date when road paving became more prevalent.

There is a location Lucia mentions that has a chapel, a convent, a retreat house, a hospital, and a shrine that dominate the area.

XIV. Lucia's Mission

Daughther: daughter, a female child when considered by her parents, a female descendant, reference to a girl or women of a younger age when addressed by a priest. Young Catholic girls are the daughters of Catholic men and women. When you attack Catholic virgins, you attack the entire Catholic community and the Church, not to mention the head of the Church, Jesus Christ. Jesus may be one suggestion of what was meant by "The Head" on page 2.

Them: for then, them, onto the parish inferring all three children went somewhere, Lucia had to stay below, at a lower height, because Our Lady wanted her too.

Maria das Dores: the name given Lucia by the bishop to allow her to remain anonymous.

Dorcas, a woman of the New Testament.

Dorbeetle, Beatles that fly with a buzzing sound.

Dorhawk, a common European nightjar, like nighthawk; any American goat-suckers; related to the whippoorwill; one who goes out late at night.

The Sisters of Dorothy, Lucia's new Order.

The remaining secret of July 13 has yet to be disclosed; it might be the catastrophe of 9/11. You get the idea of the general topics of the text and the sins. There is seduction, moral teaching, immorality, physical positions, restraint, threats, attack, anger, highjack, faith, religion, government, flower's as children, hints at 9/11 and of some other location, a mirage and more. As a whole, what exactly is the message Lucia is hiding yet trying to communicate?

CHAPTER 7

Hyphenated Words Are Clues to the Cause of 9/11

Lucia leads us to her misspellings as the important unfound words. There is no telling where they are or how to know them if they were found. Research is the logical choice for discovery of the words meant to be included to draw a conclusion, they could be anywhere so all possibilities were checked. She may have provided more information and hidden meaning with the definitions found by researching halves of words hyphenated in the *Crusade.* The names of people and places are also telling. The results when deciphered shine more light on Lucia's secret message. It is not known if they are actually some of the unfound words at all. If they are, so detailed and clever was she in dropping hints and clues, even these hyphenated words provide further testimony of 9/11 as one of the mystery presages and her sheds light on Our Lady's cause. Lucia's word selection peppers the mind with hints and directives. The definitions of the words warn against the evil in pornography and abortion, child abduction, and rape. Lucia is slowly leading us into understanding. She wants action, and she deliberately provokes the guilty with truth. Taken together, the important unfound words whatever those may be, should project cause and effect and a call to unity of all Christian faith denominations, one giving honor to the Immaculate Heart of Mary and the Sacred Heart of Jesus. Interpret the meaning of these definitions and the suggestions offered of hyphenated terms and names of people and places, in some cases full words, and decide if they could be some other unfound words and arrive at conclusions of your own. [121]

1. Portu-: a port or harbor for ships or aircraft.
2. -gal: a woman or girl.
3. Serra-: having notched tooth-like projections. Having an edge or margin notched with tooth-like projections. Similar to a serrated knife.
4. De-: reversal or undoing as in decrease or destroy. Removal. Degradation, or reduction as in declass. Disparagement; for example, to Demean. De: used in personal names originally to show place of origin.
5. Aire-: air-drops of supplies or troops by parachute from aircraft. This word is repeated as a location. Airliners were involved in 9/11.
6. Lu-, Lu'cia, L'ucia, Lucia, Lucy: all different ways Lucia's name is typed in the *Crusade*.
7. -CIA: Central Intelligence Agency; ucia, you the reader as CIA, a hint to investigate things further.
8. Remain-: to continue in a specified condition, quality, or place. To stay or be left over after removal or departure, loss or destruction of others. To be left as still to be dealt with. Remains; a corpse.
9. -ed: a movement or doctrine promoting unity among the Christian churches. A movement or doctrine promoting worldwide unity of religions through greater cooperation and improved understanding. It is a call for all to become

---

121 *Tormont Publications Inc., Webster's illustrated Encyclopedic Dictionary,* Tormont Publications Inc. 1990 edition. 338 St. Antoine St. East, Montreal, Canada, H2Y 1A3. 514-954-1441. ISBN 2-921171-32-5.
Webster's Seventh New Collegiate Dictionary, G. and C. Merriam Company, Publishers, 1972 Edition

Christians and members of the Catholic Church, as were the children. Edacious: gluttonous or voracious, as in appetite to eat.

10. Compan-: companions, friends, or playmates.
11. -ions: negative or positive charged particles or molecules. A key clue, indicating the images contained in the *Crusade* can be viewed as negative film or positive film.
12. Playmates: a companion in play or recreation. Playboy playmates.
13. Cabe'co: cabby, taxi driver. New York, New York, is famous for its taxi cabs.
14. Oak, pine, and holmoak: the initials together, *OPH*s, sounds like opiates or drugs.
15. Casa-: Casablanca. Arabic, Dar-al-Bei-da, a seaport on the Atlantic coast of Morocco, founded by the Portuguese in sixteenth century, taken by the French in 1907.
16. Velha-: verlger, free-swimming larva, like an embryo. Sounds like vail, to doff as a token of respect or submission. Old French, avaler, to lower; from vulgar Latin, advallar, to the valley. Vain: not yielding the desired outcome, showing undue preoccupation with or pride in one's appearance and accomplishments, conceited, without due respect or piety; profanely, used chiefly in "take the name of God in vain."
17. Des-: descant, a melody or counterpoint sung above the plain song of the music. A superimposed counterpoint to a hymn, tune, or other simple melody. A discourse or comment on a theme.
18. Im-: imp, the devil; intramuscular injection.
19. -pression: press, *a stamp*, a thrusting force to mark or emboss; to smooth; to exert pressure on; to force into service; to oppress: to try applying pressure to persuade; pressing, urgent, and important; press, newspapers, and magazines.

20. -cribed, -cribe: a baby's bed, a cradle; a building or bin or box to store grain. A rack or trough for fodder, a manger.
21. Ap-: author's proof. Lucia has entered proof in the *Crusade* that by using the cues provided you can find her hidden message. You will see she refers to the song "Only the Good Die Young." Everything available in Lucia's *Crusade* stands as proof that Christ is King and of the divinity of Our Lady the Virgin of virgins, Immaculate Mary. Associated Press, an international press agency. Apothecary or drug store; additional premium. Aoudad; a wild sheep, also called a "Barbery" sheep. Advanced placement.
22. -proached: probabilism is the doctrine that probability is a sufficient basis for belief and action, since certainty in knowledge is unobtainable. In the Roman Catholic Church, a principle that if there is doubt as to the moral rectitude of an action, the opinion that favors liberty may be followed provided it is theologically probable, even though the contrary may be equally or even more probable. Here, Lucia expresses that in her knowledge, "OTGDY" is responsible for many acts of violence against Catholic children. The *Crusade* contains theological proof and with it demands for religious liberty from the song "OTGDY."
23. Invit-: invite, to welcome with approval.
24. -ing: suffix, the present participle of verbs, such as in going, seeing, hoping; participial adjectives, such as striking or gripping.
25. Sud-: sudd, floating vegetable masses that at times obstruct the White Nile. Sudden, unexpected, precipitous. Sudden death, sudden instant death or one game to break a tie. Sue, seek justice or right from a person in a court of law, to bring action against. A call from Our Lady to do so.

26. -denly: denizen, a foreigner permitted certain rights or privileges of citizenship. An animal or plant naturalized in a region to which it is not indigenous.
27. Con-: contrary; ex-convict; to cheat or swindle. Meaning they need to be convicted for their crime. Lucia seems to also be requesting conversion to Catholicism.
28. -version: a description or narrative or account related from a specific or subjective viewpoint of the narrator, "Her version differed from his." A translation of the entire Bible or part of it. Manipulation of the fetus in the uterus to bring it into a more favorable position for delivery. An adaptation of a work of art or literature into another medium or style, Lamb's version of Shakespeare, the film version of the novel. Deflection of an organ, such as the uterus, from its normal position. This presumed to be a call to reverse Roe v. Wade in the US Supreme Court as stated at the end of the *Crusade*.
29. Suf-: to suffer, feel pain; sue, take action against in a court of law, such as the Supreme Court.
30. -ferings: feria, day of the week on which no feast is observed. Ferine, untamed; feral, wild animal.
31. -ques: quest, the act or an instance of seeking or pursuing something, a search. In medieval romance, an expedition undertaken by a knight in order to perform some described feat. Archaic, a jury of inquest.
32. -tions: tiny, extremely small. Here alluding to tiny images.
33. Pre-: preliminary or preparatory work or activity. The blood of menstruation.
34. –sence: send, to cause to be conveyed to a destination by an intermediary. To express for conveyance. To cause or order to go; to direct to go on a mission or errand. To enable or arrange for someone to go. To direct or order to depart; dismissal. To direct or order to go or be taken. To cause to go

or move in a certain direction. To put or drive into some state or condition; the news sent him into a rage. To transport with delight. To dispatch a messenger or message.

35. The angel: the angel at the end of chapter 1 asking the girls to sacrifice themselves for the cause the angel was speaking of. They were mortified at the idea. Getting pregnant and having children is inferred in his message.
36. Pregueira-: pregnant, carrying a developing fetus.
37. Lapa-: the front region or area of a seated person; lap dance; pregnant.
38. Go-: to leave, move, act, change; to charge.
39. -ing: suffix, the present participle of verbs, such as in going, seeing, hoping; participial adjectives, such as striking or gripping.
40. Aljustrel-: alive, having life, or in existence. Life beginning at conception; "Al just rel" equaling "All just relative."
41. Casaba-: a winter melon, maybe describing the shape to come. Pregnant.
42. Contemplat-: contemplate, to think hard about. The closest word found is contempt, open disrespect, or willful disobedience, such as contempt of authority, violating rights of Catholics against the law as written in the First Amendment to the US Constitution. Contemn; to view with contempt, despise.
43. Oasis-: fertile green area in a desert resulting from the presence of water. Highlighting the prophecy of Isaiah, "out of the desert comes ..." 9/11.
44. Attrac-: attractant, a substance that attracts, especially a chemical produced by insects and other animals to attract opposite sex members of the same species. Pheromone, causing sexual arousal.
45. -tive: Tiu; the god of war and the sky. Titus; an epistle in the New Testament addressed to Saint Paul and addressed

to Titus, his disciple. Titular bishop; a bishop who normally acts as an auxiliary bishop in a diocese and is appointed to a diocese in a remote part of the world. Titular; pertaining to, or having the nature of or constituting a title. Of or designating one of the ancient churches near Rome from which a cardinal takes his title.

46. Prin-: prince, son of the king or monarch. The Prince of Peace is Jesus Christ.
47. -ciples: cypher, a mathematical symbol denoting absence of quantity; zero. Any Arabic numeral or figure; a number. The Arabic system of numerical notation. A person or thing without significance or value; a nonentity. Any system of secret writing in which units of the text of regular length, usually letters, are arbitrarily transposed or substituted according to a predetermined key. The key to such a system. The continuous sounding of a pipe in an organ resulting from mechanical failure. There is definitely a parallel message in the *Crusade.*
48. Fear-: reverence for God; an unpleasant, strong emotion created by impending danger; reason for alarm.
49. -less: fearless Francisco filled the holes in the rocks with ewe's milk to feed the snakes. Of lower rank or importance. Reference to pornography and sexual exploitation of women to feed the desire of the antichrist by legally obstructing the teaching of the Holy Church.
50. Remark-: to make an observation or make a comment; worthy of notice; extraordinary; striking; uncommon.
51. -able: having the ability to do something; physically or mentally strong enough.
52. -partitions: parity, equality as in status or value. Equivalence, correspondence, or resemblance.
53. Hail Mary: a prayer to the Virgin Mary, Mother of Jesus. "Hail Mary, full of grace. Our Lord is with thee. Blessed art

thou among women, and blessed is the fruit of thy womb, Jesus. Holy Mary, Mother of God, pray for us sinners, now and at the hour of our death. Amen."

54. Se-: symbol for the element selenium. SE; southeast. SDR; special drawing rights, extended to the artist or first to interpret meaning. Sea; a body of fresh water, such as the Sea of Galilee.
55. Fran-: franchise; freedom, immunity, or free of burden given to a person or group; a constitutional or statutory right; a privileged group; Franciscan, the First Order of St. Francis of Assisi to preach, act as missionary, and provide for charity.
56. -cisco: a white fish. this paragraph from page 39 is important: "When noon came, they felt the same joy then as they did when the angel came, except when the angel came, they felt a sort of annihilation before his presence; whereas, with our Lady, they received strength and courage. Instead of bodily exhaustion, we felt a certain physical strength. Lucia described her reaction. In place of annihilation before the Divine Presence, we felt exultation and joy; in place of difficulty speaking we felt a certain communicative enthusiasm." This may hint at a future presage or an event having already taken place in San Francisco.
57. An-: one that relates to American or Bostonian. Ana; curious or interesting information about a person or place. This might be relevant to location.
58. -tonio: tonight.
59. Erything-: erythrism, unusual redness or pigmentation as of hair or plumage.
60. Ved-: Vector sum, a vector that is the result of two other vectors as determined by the parallelogram rule. Intersecting vectors give relative position or location; used in aviation.
61. Ches-: Chesapeake Bay, an inlet 200 miles long, on the eastern seaboard of Virginia and Maryland.

62. Sim-: simar, a loose robe for women; Sim-chas-; Torah, a Jewish holiday on the twenty-third of Tishri at the end of the annual reading of the Torah.
63. -pleminded: plenary, complete in all aspects or essentials. Plenary indulgence, Roman Catholic, an indulgence that remits the full temporal punishment incurred by a sinner. The opportunity for divine forgiveness; plenipotent, powerful, or stronger than.
64. Carreira-: Carrel, Alexis; a French surgeon known for his developments for suturing small blood vessels, who earned Nobel Prize in Medicine in 1912. Carriage, a four-wheeled passenger vehicle; a baby carriage.
65. Capelinha-: Cape York Peninsula, northern part of Queensland. "In the chapel, ha!"
66. –proaching: used again for emphasis, probabilism in philosophy; the doctrine that probability is sufficient basis for belief and action, since certainty is unobtainable in knowledge. In the Roman Catholic Church, the principle that when there is doubt as to the moral rectitude of an action, the opinion that favors liberty may be followed provided that it is theologically probable, even though the contrary may be equally or even more probable. Lucia could be hinting about the probability that the song "OTGDY" has caused child abductions and rapes, even deaths, of young teens. We do know she received what she learned from Our Lady.

All totaled there over five hundred hyphenated words in *Mother of Christ Crusade*. Many are repeated to highlight a specific topic. The definitions for each word contain key words that are hints but also serve as important supporting evidence in establishing the topics Lucia addresses in the *Crusade* such as the presage of 9/11.

CHAPTER 8

Lucia's record of apparitions as the Prophecy of 9/11

The "Thrid" Apparition

First, the word third is misspelled in the chapter V heading, as "thrid", it serves as a clue. During the Third Apparition in Fatima, the children were shown visions of Hell. Lucia's description of this apparition is easily applied to the World Trade Center towers as they burned and collapsed to the ground. Lucia said she "saw as if into a sea of fire, and immersed in that fire were devils and souls with human form, as if they were transparent black or bronze embers floating in the fire and swayed by the flames that issued from them along with clouds of smoke falling upon every side just like the falling of sparks in great fires, without weight or equilibrium, amidst wailing and cries of pain and despair that horrified and shook us with terror. We could tell the devils by their horrible and nauseous figures of baleful and unknown animals, but transparent as the black coals in the fire."[122]

Our Lady explained "You have seen Hell, where the souls of poor sinners go. To save them, God wants to establish throughout the world the devotion to Her Immaculate Heart."[123]

---

122 De Marchi, *Mother of Christ Crusade*, Chapter V, p 65-66
123 Ibid.

Consider this apparition a prophetic description of what took place during the WTC attacks and the many images seen in the billowing smoke of devils and demons, which are still available; there is no shortage of them online.

The World Trade Center site would be a wonderful place for us to build a cathedral to honor the Immaculate Heart of Mary. The Lord God seems to insist on it. Our Lady said, In fact, "if people will do what I tell you, many souls will be saved, and there will be peace. The war is going to end. But if they do not stop offending God, another and worse war will break out in the reign of Pius XI. When you see a night illuminated by an unknown light, know that this is a great sign that God gives you, that he is going to punish the world for its crimes by means of war, terrorism, hunger, and persecution of the Church and of the Holy Father." Our Lady's presages began with WWII. 9/11 is very much a possibility as one of them, with others unknown yet to occur awaiting fulfillment. It depends on our action plan, if people will do what she tells us. This is enough said about this clever nuns "text message" to us in the *Crusade* predicting 9/11. There is something seriously wrong, wrong enough that God intervened to voice His outrage. Jesus Christ has proved Himself Lord of all. America is being called to protect Him from those who persecute Him and His Church. The message for us in 9/11 is Jesus has in fact risen and lives. Those who are antichrist abuse and persecute the Catholic Church as if Jesus is powerless and Christianity is a false religion, unworthy of the protection guaranteed to all faiths by the US Constitution and First Amendment.

The Sixth Apparition as the Presage of 9/11

This is how the Sixth Apparition becomes the presage of 9/11.

Chapter 9 is "continued" through chapter 10, to chapter 11, as if chapter 10 did not exist. Chapter 10 is unnecessarily inserted. There is no topic break in the story to warrant a separate chapter 10. If chapter number 10 is crossed out, chapter 9 and chapter 11 come back to back and provide the date "9/11." The date 2001 is not as simple to find when reading the text until you know the secret.

One of the Lisbon newspapers Sr. Lucy named in her book as having reported the miracle of the Sixth Apparition was *O Dia*. The acronym *DIA* could miraculously identify the main airport in Denver, the Denver International Airport. DIA airport was not even conceived of when the *Crusade* was written. When considering DIA stands for an airport, naturally aircraft come to mind—a good match to presage September 11, 2001. During the apparition of Mary, the sun looked like "a silver disc" dancing in the sky and an areola or nipple, Sr. Lucy reports. This description is very similar to the frontal view of an aircraft turbine engine fan and center cap. The center axis has a raised silver cap analogous to a nipple or areola of a breast or mammary gland. When a turbine fan is spinning, it becomes a silver disc. When placed on an aircraft, the silver disc dances in the sky. Sister Lucy further states that the pilgrimage of believers and observers were wet during the apparition but became totally dry after the apparition. It was raining ash and paper during the 9/11 attacks; when it was over, people's clothes were dry.

This may all seem to be a reach, none the less, it was the use of these analogs of given content that led to the discovery of more information and the parallel meaning. The *Mother of Christ Crusade* states on the prefix page that it contains presages from Our Lady, and there is no reason to dismiss 9/11 as not being one of them. It is a piece of Lucia's puzzle to prove the divinity of Our Lady. She would accomplish her goal if she could pass on to the world, the presage of 9/11. Predicting 9/11 would be miraculous, like predicting the Sixth Apparition in Fatima—where and when it would take place—would convince most anyone of the divinity of Our Lady and the sacred nature of Her Immaculate Heart. Lucia accomplished her mission once in 1917, and aims to do more, even after her death.

Chapter 9

Special Images and Drawings

The definition of the prefix *"Se-"* of a hyphenated word, and the peculiarities of the pictures, prompted the need a take a closer examination of the images.

"Se" - is a chemical symbol representing the element selenium. SE is short for southeast. The acronym SDR is the abbreviation for "special drawing rights." These are the rights extended to the artist or someone who was first to interpret meaning. *Sea* is a body of fresh water, such as the Sea of Galilee.

Author's proof, rights attributed to the artist is another hint to examine the pictures for clues.

What does Lucia mean by "special drawings"? The dictionary meanings suggest to us the images, pictures, or drawings in the *Crusade* have religious content, this by virtue of having the Sea of Galilee as one of the alternative definitions. The hyphenated words are open to further interpretation, but the point is "they're special".

The peculiarities of some pictures and the subject content within them serve as hints at what is hidden. What is seen with the naked eye is not always what it appears. Lucia provided clues to the techniques necessary to find her hidden messages. Page 205, chapter XIV of the *Crusade* contains Lucia's drawing of the "apparitions of December 10, 1925." In it, a white arrow points directly to her eye. It is a hint to examine the image very carefully for more details and look where she is looking. You will find 911. Directly above her head the word VIRGIN is spelled out. It is easy to miss them reading the Crusade. This subtle method allowed Lucia to slip the secret contents past the Catholic Church authorities and get *Mother of Christ Crusade* printed and distributed, before anyone found out what it actually contained, the messages from Our Lady Lucia had sworn never to "tell". This way she cleverly gets the secrets out without ever telling a soul.

Patience, time, and excellent lighting—both bright and dim—are required. You will also need a good magnifying glass and a larger, stronger lens of some type. When you begin to truly see the picture, you will understand and be amazed. Examine each picture in great detail, the light areas and dark areas have hidden content, small informative images and those all important undisclosed words Lucia referred to in the end of the second paragraph of chapter XI. These are just the beginning of the revelation you gain when knowing her secrets. Keep in mind as you examine the *Crusade* that the text does not outright state any presages or provide any predictions, so they must be hidden and need finding. Many of the presages can be found by noticing the subtle, delicate changes in the multiple shades of gray.

What drew immediate attention to her special images in the *Crusade* and led to examining them in such detail, was the image[124] with the larger-than-life hand on Lucia's breast. The hand is strangely large—as if it belonged to a man. It is not the sized hand appropriate for Mrs. Santos, seen in the same but full sized picture found in chapter X.[125] It is another sign showing that the sexual abuse and molestation of

124 De Marchi, *Mother of Christ Crusade*, Chapter II, p 15
125 Ibid., Chapter X, p 143

children, the worst form of child abuse, is part of Lucia's motivation for writing the *Crusade* from her memoirs. Finding the reason for the large hand led to further discoveries.

On page 3, chapter I, in the photo of the three Fatima Children, there is an [what can be considered an evil claw-shaped hand] on the waist of Jacinta. The hand on Jacinta's left hip in the image is connected to her arm as if were her own, but the hands claw shape, begs for and explanation, and must have a story itself. This popular photo of the three children is one of the official signature photos for the Fatima apparitions and published worldwide. It might be a sign of abduction, a prelude to rape or sexual assault, and a visual representation of the children being tricked into the magistrate's carriage and abducted. The scenario is not far removed from the epidemic going on these days in America, of children being tricked into automobiles by predators, then raped, and then murdered—an act promoted in the lyrics of "Only the Good Die Young", if a Catholic virgin resists a sexual assault. In the upper image on page 12, there lying on the ground at the end of the street, appears to be an airliners cockpit with dark windows. Using magnification, you can read the word Joel (in white letters), beginning just above the roof of the airliner cockpit. The direct association to "OTGDY" and the book of Joel is self explanatory. Billy Joel, the book of Joel and the downed cockpit of an airliner are connected. Look at the faint images in the white stone walls of the building to see the faces of men and women. In the white area, left of the far left window of the house, a man is chasing a small child. These words and images were *stamped* onto the pages everywhere including the white margins of the pages. The stamps either emboss or smooth to a shine the words and images.

Turn to page 100, to the image of the shrine at Valinhos. Look in the upper right-hand corner. The light gray area is a wasp nest or beehive, partially covered by tree leaves. At its lower tip, you can see the opening and tiny light gray bees swarming around it. Having seen the cockpit on the ground at the end of the street on page 12 and now recognizing there are bees drawn into this image leads one to think about those hidden presages. What do you think it means? There has to be presage entries somewhere. Intentionally, they are not made obvious when simply reading the *Crusade*. Closely inspecting each of the images in the book is one way the presages are found.

In the image containing the statuary setting of the children with the angel,[126] look to the right of the angel's elbow, to see the face of a man. Look below the face of that man and see a different man with a headdress of some sort. If he is an Arab, does that validate the attackers were "the unconscious instrument of God," as the Isaiah prophecy says? Directly above Jacinta's statuary head, about three quarters of an inch into the woods, you can see a smiling witch. Many other faces can be seen in the woods using magnification. All of the drawings in the *Crusade* have these faces and other small images to decipher. Included are decidedly pornographic depictions of men and women, and men attacking both women and children. Pornography, freedom of expression and God's Will are clearly at odds; restricting pornography or eliminating it needs to occur.

In the Image chapter VI, Sacrifices and Sufferings, is the picture of the Church of St. Anthony in Fatima. It has a special inclusion, 911. Examine the bell tower, on either side of the cracked bell, in the stone, two darker vertical lines or 1's can be seen in a darker shade of grey. To the left of the tower a 9 can be seen, in the form of a bubble number, an angel, 2" tall is to its left. This is only the tip of the iceberg. "911", the emergency call and date of the WTC and

126 De Marchi, Chapter I, p 6

Pentagon attack is entered throughout the *Crusade* in the photos. Once you begin seeing them you can find them easier. It was written this way to hide her secret from casual scrutiny, she could not tell the secret, but as it turns out, there was no objection to writing it down! Remember how Our Lady said Francisco had to pray the Rosary in order to see Our Lady in the first Apparition? It might come in handy for your search. It may even be necessary for some, Lucia and Our Lady's way of spreading a devotion to Her Immaculate Heart and the Rosary.

To confirm this 9/11 message was part of Lucia's mission, on the second page of chapter XIV Lucia's Mission, the photo of "The great esplanade before the Fatima Basilica...", the vertical tower to the left is her conceptualization of the WTC towers, the flash in the middle is the point of impact. Look closely to the left in the black to see 2001 and more 911's.

On page 185, chapter XII, there is a picture of coroner Rev. Dr. Luis Fisher examining Jacinta's exhumed body on September 12, 1935. In some issues, he is using a magnifying glass similar to Sherlock Holmes. You can see in the top center what could be Lucia's drawing of one of the WTC towers as she understood it would look before it was built, complete with a broadcasting antennae on top. Adjacent, to the right you can see two tall narrow towers. With magnification, examine the building at its base; there is a house, or rather, the remains of perhaps the other WTC tower after its collapse. Notice the date of the examination is one day after September 11, when indeed the trade center towers would be reduced to rubble and lying on the ground. Glancing at the face of Jacinta, doesn't the way her hair sticks out like horns in this picture look familiar? It may be Lucia's effort to represent what the devil in the smoke might look like when it appears on 9/11. Strangely, the tower also looks like a syringe and hypodermic needle. There is a reason for it to resemble both. This picture holds many presages. Included in it is a profile of John Lennon singing. He is looking right from the left side of the page, with his chin resting on Jacinta's head. His head is one and one-half inches tall. A virtual song list of some of his works are illustrated in the picture. Look closely at where the antennae or needle is pointing. It ends in someone's eye. The point: could realistically be imagined as "John Lennon will be shot", not hoped for, just presage. This also helps to identify New York, New York, as the place, since that is where he lived.

Take a close look with a magnifying glass at the magistrate's house, found on the opposite side of the preface page. On the right corner of the roof of the house, there appears to be a priest. These presages, having originated from Our Lady, are beneficial to the priesthood. This photo could be presage of what I expect is becoming past history, that is, the suing of the Church for past offenses against children. Its location in the book can mean several things. Most important is that Our Lady holds priests close to Her Heart, though they are not perfect. Needless to say, concerning priests, things haven't changed for years in some respects. The Church has been continually under secular attack. The religious freedom once assured for all is now being oppressed more strongly. Media continues to bash the Church and religion, and there are suspect claims made against priests for profit.

In another example that suggests sin, after Francisco learned from Lucia that 'Our Lady promised that he would go to heaven, bursting with joy, he folded his *handes* in front of his breast and exclaimed aloud, "Oh MY Lady, I will say as many Rosaries you want."' "handes"[127], and . . . in Senhor Marto's words, "the whole affair," draws attention. The misspelling of the word *hands*, tells us exactly

127 De Marchi, *Mother of Christ Crusade*, Chapter III, p 33

what to look at, and the subject in Lucia's story of Fatima. Looking closely with magnification at the images that show the children's hands confirms all innuendo about the topic involving child abuse and ends speculation about whether or not Lucia's manuscript has an alternative meaning. Check the fingers of the children on pages 3, 15, and 16. All three of the children have their fingers looking like penises. The large hand on Lucia's breast in the photo page 15, of chapter II, is too unusually large not to be a clue to this alternate interpretation. The white horizontal line found beneath Lucia's feet of the same photo is made to be the mouth of a predator alligator or crocodile, headed at a small child on the ground between Francisco's feet. The children's odd shaped fingers begin to gain more meaning.

Use magnification, up to twenty times power, keeping in mind a parallel, non-factual, interpretation that the children were verbally sexually assaulted or worse by the invisible man at the Cova da Iria by music. The revelations offered in these images were one of the first clear indications that the innocent story of the *Crusade* was only a superficial cover for Lucia's important work of documenting a causal relationship with the sometimes catastrophic predictions given her from Our Lady and the sins responsible.

On the right side of page 12, there is an image of a person standing in what could be a shower or dressing area behind a transparent curtain, the folds of which create two white vertical lines. Looking just left of the curtain, in the dark area you can see the 9 of what then becomes 911. The 2001 is vertical; the circle of the 9 is part of 2001. Two things came to mind, prison bars and 9/11. Knowing this and examining the clothing worn by the person behind the curtain could be the clue to their real life identity related to 911. Examine the walls with higher and higher magnification to see other figures. Who could be the man behind the curtain? Ring a bell?

On page 13, determine see what clothes the woman standing in the front yard is wearing. She appears topless. Check the picture again and notice there is a little man standing next to her and looking up. Check the right wall of the veranda, and see the man with his head in the medieval stock. It explains the misspelling of down as "dow." The stock is low, low to the ground in the rocks! Is it a hint at something, like a stock market crash for example? There was a big one after 9/11, therefore it was presaged. Who might be locked up in the "stock"? It could be a lot of people. They were used in colonial American times for physical punishment and public humiliation, mockery and ridicule. There is a name written just below the stock in the darker area. The presentation is in both white and black, colors reminiscent of the pastor's words "sometimes white and sometimes black." Letters of the many words hidden in the pictures are printed this way. It may be best to confirm yourselves the name Lucia wrote.

Page 194 of chapter XIV,[128] when looked at vertically, contains a picture that is a relative likeness of one of the twin towers being hit by the airliner. Held up to the light, it becomes clearer. The white specks look like the shower of papers that rained from the sky. You can see Lucia's depiction of the "devil in the smoke" above the white flash mark, his face profile in white. A black **2** is left of him, a **Y** is right of him.

The caption on page 198[129] reads, "American boys at Fatima walk the pilgrim's penitential path on their knees." Why Americans, anyone could have been pictured. It would identify America as the location of 911 and penance.

---

128 De Marchi, *Mother of Christ Crusade*, Chapter XIV
129 Ibid, p 210

Jump to page 210, to the image of the basilica at Fatima. Here Lucia gives a clue where to look when she writes, "Beneath the nearby oak tree ..." Examine the tiny, finely-drawn image of a tower with an *X* on it, which can be seen beneath the oak tree as she directed. It appears there are two, the one with the *X* looks especially like the Sears (Willis) Tower in Chicago. Remember how the children were referred to as "Seers." Is there a message here—a prediction or presage? "Seer" means prophet. Did Lucia use it to prophesize something about the Sears Tower in Chicago? One could speculate without further evidence that the Sears Tower was the actual intended target of flight 93, the flight that passengers retook control of with the battle cry, "Let's roll." One could extrapolate and say the meaning of the *X* makes it one planned target.

Higher magnification yields an entirely new dimension and set of images, arguably of miraculous nature. Focusing on the darker areas in each image in excellent light, first identify a small image and then focus even closer. The images transform into new, deeper images of people and things, body parts become visible. Examine the pages for tiny images of faces, people, and more identification of everything involved with 9/11. It is all rather miraculous. Most pages are stamped with images in the open margins. When letters in print have dots in center of the O's or e's, it is an indication something is there to be found. Odd ink marks also mean something more can be seen nearby. The word discipline, bottom of page 14 has a mark that points to the first four letters of the word, disc. She refers to records and CD's. They are lined up on the bottom of the picture on page 15 under magnification, with the crocodile. There are several other ink marks on this same page. Look between the lines and see tiny stamped images. Perhaps on every page of the Crusade you will find, OTGDY, Joel, 911, WTC, 2001 and more.

Chapter 10

Trans-illuminate the Images to Yield a Visual Revelation

Twice Lucia wrote "When you see a 'night' illuminated by an unknown light, know that Our Lord is going to punish the world for its sins." In the image the "Shrine at Valinhos," found on page 100, beneath Our Lady's hand is a "knight" standing guard—standing "honor guard" to be more exact. Our Lady's hand points to the knight, recognizable as a Fourth Degree Knight of Columbus in honor guard regalia. The knight can easily be made out with the naked eye tilting the picture to reflect the light. A lady stands next to him on the left. There is a tall candle on his head; its flame is the face of Our Lady. With this clue found, the presage of 9/11, the whole story of the terror attacks on September 11, 2001, and the condemnation of the song "OTGDY" are brought to life, using the information the picture tells. If the stamped words are not enough there is much more to prove Lucia and Our Lady's message. The method to find more evidence of Lucia's secret message is backlighting. By holding the picture pages or even pages with only text up to a candle or "knight-light," many new images are revealed. Backlighting used in combination with magnification yields written words, phrases, letters, dates, the faces and hands of analog clocks and more, in picture pages. Even pages with print only, have names, dates, initials and images in them when trans-illuminated, some black and some are white. Use dim light and look through the pages to view these.

Consider these other clues. One hand of the pope is white, the other black, in the picture of the pope and Lucia on page 191, the last page of chapter XIII. There are images on them. This page has presage within it. The pastor's expression again, "sometimes it is white and sometimes it is black"[130], together with the use backlighting are priceless clues. It is how to "read into" *Mother of Christ Crusade* to discover the theme, topic and purpose of Lucia's talented and clever work of miraculous art, and the presages the Immaculate Heart of Mary has prepared for the world.

In a pitch-dark room, with a candle or night-light to backlight, look through the pictures to see different images and key words revealed. Looking through typed pages reveals letters large and small, initials, words, and new images of their own. It takes time and patience. Rocking the images slightly in the light and viewing them from different angles will show you what is to be found, more of the unfound words. The content is more than the work of a super nun—it has to be miraculous. This is another reason to believe the predictions were made by Our Lady, the images, and their multi-dimensional content must have required divine intersession.

Examine the initials, words, and new images. Not only do they foretell 9/11, but they provide other presages as well. The very method in which some of the presages are entered—created by the blank spaces between the typed letters when looking through the printed and picture pages—is a miracle in itself.

These words can all be seen looking through several picture pages: JOEL, SCREEM, VIRGIN, OTGDY, RAPE, 911, WTC, NYC, USA, 2001, MMI, KC, NYNY and Columbus. Letters are not always capitalized, words like Joel, Virgin and rape sometimes are and sometimes

130 De Marchi, *Mother of Christ Crusade*, Chapter IV, p 42

not. The initials TV, CD, and more are visible and reference media. The picture of the small chapel that was blown up in Fatima found on the last page of chapter XIII, has a movie screen, the left square white wall represents film and TV programs. Look to see what is playing on it, the letters or numbers and people with magnification.

By rotating the individual picture pages, other images may appear. Tilting the pictures back and forth in front of the dim light will make the secret message come into view. You will see images of past rock and rollers in days of old. They are not exempt from Lucia's firm criticism. The pictures are repetitive about Joel though. The piano, virgin girls, scream, 9/11, WTC, NYC, and USA all appear together on the same page. The text pages are also very important. They, too, when tilted in the dim light reveal more words, initials, and presage—sometimes black and sometimes white.

You will see the twin towers, including some images of when the airliners impacted. You may find the analog clocks on which you can make out the time. Most prevalent are all things relating to 9/11 and the song "OTGDY." Images of a man at the piano (some with a microphone shaped like a beer bottle), a virgin or the word VIRGIN nearby or a *V* coming from the mouth of the musician, and a jar on the piano are all visible using this technique. There is no need to say more. It is Lucia Santos that entered these images, and as she stated, with the help of Our Lady and at Her direction. What Lucia has written is not shear speculation. It is part of Lucia's mission. The mission she started continues and with Our Lady's help, will come to completion soon. All the hidden information is part of Our Lady's peace plan, 911 expressing the urgency, the emergency call for your help in Our Lady's cause to gain world peace, is requested. It was only the call for help. Further consequences seem to be part of the *Crusade*.

What of the Liberty Bell, cracked, as can be found in the church towers in some photos using magnification? Our Catholic religious liberty is being cracked apart, it being oppressed by the song "OTGDY." "OTGDY" is Our Lady's way to bring the issue of Catholic religious liberty forward. Lucia documented Our Lady's disgust with the song. There are indications that the song is directly responsible for the deaths of many Catholic virgins. The lyrics and in public broadcasts continued use of them are implicated in the abduction, rape, and murder of Catholic virgins and other little children. Through media, Joel and OTGDY has encouraged promiscuity and pedophilia and though impossible to prove, successfully produced nothing short of Catholic genocide. The word probablism addresses this point. Read it on page 8, in the image drawing of "The Well." Illuminating the page reveals small caskets with crosses on them lined up across the bottom and the word RAPE is found written in white letters in the trees, top center in white with back-lighting. The layout of the caskets with white crosses on them seen at the bottom of the page could also be boxcars full of dead, not just caskets in a row. Lucia included this because Our Lady told her too, so improbable are they Our Lady may have contributed to them. Turn the page counter-clockwise and see faces made with the tree branches, looking right with regular light, no magnification. Enough said.

On page 208, chapter XIV, there is a drawing representing the premise that Catholic religious liberty is under attack by those who are actively antichrist. In the upper right corner of the page is a face looking right. By turning the page counterclockwise 90 degrees, the arm of the crucifix becomes one of the WTC towers. Smoke is seen above it. If the image is inverted, a small Liberty Bell will be seen in the lower left corner. The bell in the tower on page 78 also has a crack in it. Both pages have the numbers 911.

Chapter 11

The "Secret Proper"

Lucia held the predictions of 9/11 sacred and secret. She documented them but did not make them known to anyone; for whatever reason, they were left to be discovered. They were written from her memoirs and dated December 8, 1941, the day after the Pearl Harbor attack, long after she left Fatima. The children's inclination to keep the presages they learned secret was an act of faith; they felt God moved them too keep the secret. Their inclination to silence was confirmed by Our Lady, when on July 13, she told them they needed to not tell about what they had seen. But Lucia did write about it in the *Crusade*. What Lucia said was this "is know as" the "Secret proper."[131] It was only after many years that the public was allowed to "know" any of the substance of this secret. Even to this date, there are important words of Our Lady yet undisclosed. The secret proper is 9/11. Twice Lucia spelled the word *known* as *know*. That was to indicate that there is a way to know the secret proper and find the undisclosed words. The presage of Our Lady about 9/11 is in the *Crusade*. Could anyone have found the prediction of 9/11 and prevented it from happening? It is doubtful. The events of 9/11 had to occur; Our Lady presaged it. The vision of Hell in the second apparition, by the way Lucia describes it, was there to predict what the catastrophe of 9/11 would look like.

131 Ibid, Chapter XI, p 145

For clarification, Our Lady's presaged events do not necessarily represent an Act of God like the Book of Isaiah describes; rather, they simply foretell something like this will happen and fulfill the presage. The devil in the smoke and the cross of Jesus (the Cross of Hope) is beyond a doubt the work of God's hand. His message to us and the whole world has been received loud and clear. The antichrist, those harming the reputation of Jesus and the Virgin Mary, were not deterred by 9/11 at all. Things have gotten worse, much worse. Public broadcast media has defiantly continued to air the anti-Catholic song "Only the Good Die Young" as if they have special privileges, arrogantly seeing themselves as better than Catholics, even above the declaration written in the First Amendment to the US Constitution, immune to lawful prosecution even if knowingly guilty. They remain steadfast in believing they somehow have been endowed with special rights not afforded to Christians that allows them to demean, denigrate, and mock everything Catholics hold sacred. The teachings of Jesus Christ, the Gospels, and the Catholic Church have been made out to be a third-rate religion. Now the Holy Church as Jacinta called it, is being legislated against and federal funds withheld for non-compliance with anti-Catholic doctrine. Proper marriage has been redefined by legislators. Electing representatives is the peoples business, vote.

Catastrophes matching the same descriptions provided by the prophets Isaiah and Joel could happen again. They can be used more than once—and will, if those antichrist refuse to stop bashing, and undermining the Catholic Church. If the sins repeat, so can catastrophic prophecy.

Other Presage

You have to decide yourselves the true messages written into the *Crusade*, its real divine purpose. Some, but not all presages are presented using caricatures and faint lettering. Lucia gives many presages, some are found in chronological order, with the year given as well. An example to contemplate is the possible presage of the life, wedding, death and music of John Lennon on page 185, in the photo of the exhumation of Jacinta. You can also find the word *imagine* in the *Crusade*, the title of a song which suggests if there were no religion practiced by anyone, it may bring peace. Having no religion, would not be something Our Lord would desire. What happened to Natalie Wood might be answered. Examine the wooden planks (of the basket) above the head of the middle child on page 31, chapter III. Rotate the image upside down and the little one will be headed for the water. To see the yacht in the upper right-hand corner, use trans-illumination. It is in white, a crude replica, but there. The girl's dresses on page 15, of chapter II, look like mop tops. The images seen are not always meaning something negative; some are neutral, and some give praise for events taking place before they even happened. Using the techniques Lucia hid in clues will reveal many more events that had not taken place when the Crusade was written. They are the presages of the Immaculate Heart of Mary. The point isn't entirely the content of these found images; the significance and importance is Our Lady predicted them, proving her divinity, making it strictly forbidden for musicians and media to mock and discredit her. Doing so is an insult to Our Lady, Our Lord God, the Catholic Church and all its members, and a violation of Catholic religious liberty. As the insults continue, the consequences for doing it may yet to be seen.

Chapter 12

Lucia's Journey

Mother of Christ Crusade ends with Francisco and Jacinta Marto going to heaven and Lucia fulfilling her promise to Our Lady by leaving Portugal to attend a convent school, the secret place never disclosed in the book.

When you finish the *Crusade* book, you can't help but wonder where she went. Such a holy young lady would be an inspiration; why would she just disappear without telling the world what she knew of Our Lady and Our Lord. It would help humanity to have everyone believe in God the Father, His Son Jesus Christ, and the Holy Spirit. It would straighten out a lot of religious controversy and answer many questions if Lucia shared her experience with world, and revealed "the secret message" everyone tried so hard to find out. Now, she has.

Between the oversized hand on Lucia's breast on page 15 and her disappearance to an unknown destination, the ending was completely shocking yet thoroughly intriguing. These are what began this journey. There had to be clues. It was Jesus who illuminated the way to know many answers.

Figure 2

The faces of Spain and Portugal[132]

It was because of Lucia's experiences, she was mobbed continually, that she needed to leave and go to some undisclosed location. She tells of at least one but another she promised never to tell.

Lucia's mission was to start a devotion to the Immaculate Heart of the Virgin Mary and fulfill the request of Our Lady for her to accept a vocation in the Sisterhood. She did both. She made plans with the help of the bishop, who arranged for her to attend an unnamed convent school. At the bishop's instruction, she left Fatima within five days, promising never speak about her time in Fatima, to protect her identity. She snuck out of Fatima in the cover of night. Originally,

132 CIA Maps.gov

she went to a convent school at Villa de Porto on June 17, 1921, then Tuy, Spain, but these we were told, so it wasn't her final secret destination. The question remains: where did she go?

After leaving Fatima, Lucia de Jesus dos Santos soon was admitted into the Sisters of Dorothy at the Convent of Miracles. Therefore, she did indeed go to a convent school and become a nun. On the contents page, her name became Sister Maria Lucia of the Immaculate Heart. It seems becoming a Sister endows one with extraordinary powers of perception and more.

You can read and reread her book to answer the question of where she finally ended up. The place she vowed not to tell of still remains an open question. There must have been a purpose for this secrecy: she could do the work of Our Lady without anyone knowing what she was doing. Now knowing what secrets are held by the *Crusade* one might expect the secret location to reveal additional presage and worth searching out, by necessity requiring she leave clues to find it. Indeed, Lucia had hidden clues to the location of her convent school. The path she took is mapped out from Fatima, Portugal, right to the convent school, through a host of identifying hints allowing the reader to narrow it down. The early and biggest clues came from examining the *Mother of Christ Crusade* preface page. The *Crusade* carries no copyright, a deliberate omission necessary to allow the discoverer of its secret contents to reveal them and help spread the devotion to the Immaculate Heart of Mary and continue Our Lady's peace plan.

The acknowledgments on the very first page of the *Mother of Christ Crusade* book read this way:

> MOTHER OF CHRIST CRUSADE
>
> *Nihil Ostat:*

Francis J. Maloney, S. T. L., *Censor Librorum*

Imprimatur:

+ James E. Cassidy, *Bishop of Fall River*

August 11, 1947

Fall River, Mass.

By

John De Marchi. I. M. C.

DECLARATION

In conformity with the decree of Pope Urban VIII, we do not wish to anticipate the judgment of the Church in our appraisal of the characters and occurrences spoken of herein. We submit wholeheartedly to the infallible wisdom and judgment of Holy Mother Church.

What has happened in Portugal, proclaims the miracle. It is the presage of what the Immaculate Heart has prepared for the world.

His Eminence,

The Cardinal Patriarch of Lisbon

Looking up the names from this page and the city of Fall River, Massachusetts, might provide some clues. The results were amazing.

Nihil Ostat: means “no objection.”

Censor Librorum: reviews texts for doctrinal accuracy concerning the Catholic faith.

Imprimatur:

James E. Cassidy, Bishop of Fall River Mass.

Take a look at this revealing image of Fall River, Massachusetts. It is miraculous—incredible for its simple existence. How would a young lady from Portugal know this image even existed to leave it as a clue? A search of Fall River on Wikipedia, Map Quest and free Mass. State documents came up with this same image for Fall River, Massachusetts.

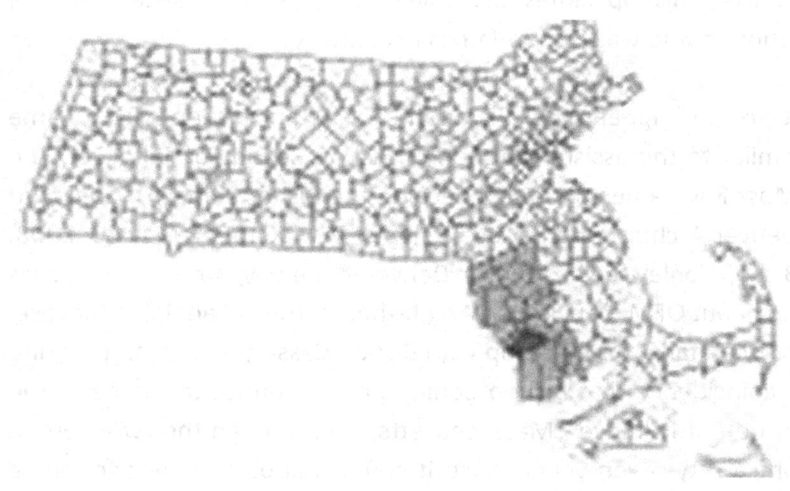

Figure 3

The skier of Fall River, Massachusetts[133]

133 Fall_River_ma_highlight.png, en.wikipedia.org

When the image of Fall River is highlighted, the remaining east coast of Massachusetts looks just like a female skier facing east! She appears to have goggles on. She could be anywhere around the world, but this clue being on east coast of America, hinted the location was in America.

Fall River, Massachusetts, had a bishop named Cassidy. Lucia had already become a nun. Here are the results from the search for Bishop Cassidy of Fall River, Massachusetts.

Bishop James L. Cassidy, August 1, 1869–May 17, 1951,[134] was the person responsible for censorship and giving his permission for Sister Lucia to publish her book, approved as presented, containing nothing harmful to the Catholic Church.

In 1945, Bishop James L. Cassidy appointed an assistant bishop, whose name was Bishop James L. Connelly.

It just so happens there is another assistant bishop with a name similar to the assistant bishop of Bishop Cassidy of Fall River. The Most Rev. James D. Conley became the Bishop James D. Conley to Denver Archbishop Charles J. Chaput OFM, Cap, on May 30, 2008. Bishop Conley can be found in Denver to this day, Archbishop Charles J. Chaput OFM, Cap. is now Archbishop of the Philadelphia Diocese. You can take this matchup with Bishop Cassidy as a sign. It is quite a coincidence that Bishop Conley's name sounds the same as the bishop of Fall River, Massachusetts, even though the two were in office fifty-seven years apart. It could well be the presage dating the approximate time when the contents of the *Crusade* would be discovered.

---

134 the diocese of fall river, James E Cassidy of Fall River Mass.,www.fallriverdiocese.org/glance.asp?display=history

Lucia de Jesus dos Santos wasn't exactly looking through travel brochures to decide where she was going for vacation when the bishop whisked her away to a convent. She most likely hadn't a clue where she was headed until she arrived, and she promised never would she tell where she was going or where she was from. Surely, she would not have known there would now be a Bishop in Denver named Conley when she published the *Crusade* in 1947. This coincidence could be thought of as some sort of Church hoax, but I assure you it is neither a hoax nor a joke—it is serious work Lucia has to accomplish.

> "In conformity with the decree of Pope Urban VIII, we do not wish to anticipate the judgment of the Church in our appraisal of the characters and occurrences spoken of herein. We submit wholeheartedly to the infallible wisdom and judgment of Holy Mother Church."[135]

Pope Urban VIII was actually the pope from 1623 to 1644.[136] How could a pope leading the Catholic Church around 370 years ago possibly enter into Lucia's story?

From 1931 to 1941, there also happened to be a bishop named *Urban* John Vehr, bishop of Denver. The word *Urban* is the clue. Bishop Vehr then became the archbishop of Denver, 1941–1967, appointed by Pope Pius XII. Later, Bishop Vehr advanced to titular archbishop (1967–1970). *Titular* and use of the word *utter* so many times connected with the large hand over Lucia's breast in the picture of the three seers in chapter II. At least it brought it to mind. Plus, a bust of Pope Pius XII can be found in the Cathedral Basilica of the Immaculate Conception in Denver, Colorado.

---

135 De Marchi, *Mother of Christ Crusade*, preface page

136 The American Conference of Catholic Bishops, *New American Bible, appendix of pope timeline, Pope Urban VIII*

This Bishop Urban Vehr of Denver had an assistant bishop, David M. Maloney, who shares the same last name as the *censor librorum* in the *Crusade*: Francis J. Maloney. Since Lucia was writing the *Crusade* at the time, she would have known about this to leave it as a clue.

If the theory is correct, Lucia would have been in Colorado when Bishop Urban Vehr presided. She was able then to use Pope Urban VIII to help lead us to Bishop *Urban* Vehr in Denver, the location confirmed by the presence of Bishop Conley and past Bishop Maloney. However, it could have been there would never be a Priest named Conley for years or ever come to Denver as Assistant Bishop, or one with a name that even sounded the same. I call it divine providence and a miracle that after Lucia's time Bishop Conley would arrive. Lucia could not have known this fact.

Analyze the next section of text on the prefix page.

> *What has happened in Portugal proclaims the miracle. It is the presage of what the Immaculate Heart has prepared for the world.*
>
> His Eminence,
>
> The Cardinal Patriarch of Lisbon

This is located on the inside of the back cover:

> **EXACT TRUTH**:
>
> "This book is written by Sr. Lucy and Fr. John de Marchi together. He spent 3½ years in her company gathering all the facts and she carefully verified them in every detail personally."

This information was convincing enough to look for traces of Lucia's presence in the past cathedral parish of Archbishop Charles J. Chaput OFM, Cap, at the Cathedral Basilica of the Immaculate Conception in Denver, Colorado. The statues and other holy icons found within the cathedral happen to match those pictured or written about in the *Crusade*. The hidden contents of the Crusade slipped right by the Church representatives who approved it for publication in 1947 or Lucia may in fact have added the presages after they approved it. It is because Lucia wrote "fifty years had passed since the apparitions in Fatima" in the *Crusade* that lets you know that she secretly added to the manuscript after it was approved.

Chapter 13

Cathedral Basilica of the Immaculate Conception in Denver, Colorado

Many of the images of statues in the *Crusade* have a striking resemblance to those found at the Cathedral Basilica of the Immaculate Conception in Denver. Lucia would have needed to see the statues firsthand for her to enter pictures of them in the *Crusade*. They serve as more clues to establish her destination. We were already prompted to make a connection between Fatima and Denver, Colorado, because of the coincidence of the name of the newspaper in Lisbon, Portugal, the *O Dia*, and DIA, Denver International Airport. Lucia could not have known there would be a DIA airport when she released *Mother of Christ Crusade*. Suddenly the coincidence of the two names is looking more like the miraculous connection. The following pictures taken of statues and artifacts were taken at the cathedral and demonstrate their similarities with the images of Fatima in *Mother of Christ Crusade*, providing more clues to establish her travels included the Cathedral Basilica of the Immaculate Conception in Denver, Colorado.

Figure 4

The Cathedral Basilica of the Immaculate Conception

Figure 5

An angel holding a chalice

Upon entering the cathedral, walk forward to the steps of the sanctuary and then turn and walk left. You will approach two angels facing each other; one angel is holding a Host, the other a chalice. The angel pictured on page 6 of *Mother of Christ Crusade* who gave the children Holy Communion is similar to this angel in the cathedral.

Figure 6

The crucifix of Jesus Christ

In the northwest corner, to the left of the sanctuary, is a crucifix of Christ, looking very much like the crucifix found on page 108 of the *Crusade* in the picture entitled "Our Lady's Apparition: 1929." Our Lady and St Francis are in the bright light.

Figure 7

An angel guardian of a young child

Figure 8

Our Lady stands over the holmoak tree

This statue of the Blessed Virgin Mary can be found to the right of the sanctuary, on the east side of the cathedral. She looms large above a little tree, the holmoak tree in this possible version of Shrine at Valinhos. The tree in foreground matches the condition of the little holmoak tree after the second apparition, chapter IV, at the Cova da Iria. It is inclined toward the East (Lucia always capitalized this when Our Lady departed), stripped of its leaves, and its lower branches broken off, with Our Lady standing above, just as Lucia described the tree in Fatima. This scene recreates content wise, what the visions of Our Lady looked like during the apparitions in Fatima, Portugal.

This life-sized statue of Our Lady is surrounded by pillars. When viewed from the west side of the sanctuary, it looks very similar to the statue and scene of Our Lady seen in the photo on p. 100 of the *Crusade*, chapter VII, "Shrine at Valinhos", the same picture that has the knight dressed in Fourth Degree regalia with a candle on his head. The Knights of Columbus, Fourth Degree honor guard have had a regular role during the past celebrations at the cathedral, making another match.

Construction of the Cathedral Basilica of the Immaculate Conception's two towering spires was completed in 1911, six years before the Fatima apparitions.[137] Compare this structure with the identifying words mentioning "the spire of the church" in the caption for the photo on page 25—a fit with the cathedral's spires. It would not have been known when Lucia wrote the *Crusade* that on June 23, 1997[138], one of the spires of the Cathedral Basilica of the Immaculate Conception would be struck by lightning. Lucia had described the start of the First Apparition as "a sudden bright shaft of light," a flash

---

137 Cathedral Basilica of the Immaculate Conception web site, www.archden.org/

138 Ibid

of lightning, after which they soon became "immersed in the glorious light of splendor that shown from the Lady."[139] It was a "flash" of lightning that struck the east spire, shattering its tip. On the same side of the cathedral, above Our Lady in the Cova, is a stained glass window showing Our Lady entering Heaven, with Her foot almost caught in the door. The cathedral has the statue of Our Lady over the holmoak and a view of Her departure, like that described in the *Crusade,* in the stained glass window. The lightning could be taken as a sign from above, not simple coincidence, and another prompt attracting publicity, to take a closer look at the image of Our Lady in the stained glass on the same east side of the cathedral. The lightning strike could be divine intervention to confirm Lucia's visit at the cathedral. If God intentionally struck the spire, since it did, it would provide a validation as well as divine endorsement of the truth that Lucia's message to us is authentic. It could have been a coincidence that lightning struck the east spire, the same side of the cathedral with a statue of Our Lady and this stained glass window with her entering heaven, though the chances of all three tied together recapitulating the *Crusade* could also be easily thought of as miraculous since the lightning was an act of God.

139 De Marchi, *Mother of Christ Crusade*, Chapter III

Figure 9

Our Lady in the doorway to heaven

In the depiction in this stained glass window, Our Lady enters heaven through an opening in the sky. Her feet are not yet completely inside the opening leading into Heaven. Jacinta remarked after the First Apparition that when Our Lady departed, the door to heaven closed so quickly that She almost got her feet caught in the door. Our Lady is the central and brightest figure in this stained glass window. She is surrounded by a clean yellow, strikingly brilliant aura when the sun shines through on a clear, bright Colorado day. The floor of the cathedral also slopes downward in the east aisle as you walk toward the statue of Our Lady surrounded by the pillars.

> When Francisco could not see Her immediately like the girls, Lucia asked "the Lady" to allow Francisco to see the apparition. She replied, if Francisco will pray the Rosary, "in that way he too will see me."
>
> Francisco quickly took his Rosary from his pocket and prayed. Only then he could see -"the Lady with almost blinding splendor more brilliant the sun, shedding rays of light clear and stronger that a crystal glass filled with the most sparkling water, pierced by the burning rays of the sun."[140]

Glass is included in the description. The scene in the window recollects the First Apparition, when the children had headed down the slope, took a few steps, turned right and there stood Our Lady. In this case, Our Lady is above a holmoak seen in the stained glass window to the right.

In the *Crusade*, Francisco asked Lucia to throw a stone at Our Lady's image to see if it was real. "Never,"[141] Lucia replied. Was she afraid that throwing a stone would be disrespectful of Our Lady, or it could

---

140 Ibid
141 Ibid

have been an addition to the Fatima story to help see the analogies at the cathedral, with Fatima. One can assume she would never throw a stone at a stained glass window either, this providing another hint she was at the cathedral in Denver, to advance and promote her mission.

The Cathedral as Presage to September 11, 2001

There is evidence that Lucia either managed to do some designing inside the cathedral and had arranged things to reflect Fatima and the presage of 9/11 or it is an act of God. She kept her secrets but did still need to document information for her mission further, just to prove the Crusades presage of 9/11. The *Crusade* has many things in common with the cathedral.

A couple Pope Pius' were mentioned many times by Our Lady and Sr. Maria Lucia when explaining the dates of presage provided her by the Virgin Mary. These were dates when war would break out if men did not mend their ways. The world did not heed the warning from Our Lady in Fatima. Some countries refused Consecration to the Immaculate Heart and as a result, according to Lucia, World War II broke out.

In the southeast narthex area, you will find the busts of four popes. Three are of a Pope Pius and one is of Pope Benedict XV. Our lady mentioned Pope Pius XI in chapter III and both Pope Pius XI and XII in chapter XIV. Beside these two Popes Pius there is one of Pope Pius X. These four busts along with the bust of an unnamed pope, found in the southwest narthex area, are the only five busts of popes in the cathedral.

In the southwest narthex area, is the unnamed bust of a pope. His coat looks as though the bust could be of another Pope Pius. The robe he is wearing is in the same bust style to match the other Popes Pius in the southeast side of the narthex, providing another clue that it could be another Pope Pius. Only Popes Pius were named in the

Crusade. The pope standing with Lucia in the picture on page 191, chapter XIII, is unidentified—other than saying he was a pope—the same situation as in the cathedral. The pope in the picture actually wears the same type collar as the unnamed bust in the west narthex. Why so many Popes Pius? Was it meant to jog the memory of those who have read the *Crusade*? There has to be a reason.

The four busts of popes in the southeast narthex have an asymmetry about them, which appeared to be a clue when assessed in light of the transposition of the letters *r* and *i* in the misspelling of the word "Third" in the title of chapter V, spelled "Thrid". The "Thrid" Apparition's transposition of the letters brought to mind, what if the statue of the untitled pope in the southwest chamber of the narthex would be of a Pope Pius also, it ought to be transposed as well. Switching it with the only dissimilar bust, of Pope Benedict XV in the southeast chamber of the narthex would then put all four Popes Pius together.

Figure 10

The unnamed pope in the southwest narthex of the Cathedral of the Immaculate Conception

Trading the bust of the unnamed pope assumed to be a Pope Pius, with the bust of Pope Benedict XV, would bring all popes named Pius together in the southeast narthex. It is because the unnamed pope is adorned in the same robe style as Pope Pius XI and XII, he could be designated Pope Pius IX. When done in this way, Pope Pius "IX" (9) is directly "across" from Pope Pius "XI" (11), the sequence now reading IX/XI, or 9/11. The bottom two would remain as they were, Pius X and XII, this date now references 10/12—one day short of the Sixth Apparition of October 13. Recollect that the date 10/12 was stated inaccurately in the *Crusade* as the "last day of the public apparitions." The last day of public apparitions was actually October 13, and proved to be the greatest of them all, when some seventy five thousand plus people witnessed the miracle in the skies over Fatima. It also is related to 9/11. This may have occurred by chance, divine providence or managed by Lucia for supporting evidence to connect the cathedral directly to the *Crusade* and provide additional presage of 9/11. *Mother of Christ Crusade* refers to 10/13 as 10/12,[142] an error made intentionally to match the current arrangement of the two popes on the lower section of the shelves in the southeast narthex at the Cathedral. This also confirms we are on Lucia's secret journey.

The unnamed statue guessed to be of Pius the IX is already "across" the narthex from Pius XI. The peculiarity of dissimilar Pope Benedict XV bust, switched with the unnamed pope in the west narthex becomes relevant to the present reign of Pope Benedict XVI and a cross on the rubble of 9/11. Either way, it could be thought of as the miraculous presage of 9/11 put in place by Lucia de Jesus dos Santos, now Sr. Maria Lucia of the Immaculate Heart of Mary, exactly as Our Lady had ordered. Retrospectively, it seems obvious, given the trail of connections between the names of the bishops, popes and the *Crusade*. The awareness of the possibility of the busts being

142 Ibid, Chapter XI, p 149

presage could only be understood after September 11, 2001, when the term *9/11* had already become infamous and understanding the *Crusade*. She knew the presage, but kept it secret just as Our Lady said. How she was allowed the liberty to arrange things in the cathedral remains a mystery. It had to be her way or divine assistance involved.

Figure 11; Figure 12

Pope Benedict XV is above Pope Pius X (left) and Pope Pius XI is above Pope Pius XII (right) in the east narthex at the Cathedral of the Immaculate Conception

Although Lucia de Jesus dos Santos may have visited the cathedral, or even lived there during the winter months, it had no convent school—her final destination. Recall the word "Aljustrel"[143] in the opening paragraphs of *Mother of Christ Crusade* listed as the name of a small hamlet near Fatima, Portugal, is also intended to mean "all just relative." It must have been intended that *Mother of Christ Crusade* would have a real parallel location, matching the cities, the hills, the statues, and more in her memoirs of Fatima, Portugal. Lucia provides more clues for us, to follow in her footsteps to the convent school.

143 De Marchi, *Mother of Christ Crusade*, Chapter I, p 1

Chapter 14

The Mother Cabrini Shrine, Golden Colorado, a the Sister City of Fatima

When Lucia arrived at the convent, she remembers the request of the bishop, per her agreement, not to speak of Fatima or give her true identity to anyone. She was fulfilling the request of Our Lady to become a Sister in Faith, a nun, and complete the important mission of spreading a devotion to the Immaculate Heart of Mary.

Lucia wrote in the *Crusade* that she went from Fatima to Tuy, Spain. However, she had already promised never to tell anyone of some undisclosed location. That would mean she could not write it into the *Crusade* either; so for this, you can take her at her word she did not tell where she went.

In Fatima, Lucia received instruction and direction directly from Immaculate Mary, some of which she may have still kept secret. What is not widely known, however, is the fact she experienced more apparitions after leaving Fatima. These she kept to herself, but she recorded some of them in the *Crusade*, and in a clever way, at the Mother Cabrini Shrine in Golden, Colorado where the residents are the pious and delightful Missionary Sisters of the Sacred Heart of Jesus. The Sacred Heart of Jesus, Lucia points out is the ultimate destination, the goal that should be for everyone, to live in Heaven with Jesus Christ the Lord. The miracles of 9/11, those of presage in the Crusade and found at Mother Cabrini Shrine are a gift to the world and our open invitation to peace on earth, good will toward men and the realization of eternal life after death.

The Cabrini Shrine, using the following evidence was her destination at least for a time.

Back to the Crusade, reports have it that the two younger of the three children who also experienced the miracles and visions at Fatima—Francisco and Jacinta Marto—died. They since have been canonized as Saints. There is something they said that draws attention. They kept saying they were going to "heaven." It was all they wanted to do, "just die and go to Heaven."[144] Lucia was not foreign to creative thinking or above disappearing in spite of her knowledge. The *Crusade* has one date on the prefix page of the imprimaturs approval date of 1947, yet she entered in the *Crusade* that fifty years had passed since the apparitions, making the date 1967. It is possible she could have also aided in protecting the privacy of her cousins, the Marto children, maybe they too snuck away from Fatima using a casket as cover. No one would look for them if they had died. Not much of Jacinta's face is shown in the coroner's examination photo of chapter XII, p 185, to be sure it was her. The whole presentation is unusual. There was also a Dona Estefania hospital in Denver at the time of her death, though caption under the photo of her on p 180 is designated as Lisbon. When the characters in each photo are examined carefully the theory is much more plausible.

At the main gate entry to Mother Cabrini Shrine there is a stone house. Curiously, it is named the "Queen of Heaven Orphanage." It has a backyard with a fence of iron bars. This fence may relate to

144 Ibid, Chapter XI, p 148

Barrerio—an odd word from the *Crusade*—used to help identify her true destination.

Is this the uncapitalized "heaven" they really meant: the Queen of Heaven Orphanage? When Jacinta was ill, she told Lucia "she" was going to come for her and take her to Heaven.[145] Since the word she was not always capitalized, she did not mean Our Lady was taking her to the real Heaven necessarily. Some other lady named Mary not Our Lady, may be taking her somewhere else—quite possibly to the Queen of Heaven Orphanage. This way she wouldn't lie technically. She said that I should not be afraid since she will come to take me with her to Heaven.[146] It is quite possible Jacinta and Francisco did not die, but could have been just secreted away using a pretend death as their cover. The two of them could have been practicing laying perfectly still in their beds as they did, to enable them to fool the public as they lay in their caskets, at least for short periods of time, before they were quickly brought into the sacristy, where only women, family, and authorities were present to seal the caskets. Once in the sacristy, they could have gotten out of their caskets and been secreted away with the help of the authorities. The caskets would then be closed, and no one would know they were no longer in them. The empty caskets would be buried while they ran away to "heaven," Queen of Heaven Orphanage. After all, the three had each received a calling in a vision of Our Lady, when they saw themselves as if in a mirror—a vision of their futures! They had the same motivation as Lucia to leave Fatima to an unknown location. It explains why Jacinta said to Lucia that she will be going to heaven soon, but Lucia must stay "down below"[147] for a while, meaning at the convent and cathedral down in Denver as opposed to up at Cabrini Shrine in the foothills

145 Ibid, Chapter XII, p 168
146 Ibid
147 De Marchi, *Mother of Christ Crusade*, Chapter XII

of the Rocky Mountains. Here the transposed h and t for height and elevation on p. 2 have purpose. Our Lady wanted the girls to become nuns and Francisco to become a priest, but only Lucia was old enough to enter into formation for the Sisterhood. The two Marto children would have stayed at an orphanage of Mother Cabrini and at Mother Cabrini Shrine part time until they were old enough to begin the training in their vocation. There would be no sense in showing each their vocation as if in a mirror if they were not going to live or be able to become a priest and nun as Our Lady asked of them during the apparitions. It was a secret plan for these Holy children to slip away.

Since Francisco was born in 1908 and Jacinta in 1910, they would have to be 103 and 101 years old, respectively, in 2011. I suppose it is possible both are alive today, especially since they were blessed and Holy children. Perhaps the Crusade was not divinely assigned to be found before they indeed did go to Heaven.

These parallel terms, phrases, and locations from *Mother of Christ Crusade* confirm Mother Cabrini's Shrine and the cathedral in Denver as at least Lucia's destination from Fatima for some of her years. The shrine recreates chapter thirteen, "The Chapel at Cova da Iria." They went to a place that has a great shrine, a convent school, a retreat house. The Shrine also has an area one might consider a second, made to order Cova da Iria. Mother Cabrini Shrine has all of the above. The stone house has since been converted from a summer orphanage residence into a rentable retreat house (a flash rent the air). There are other similarities with the *Crusade* that support the premise Lucia meant to leave a trail to her whereabouts.

Figure 13

St. Francis written in stone, seen on the road to Mother Cabrini Shrine, Golden, Colorado

The shrine area is named for St. Frances X. Cabrini. When you arrive at the shrine, the hill across from the stone house has St. Francis written out on it with stones—a likely play on words paralleling "Francisco Leads the Way,"[148] to the shrine and orphanage.

148 Ibid, title Chapter XI, p 144

Figure 14

The Stone House with fenced yard of the Queen of Heaven Orphanage at Mother Cabrini Shrine

At the main gate entry to Mother Cabrini Shrine there is a building titled the "Stone House" in pamphlets with hay bales next to it. The sign in front says it was the Queen of Heaven Orphanage. It has a backyard with a fence of iron bars, "Barrerio." This was possibly a place Lucia visited when she arrived down below in the Denver area. A portrait of Lucia hangs on the wall inside the stone house.

Figure 15

The Stone House was the Queen of Heaven Orphanage. It is now a rentable retreat house. A well is positioned near the front door. This well has a special bolt; the head is a five-pointed star. In the picture of the pope and Lucia, a magnified examination reveals Lucia has a five-pointed star on her cheek—a direct connection to the Queen of Heaven orphanage.

Figure 16

"A globe of Light"[149] is an important phrase in the *Crusade*. The world sits atop the gazebo in the backyard of the stone house. Sometimes Our Lady would come as a globe of light.

Figure 17

This is the barn and a wagon wheel fixed in mud along the road into the Cabrini Shrine. It was mentioned often that the children led their sheep in and out of the barn. On their way to see the sixth apparition, some had the wheels of their carriages stuck in the mud.

149 Ibid., Chapter XII, p 174

Figure 18

This wagon wheel is fixed in mud, next to the parking lot (which is related to the word Cabe'co). Losing a wagon wheel was one of the problems the pilgrims encountered when traveling to Fatima to reach the site of the Sixth Apparition of October 13, 1917.

Figure 19

The chassis of a carriage is reminiscent of the magistrate's kidnapping of the children to learn the secret and the transportation used by some pilgrims traveling to Fatima to experience the Sixth Apparition

Figure 20

The huge Sacred Heart Statue stands tall on top the mountain. In Mrs. Santos's words, "Oh, what a big man"[150] carried Lucia. The *Crusade* also mentioned St. Mary Margaret who began a devotion to the Sacred Heart of Jesus.

150 Ibid, Chapter V, p 68

Lucia de Jesus dos Santos leads us, the sheep, in her clever way, to the Mother Cabrini Shrine. The list of parallels includes the Sacred Heart Statue, the main feature of the shrine. The Sacred Heart is referenced in the *Crusade* when Lucia mentions Saint Margaret Mary of the Sacred Heart, who had visions of Jesus that began her devotion to the Sacred Heart on December 27, 1673. Lucia was called upon to begin a devotion to the Immaculate Heart of Mary and said Our Lord wants the people to venerate His Sacred Heart and Mary's Immaculate Heart together. The following are word clues from the *Crusade* that parallel and identify Cabrini Shrine and the convent school as Lucia's new location and hint at the presage of 9/11.

Caba'co, or taxi driver: I concluded this word relates to where cars park, or parking lot. New York is famous for its taxis, providing more identification as to the location of the 9/11 terrorist attack. Terrorism is listed as a presage on the second to last page of the *Crusade* under the heading, "AN EMERGENCY PLAN."[151]

"The Head": Found on page 2 of the *Crusade*, this helps identify Mother Cabrini Shrine by referencing the fact that Mother Cabrini's head is truly in Rome, while her body was laid to rest in New York State.

Wooden Saint: Lucia's mother said to Lucia, "what a little wooden Saint you are."[152] The statue in the parallel Cova da Iria, with a likeness of Lucia in the shrine's chapel, is made of wood.

Grapes: Jacinta's mother brought Jacinta some luscious grapes once when the children were playing. Luscious grapes like those described by Jacinta are found on another sign hanging above the parking area, or Cabe'co.

151 Ibid, Chapter XIV, p 218
152 Ibid, Chapter V, p 61

The Well: Not only is the miraculous well found at Cabrini Shrine, there is the half round of a well at the entrance of the Queen of Heaven Orphanage, where Lucia lived part time after leaving Fatima. The water source is fitted with a hose and a peculiar bolt. The head of this bolt is a five-pointed star, not a hexagon as is the norm. It ties in with Lucia because of the star on her cheek seen with magnification in the image of her with the pope on page 191 of the *Crusade*.

The Great Divide: In the United States, the Continental Divide traverses through Colorado, very near the Cabrini Shrine. It is visible from the shrine complex when looking to the west. The chapel and convent home looks like a ski chalet. The many Colorado world-class ski areas are just over the Continental Divide, explaining Lucia's clue when looking at the map image of Fall River, Massachusetts.

Sr. Bernadette: Jacinta's Mother Superior at the hospital. For many years, Sr. Bernadette was the Mother Superior of the Mother Cabrini Convent. In Fatima, Lucia had encountered a Mother Superior named Bernadette.

A Sacred Heart Holy picture: You will find one available in the shrine's gift shop, like the one Jacinta kissed so earnestly. Jacinta asked Lucia to find a picture of the Immaculate Heart of Mary for her to keep also, but Lucia said she could not find one anywhere. You will not find a picture of the Immaculate Heart of Mary in the Cabrini gift shop.

A charity donation statue: One stands just outside the convent reception desk near the entry doors of the Cabrini chapel. Above the deposit slot, the word *charity* is printed. It has always been missing the letter "i", thus making the word *Char ty*. *Ti* is the short form for

Antonio Marto. The missing *i* may mean your charitable contribution is needed, similar to; "needs your dime"[153] for the Crusade.

Two cents: Two pennies have been found routinely when walking the stairs up to the Sacred Heart statue. If you take them, there will be two more when you return. Lucia's friend John in the *Crusade* was given two pennies for going to fetch Jacinta. If he came back with her, Lucia told him she would give him two more pennies. [154]

A cemetery: Now gone, it was sure to have had the names of the deceased in the *Crusade*.

Francisco's flute: A flute plays as background music in the instructional video room, below the small lower chapel, near the miraculous well.

The angel: There is an angel statue near a statue of the Immaculate Conception at Cabrini found east of the lower chapel in an area covered with small stones.

A Balcony off the Rectory: A balcony is just outside the Cabrini chapel along with another down below at the smaller grotto chapel. The latter also has an altar rail.

Big man: In the final paragraph of chapter V, the "Thrid" Apparition, "Lucia was being carried away by a very tall man, so tall in fact that Lucia's mother was distracted from her worry, saying 'Oh, what a big man.'" It seems either the mosaic of the Risen Jesus of the Cabrini Sanctuary or the towering statue of the Sacred Heart on top the mountain could be the "Big Man" Lucia's mother referred too.

153 Ibid, A GOOD START, final page of the *Crusade*
154 Ibid, Chapter IV, p 48

Myriad of stars: The base on which Our Lady stands in the chapel of Cabrini is covered with a myriad of stars; reminiscent of those in the First Apparition describing Our Lady's returned to heaven.

On June 17, 1921, the day of Lucia's final farewell, she took a tour of her favorite Holy spots at Fatima. Before leaving for the unknown convent school, she walks a path, first to the angel and then to a spot of a vision of Mary. This may be in reference to the white statue of the Virgin Mary in the video room, exactly like the cover of the Crusade and Jacinta's first description to her mother and father after the first apparition. She then went to the bog, the pond, and then finally to the Cova da Iria. Jacinta and she went to the altar rail found in the lower chapel, above the video room, as well. All the above and more are recreated at the Holy Mother Cabrini Shrine. You can walk in her footsteps by following the path she described, beginning at "the angel" with the little girl.

The Sisters of Dorothy: Lucia called the order of the nuns she was joining the Sisters of Dorothy. "Toto" is the brand name of a fixture in the men's room on the second floor. It is also found at the shrine on a nameplate fixed to a bench on the platform of the great statue of the Sacred Heart. The names Dorothy and Toto remind one of *The Wizard of Oz*[155] and Dorothy's expression when speaking to Toto, "I don't think we're in Kansas anymore." Correct, but right next to Kansas is Colorado. It is true, that Mother Cabrini Shrine is a magical place. In the photo p 6 of the Angel, directly above Jacinta's head in the background there is a witch, pointed hat and all. It is a clue to confirm that *Mother of Christ Crusade* and Mother Cabrini Shrine have a common connection, establishing that Lucia de Jesus dos Santos did spend some time at the Mother Cabrini Shrine, at least in the summers. There is also a convent school with an orphanage in Denver, which was founded by Frances X. Cabrini, where they could have lived also.

155 Metro-Goldwin-Mayer, *The Wizard of Oz*, 1939

Chapter 15

St. Sister Maria Lucia Switches with Mother Cabrini

Figure 21

The statue of Sr. Maria Lucia in the Cova

Lucia said she began to go to the Cova da Iria every day after the Second Apparition. The far left corner of the Cabrini chapel has this little replica of the Cova, with a wooden statue assumed to be Mother Cabrini. However it looks nothing like Mother Cabrini, who often suffered from illness and was frequently infirmed. She was a frail woman with a long, narrow face.

This statue looks nothing like the bust or photos of St. Frances Xavier Cabrini, the "Mother Cabrini". This statue looks like the description given of young Lucia Santos from chapter 2, "The Children of Fatima." Sister Maria Lucia's facial bone structure would remain basically the same as she grew. Her childhood picture is on page 14, chapter 2, of the *Crusade.* It shows her "having a flat nose and heavy mouth, with a pair of beautiful dark eyes that glistened under heavy lids, making her most attractive." This statue is of an attractive woman. Her eyes are made of glass and are absolutely spectacular— dark green, but dark nonetheless—fitting the image of Lucia. A reliable source said Mother Cabrini had blue eyes, though not confirmed. This statue in little "Cova" would make this little cove in the chapel the new Cova da Iria, the "cove of the eyes." The fact that the statue is wooden explains Lucia's mother telling her, "What a little wooden saint you are. . ."[156] This statue really is of Lucia, switched with Mother Cabrini. The Cabrini Shrine is now hers to design. Lucia came to the convent school in Denver and to the Mother Cabrini Shrine. There she recreated the "Cova da Iria" of Fatima at the Cabrini Shrine; in fact, most of her memories of Fatima and the visions of the apparitions are represented at Mother Cabrini Shrine. It must have been her mission to leave a trail and record the presage of September 11, 2001, secretly.

156 Ibid, Chapter V, p 61

Figure 22

Mother Cabrini's arrival in New York, New York

St. Frances Xavier Cabrini traveled through and worked extensively in New York. Young Lucia Santos, too, probably immigrated to the United States through New York City harbor. The image above has a crane, a ship, and the Statue of Liberty in it. The Statue of Liberty shines light on her cause of religious liberty. Its presence at the shrine could be taken as a clue, helping to identify where catastrophe will occur, part of the presage of 9/11. Before 9/11, it could have been passed over as insignificant. As with the images in the *Crusade*, this collage drawing of Lucia at New York Harbor has other smaller images within it.

Figure 23

This interesting image of a young nun at the entrance of the memorial garden is not of Mother Cabrini. On closer examination, she has her fingers on "a little light switch" behind the cross she wears, a telltale sign the pictures and statues of Mother Cabrini have been substituted with those of Sr. Maria Lucia.

Having her fingers on a light switch is a decisive clue indicating the young woman of the marble is not St. Frances X. Cabrini at all, but rather Sr. Maria Lucia of the Immaculate Heart. The X, of St. Frances X. Cabrini helps to understand the X on one of the two towers seen with magnification under the tree in the picture on p. 211 of the Crusade. The Shrine like the Crusade must also hold the presage of 9/11. This isn't the only image of Mother Cabrini with her fingers on a light switch, there are at least three. Throughout the shrine, images and statues of Sr. Maria Lucia of the Immaculate Heart have replaced those of Sr. Frances Cabrini. Two depictions of Mother Cabrini remain to compare with the other statues.

They made the "switch" sometime after Lucia arrived at the convent school and Queen of Heaven Orphanage in Golden, Colorado. Frances X. Mother Cabrini died December 22, 1917—the year of the apparitions. It would be after 1929, when Lucia was known to be in Tuy, Spain.[157] If you remove the oddly shaped *S* from the word *saint* in this image, you are left with "aint Frances Xavier Cabrini."

157 Ibid, Chapter XIV, p 209

Figure 24

St. Frances X. Cabrini, Mother Cabrini, has a narrow face and more prominent nose

The facial features of Mother Cabrini and Sr. Maria Lucia and are very distinctive and not at all alike. This sculpture of the real Mother Cabrini can be found behind the main chapel. The picture signs in the parking lot, the statue in the new Cova da Iria of the Cabrini chapel, and the marble image at the entrance to the memorial garden do not match the facial features of this sculpture of the real Mother Cabrini. There is another statue like the one seen in the new Cova da Iria and a portrait that fit the description of Lucia given in chapter II of the *Crusade*, to be found in the Stone House. They are not Mother Cabrini. By taking the place of Mother Cabrini, Lucia became the principle subject of the shrine. This allowed her to use the shrine to advance her mission of establishing a devotion to the Immaculate Heart of Mary. Here she secretly recorded the predictions Our Lady passed on to her, including the details regarding September 11, 2001.

Figure 25

Lucia has her fingers on a small light switch

Above is the second image of Lucia with her fingers on a small light switch. It confirms the other marble image is not an error—Sr. Maria Lucia, not St. Frances X. Cabrini, is represented at the shrine. Noticing the small details in the *Crusade* and those at Cabrini Shrine is the path to discovery.

Figure 26

This third portrait of Sr. Lucia in place of Mother Cabrini with her fingers on a light switch hangs along the staircase just outside the Cabrini chapel

There is no other logical explanation for the inclusion of a light switch in these portraits, accept to directly say Sr. Maria Lucia Mother Cabrini is substituted in place of St. Frances X. Cabrini. Therefore, all the images and statues around the Cabrini Shrine are really of Sr. Maria Lucia of the Immaculate Heart of Mary, with the exception of the bust of the real Mother Cabrini behind the chapel and the photo of her in the conference room to compare the two women. These three light switch images end all speculation about whether or not Lucia came to Mother Cabrini Shrine.

The question is why hide Lucia's secret location in *Mother of Christ Crusade* and then confirm the shrine was Lucia's new hideout through these clues? Now that we know, what else does Sr. Maria Lucia want us to find? Whatever it is will be as cleverly hidden on the grounds of the shrine as the prediction of 9/11 was hidden in the *Crusade*. It is sure to include another way of documenting Our Lady's miraculous presage of 9/11. A search for key "unfound" words and misspellings is a start. A closer look at the special images, like checking the portraits of Lucia to see her fingers on a light switch, will be required.

Chapter 16

The Apparitions in *Mother of Christ Crusade* Were Recreated by Sr. Maria Lucia at Mother Cabrini Shrine

The First Apparition

After Mass, the three children were "playing, building, making castles out of rocks, with Francisco as the mason and architect, while Lucia and Jacinta gathered the stones," when the First Apparition began. Suddenly, the children are distracted by a bright shaft of light, like lighting, though the weather was clear and bright and no breeze stirred the air. Thinking a storm was coming on, they gathered the sheep and headed down the hill, took a few steps, turned to the right and there standing over the holmoak was a "most beautiful lady. . . . It was a lady dressed all in white."[158]

158 Ibid., Chapter III, p 27

Figure 27

This is the slope or ramp the children were walking down when they saw the first shaft of light

The narrow light pole without a hood, the bare light bulb on the near left as you descend the slope, is the "shaft of light" that pierced the air signaling the beginning of the First Apparition. Further down the slope, turn to the right and you will see this statue of Our Lady, white, hands folded in prayer just like Jacinta described.

Figure 28

Our Lady dressed all in white, to the right of the sloping ramp

The children already knew why Our Lady had come to visit. The angel told them in this prayer before he gave the children Holy Communion, the True Body and Blood of Our Lord, Jesus Christ. "Most Holy Trinity, Father Son, and Holy Ghost, I adore You profoundly and I offer You the Most Precious Body, Blood, Soul, and Divinity of Jesus Christ, present in all the tabernacles of the earth, in reparation for the outrages, sacrileges, and indifferences by which He Himself is offended. And by the infinite merits of His Most Sacred Heart and the Immaculate Heart of Mary, I beg of You, the conversion of poor sinners."[159]

159 Ibid, Chapter I, p 10

Second Apparition

These specifics are spoken of in chapter four. When Our Lady departed from over the holmoak tree at the Cova da Iria, the crowds had left carnations and a bit of a mess, so Lucia began cleaning up the Cova.

She stated, "I removed all the stones that were there and pulled out, or cut away the thickets and furze. I gave the place the shape of a round thrashing floor. I also tied a silk ribbon on the branches of the holmoak and I was the first one to place flowers on it".[160] This is also a description of the sanctuary floor and appointments of Cabrini chapel.

160 Ibid, Chapter IV, p 55

Figure 29

Our Lady stands above a floral arrangement in the Cova. It could be considered the thickets and furze. A similar arrangement with Our Lady over the holmoak tree was seen at the Cathedral of the Immaculate Conception in Denver fig. 9.

On the left side of the mosaic sanctuary, set on a small shelf of the sanctuary wall, is the statue of Our Lady with the base displaying the myriad of stars. This is the vision of Our Lady of the Second Apparition. At times there is a small tree adorned with a ribbon representing the holmoak, with or without leaves or flowers, placed directly beneath Our Lady. It is very similar to the tree seen in the photo of Our Lady above a holmoak at the cathedral. Usually there are vases of carnations perched on nearby pedestals on either side of the sanctuary behind the altar. The sanctuary floor is rounded, a semicircle, just as Lucia described the thrashing floor she made after this Second Apparition. It is reasonable to conclude Sr. Maria Lucia not only spent some time at the shrine, but she helped design and build it as Our Lady instructed her—to parallel Fatima.

Figure 30

The statue in the Cova da Iria

Lucia said in the Second Apparition that she was the first to put flowers on the leafless holmoak. In front of this statue of Sr. Lucia as Mother Cabrini in the new Cova da Iria, there are leafless branches with only flowers on them. This statue of Sr. Lucia has her hands folded in the identical fashion of the hands of the children in the picture on page 15 of the *Crusade*. Here in the parallel Cova da Iria of the main Mother Cabrini Shrine chapel, Lucia prays near the statue of the Blessed Mother (center) who stands right of her statue on one of two small shelves of the sanctuary wall. The statues simulate the apparitions. "Was the Lady as beautiful as so-and-so? Her sisters asked.

Much more beautiful.

Was she like a little statue in church with the mantle of stars?"[161]

Figure 31

Our Lady on a pedestal to the right and above St. Maria Lucia in the corner of the Cova da Iria of the chapel

161 Ibid., Chapter IV, p 56

This particular statue of Our Lady does not match the description of Our Lady of the apparitions that Jacinta gave to her mother. Another statue of Our Lady, a bit larger than this one, can be found in the video room, found below the lower Cabrini chapel, near the miraculous well. It looks exactly like Jacinta's description and also matches the image of Our Lady on the cover of *Mother of Christ Crusade*.

Figure 32

Our Lady in the video room, below the lower chapel, as she appears on the cover of the *Mother of Christ Crusade*

Jacinta gave this exact description of this statue of Our Lady when she explained the vision of Mary to her mother after the first apparition.

> "It was a lady so beautiful, so pretty ... dressed in white with a chain of gold around her neck extending down to her breast ... her head was covered with a white mantle, yes, very white ... I don't know but it was whiter even than milk ... which covered her to the feet ... all embroidered with gold ... how beautiful! She kept her hands together, in this way. The Child rose from the stool, joined her hands at the breast, imitating the vision."[162]

This statue imitates the vision, the cover of *Mother of Christ Crusade*, and Jacinta's description of the vision of Our Lady at Fatima.

162 Ibid, Chapter III, p35

Figure 33

Lucia de Jesus dos Santos, "the Jesus of two Santa's" standing on the world. The tipped red Fedora can be seen right of Jesus' head, on His copper colored halo. He is removing His hat in church just like Jacinta insisted. The white sanctuary wall, taken together with the glowing stained glass window, is the rocket.

The statue of Our Lady outside with the nameplate Sam A. Carpenter identifies this mosaic as a SAM (surface-to-air missile).

At the feast celebration given at the St. Anthony Church in Fatima, Mrs. Santos reminded Lucia there would be rockets and rolls and a band at the church celebration, tempting her to stay away from the Cova da Iria. The Resurrected Jesus together with the pointed stained glass window above Him forms a white rocket with a glowing tip. The sun shining through the stained glass window is so bright at times that the rocket reminds one of a warhead. No distractions could keep Lucia from the Cova da Iria at the appointed time. The rockets and rolls available at the feast at their church in Fatima have purpose. After seeing signs like this associating Lucia's presence at both the cathedral and the convent connected with Cabrini Shrine, Lucia's secret work at the direction of Our Lady seems to have included her personal arrangement of the many statues at both places. The children's favorite form of play, singing and dancing, combined with the rockets and rolls and the band at the church's feast day celebration in the *Crusade* and the Cabrini Shrine Sanctuary, serve notice to rock-and-roll musicians of the outrages and sacrileges offending Our Lord, including having demeaning lyrics and contributing to the abuse of women. Music lyrics were from the invisible or transparent man. They are what mortified them when they heard them. Lucia, after hearing the lyrics of "OTGDY," totally lost interest in bands. Jacinta condemns many rock-and-roll song lyrics herself, terming them repulsive and grossly offensive. Our Lord condemns them as an outrage, especially those songs involving the indecent treatment of virgins and demeaning everything sacred of the Catholic Church.

Figure 34

The church sanctuary at Mother Cabrini Shrine

The sanctuary mosaic of the Risen Christ is made of tiny stones.

The vigil lanterns in the sanctuary are gold, just as described in the Fourth Apparition. The world is just below the feet of the Risen Christ. When she was ill, Jacinta described a different way Our Lady sometimes visited her using these words, "sometimes she appears as the globe of light. But this was different than up in Fatima."[163] Notice the anchor, chalice, and cross on the banner hanging on the pulpit.

In the Sixth Apparition,

"The sun was now pale as the moon. To the left of the sun, St. Joseph appeared holding in his left arm the Child Jesus. St. Joseph emerged from the bright clouds only to his chest, sufficient to allow him to

163 Ibid., Chapter XII, p 174

raise his right hand and make, together with the Child Jesus, the Sign of the Cross three times over the world. As Saint Joseph did this, Our Lady stood in all her brilliancy to the right of the sun, dressed in the blue and white robes of Our Lady of the Rosary.

Meanwhile, Francisco and Jacinta were bathed in the marvelous colours and signs of the sun, and Lucia was privileged to gaze upon Our Lord dressed in red as the Divine Redeemer, blessing the world, as Our Lady had foretold. Like Saint Joseph, He was seen only from His chest up. Beside Him stood Our Lady, dressed now in the purple robes of Our Lady of Sorrows, but without the sword. Finally, the Blessed Virgin appeared again to Lucia in all her ethereal brightness, clothed in the simple brown robes of Mount Carmel."[164]

Jacinta said she wanted to go to the Cova everyday like Lucia did. Lucia or her statue, is there everyday. Jacinta however living in the summer orphanage, the Stone House (the Queen of Heaven Orphanage; Heaven is capitalized))at Cabrini, was not allowed to go in the winter, her parents wouldn't hear of it.[165] The Queen of Heaven Orphanage was closed in the winter, Jacinta couldn't go there, but could go to Mass down in Denver.

Behind the convent and Cabrini church, a statue of Our Lady of Sorrows is dressed in purple with two St. Josephs, one holding Jesus, partially blocked from view by a closely placed rock (Fig. 38).

164 Ibid., Chapter X, p 130-131
165 Ibid., Chapter XII, p 164

Figure 35

This sign with Lucia's fathers name on it, can be found along the steps leading up to the Sacred Heart. It is intended to convey the message, "We love you, Daddy." *Tatay* is the affectionate word for daddy in Portuguese. It could only be there to show the children's respect for Antonio Santos.

Jacinta said to Mother Superior that Our Lady would like for her sisters to become nuns very much. "Mother does not want it and Our Lady will take them soon to Heaven."[166] They also would be going to the Queen of Heaven Orphanage. It seems the whole family made the trip to America with the young children too.

166 Ibid., p 176

Figure 36

The miraculous spring at Cabrini Shrine

Lucia said, 'Mother wanted to do what was right, but she didn't understand. "If it were Our Lady, mother lamented, she could have performed a miracle already, starting a spring or something else. Oh, how would this all end." '[167] Mother Cabrini discovered a source of water at the shrine site while walking the property. Led by the Holy Spirit, she stopped and pointed at a stone with her cane and asked for someone to move it. Just below the surface was a spring. It is miraculous that Mother Cabrini knew there was water under the stone she pointed to, the same spring referenced in Lucia's mother's remark in the *Crusade*.

167 Ibid, Chapter X, p117

Figure 37

Our Lady told Lucia what she could expect during the Sixth Apparition. "And Our Lady of Sorrows will come too."[168] She is pictured above. The name "Maria dos Anjos"[169] is the equivalent of "Mary and two Josephs." The Shrine to Our Lady of Sorrows has two smaller statues of St. Joseph, one on each side, one holding the Child Jesus.

168 Ibid, Chapter VIII, p 111
169 Ibid, Chapter III, p 37

Figure 38

A young Jesus holding the world in His hand

After Lucia arrived at her convent school, she continued to have apparitions. One visit was on December 10, 1925, and included a visit by a young Jesus. Young Jesus is pictured on page 205 of the *Crusade*. Lucia and her Superior both wanted to spread a devotion to the Immaculate Heart. Their confessor told them they could do nothing on their own. To this, Jesus replied, "It is true your Superior alone can do nothing, but with My grace she can do all." Compare these words with "Omni possum in eo, qui me comfortat," meaning "I can do all things through Christ who gives me strength," an expression etched on a window along with another reading "Go East Not West", both near this statue of young Jesus in the Cabrini chapel. Our Lady always departed to the *east*.

Figure 39

The Stone House

The stone summer house has a second statue of Sr. Maria Lucia, identical to the one that is in the replica of Cova and a larger than life size statue of Jesus, the Sacred Heart. Jacinta said she is going to live in the same place as Jesus. There is a large statue of Jesus standing on the landing of the stairs leading to the second floor at the Stone House. It is about a ten minute walk to get from the Stone House statue to the new Cova da Iria—the same amount of time it took to walk to the Cova da Iria in Fatima.[170] The Stone House is now a retreat house available for rent. Inside is a portrait of Lucia with exaggerated thick, full lips. They are a key feature that completes the full description of Lucia's facial features to match the description of her; "Although her features, a rather flat nose and a heavy mouth suggested a frown, her sweet disposition and keen mind were reflected in a pair of dark, beautiful eyes which glistened under their

170 Ibid, Chapter IV, p 44

heavy lids, making her most attractive."[171] When the children revealed news of the Sixth Apparition to come, it spread like wildfire. Wildfires break out regularly in the canyons below the Mother Cabrini Shrine, one of which is named sunshine canyon.

Figure 40

The stone mosaic of the Risen Jesus Christ standing over the world

The entire white area in this mosaic, the world, and the Resurrected Jesus are made from tiny sparkling stones of different colors, each with a diameter of about 4 mm. A statue of St Joseph is in the lower left quadrant of this picture. Resting on another pedestal, right of Jesus, is Our Lady. Our Lady stands on a pedestal (a mantle) left of the altar, while the Statue of Lucia stands praying in the parallel Cova far left. Lucia began to visit the Cova every day in Fatima before she left. This statue of her is a permanent fixture, there every day—a reminder of Lucia's days in Fatima.

171 Ibid, Chapter II, p 14

In the mosaic of the Risen Christ, when looking from a distance, Jesus appears to be carrying a little person on His shoulders. The circle with the dove above Jesus is the head of the smaller person dressed in red and white. Lucia was carried by a very big man. Jacinta, when she spoke of the "Hidden Jesus," presented a dual reference, either the Sacred Heart Statue or Christ within the Eucharist, the Body, Blood, Soul, and Divinity of Jesus Christ. ". . . Our Lord dressed in red as the Divine Redeemer, blessing the world, as Our Lady had foretold. . . . Finally, the Blessed Virgin appeared again to Lucia in all her ethereal brightness, clothed in the simple robes of Mount Carmel.[7]"[172]

172 Ibid., Chapter X, p 131

Figure 41

The band, and rockets and rolls reference rock-and-roll music in the Crusade.[173] From the Altar up to the tip of the glowing stained glass, is the rocket. Visible is the raised and rounded sanctuary floor.

173 Ibid., Chapter IV, p 46

Figure 42

"Mule-heads, mule-heads"[174] of the *Crusade* refer to mule deer at Cabrini Shrine

Lucia reported in chapter 13, "The Chapel at the Cova da Iria," that those trying to break up the procession to install the statue at the Cova da Iria were greeted with resistance. The faithful chanted at them, saying "mule-heads, mule-heads." Mule deer above are ever present, roaming the rocky hillsides on the Cabrini property in Golden, Colorado. Snow is regularly on the ground in the Rocky Mountain foothills during the month of October. It accounts for the snow-white feet of the pilgrims who travelled to Fatima to see the Sixth Apparition.

When October 13 came around and the predicted miracle in the sky over Fatima actually took place as Our Lady said, the reality of all six

174 Ibid., Chapter VIII, p 109

of the apparitions the children experienced were accepted as fact, thus vindicating them of accusations of lying or imagining them. Lucia had indeed given an accurate presage. Her knowing the miracles in the sky would occur ahead of time, based on the word of Our Lady, proved the divinity of the Virgin Mary. She had given the date and time and place when the sixth Fatima apparition would happen. There would be no other way for her to predict such a miraculous event, other than with divine help. It is surprising that the Sixth Apparition, seen by seventy five thousand plus people, has never been made into a movie or documentary by major broadcast media. Such a miraculous event and testimony by those who witnessed this apparition would promote Jesus and Our Lady. It is no different from the magistrate using his newspaper to discredit the children to squelch any renewed enthusiasm of the Catholic faithful in Fatima.

Figure 43

This pitifully small chapel can still be seen behind the convent residence at Cabrini Shrine

This tiny chapel is located behind the convent residence at Cabrini. It is about the size of a bird house—pitifully small. Our Lady requested to "have a chapel built in Her honor" at the site of the apparitions. Given the details of the Sixth Apparition resemble 9/11, and the parallels between the Cabrini Shrine and the Fatima Shrine in Portugal; Our Lady may be calling upon all Americans to build a chapel at ground zero in honor of the Immaculate Heart of Mary. Building a chapel at that site would be more than just a token gesture in honor of Her; it would be a wonderful place to pray for the reparation of sins by which Our Lord is greatly outraged that caused 9/11 to begin with. She deserves one for providing the world with the presage of 9/11 in the *Crusade* and at Cabrini Shrine. Unfortunately, it is not happening.

Figure 44

Our Lady above the *greate*, the air conditioning vent

The word *greate*[175] is a misspelling needing correction in the *Crusade*. "To me, this was greate proof of the miracle." How does Lucia want the word spelled: as *great* or *grate*? *Grate* could indicate the pattern of the vertical wooden slats of the circulation vent seen directly beneath the statue of the Virgin Mary—another connection between the *Crusade* and the Cabrini Shrine and exacting a specific location. When air conditioner is running, there is a sudden of the cooling air, and it does sound a bit like a gadfly in a jug. The word *grate* helps in identifying the Cabrini Shrine sanctuary. Great proof of the miracle of presage for 9/11 is present in this sanctuary, the source is Our Lady. 'While she was with us (at the orphanage) she was visited by Our Lady more than once, the Superior continued. I remember once going to her room and standing at the foot of her bed. She said to me "Move over please dear Mother because I am expecting Our Lady!" Sometimes it was not a globe of light, as the one seen in Fatima, for then she would say, "This time, it was not like up in Fatima, but I knew it was Our Lady"'.[176] Cabrini is also only a few miles from the Great Divide of the Rocky Mountains. "One such hamlet (near Fatima) known as Aljustrel; and it is here and more especially in the surrounding rocky pasturelands that our story is centered.[177]

175 Ibid, Chapter V, p 63
176 Ibid, Chapter XII, p 174
177 Ibid., Chapter I, p1

Figure 45

Our Lady at Mother Cabrini, similar to appearance in the Shrine at Valinhos

This statue of Our Lady is located at the bottom of the Cabe'co, the parking lot at Cabrini Shrine. It has a strong resemblance to the statue of Mary in the *Crusade* on page 100, "Shrine at Valinhos". Jacinta described the vision of Our Lady to her mother stating she was wearing all white, whiter even than snow or milk. Lucia said it was a Lady dressed all in white.

Chapter 17

The Missionary Sisters of the Sacred Heart of Jesus and the History of Mother Cabrini Shrine[178]

Mother Cabrini, St. Frances Xavier Cabrini, had traveled the world around and began the Missionary Sisters of the Sacred Heart of Jesus. She deserves recognition for her accomplishments, so this brief history of the shrine in her honor is necessary to honor this tireless, fearless little agent for the Sacred Heart of Jesus. On a mission to bring ministry to miners of the Rocky Mountain region—the majority of whom mined silver—she found the property where the Mother Cabrini Shrine is now located on the side of Lookout Mountain in 1902.

There were a couple barns on the original property site, but there was no close source of water. She, by following the guidance of the Holy Spirit, knew a specific spot on the property would remedy this. She pointed at a stone with her cane one day, and asked for someone to turn it over. A little beneath the surface in that spot was a running spring. She had discovered what is now called the "miraculous spring" at Mother Cabrini Shrine. She purchased the property in 1910 to use as a Mission and develop into a summer camp for children of the "Queen of Heaven Orphanage." From this location, she was able to trek out to the mines and tend to the local silver and gold miners,

178 Mother Cabrini Shrine Colorado, www.mothercabrinishrine.org/

who she felt worked long, hard hours in very poor conditions. At times she went crawling on her hands and knees into narrow mine shafts to visit, spread the Good News, and invite the miners to Mass. Her summer camp enabled groups of girls from the orphanage to enjoy the outdoors and perform farm chores. A replica of the grotto of Lourdes was built over the miraculous spring in 1929. It was later replaced by the current sandstone grotto in 1959. The grotto, houses the Statue of the Immaculate Conception. St. Bernadette of Lourdes is mentioned frequently in the *Crusade*, and Sister Bernadette also happened to be the Superior at the Mother Cabrini Shrine convent house for many years. Construction on the Stone House, designed as a dormitory for the summer camp, began in 1912 and was completed in 1914. This summer home is about a ten minute walk away from the new Cova da Iria in the Cabrini chapel—the same amount of time it took from Lucia's house to the Cova da Iria in Fatima.

The shrine became a pilgrimage site in 1938, after Mother Cabrini's beatification. The property was established as a Holy Shrine in 1946, the year she was canonized. In 1954, a twenty-two-foot statue of the Sacred Heart of Jesus was mounted on an enlarged platform at the highest point on the property St. Frances X. Cabrini called *Mount of the Sacred Heart*. Construction on the steps to reach the Sacred Heart statue was begun on September 11, 1954. A 373-step stairway was poured, following the path Mother Cabrini took on her climb up to the mountain top where the statue stands. In 1955 the Knights of Columbus placed terra cotta benches along the stairway, thus allowing pilgrims, to rest, pray and meditate.[179] It is still used by pilgrim visitors today.

Today, the shrine is home to a chapel, meeting rooms, a gift shop, housing for the resident Sisters, and overnight accommodations for visitors.

---

179 Ibid

The summer camp for orphans closed in 1967, and the Stone House was used as a convent until a permanent convent building was completed in 1970, of the same building as the chapel. It is now available as a rentable retreat house.

Lucia entered in the *Crusade* the names Rev. Joseph Corriea da Silva / Bishop Silva as head of the new Diocese of Leiria (*the eyes*). It may be more than coincidental, given the degree of silver mining around the Shrine. Lucia's remarks about St. Margaret-Mary (Virgin AD 1690) of Burgundy, France, could be intended a clue that her final location is connected in some way with the Sacred Heart of Jesus. Mother Cabrini began the Missionary Sisters of the Sacred Heart of Jesus, the main attraction to the shrine. Mother Cabrini is said to have made her First Communion at nine years of age. St. Frances X. Cabrini's Feast day is remarkably, November 13th. In Fatima on May 13th, 1917, Our Lady told Lucia: "I come to ask you to come here for six consecutive months, on the thirteenth, at this same hour. I will tell you who I am and what I want. And I shall return again here a seventh time."[180] St. Frances X. Cabrini's Feast day, November 13 would have been the seventh consecutive 13th of the month. If it were the seventh month, Our Lady would have said come here for seven consecutive months. If the Mother Cabrini Shrine somehow records the presage of September, 11, 2001, that Our Lady confided to Sr. Maria Lucia, it follows that she must have come to the Shrine, and September 11, 2001 was Our Lady's promised seventh visit. "The Sign of the Cross"[181] and the devil in the smoke were truly messages sent by the Lord God and Our Lady.

The architecture of the Cabrini convent chapel complex building is like that of a Swiss chalet—an appropriate style, given the image of the skier highlighted when seeking the location of Fall River, Massachusetts. It

180 De Marchi, *Mother of Christ Crusade*, Chapter III, p 28
181 Ibid., Chapter X, p 130

fits the clue. Church bells call the faithful to Mass, reminding us of the St. Anthony's Church in Fatima. St. Anthony happens to be the patron Saint to help locate things you cannot find.

A visit to Mother Cabrini Shrine

The presence of reminders of Fatima and the *Mother of Christ Crusade,* at Mother Cabrini Shrine, point toward there being the second "Mother Cabrini," present after St. Frances X. Cabrini died on December 22, 1917, being none other than the little girl from Fatima, who became St. Maria Lucia.

The huge statue of Jesus is the most obvious landmark at the shrine. Mother Cabrini Shrine is centered on the statue of The Sacred Heart of Jesus, designed to honor Him and Mother Cabrini who founded The Missionary Sisters of the Sacred Heart of Jesus.

To this day, the water of the miracle spring still flows and is available to all. Curiously, few take advantage of the miraculous spring water. It is a fabulous place to baptize people into the faith of Our Lord, Jesus Christ.

Mother Cabrini herself founded the location of the shrine and developed the area, doing much of the physical labor herself. Any additional construction she could not do was done to her exact specifications. The Statue of the Sacred Heart was placed long after Mother Cabrini died. She did make a heart of white stones that now rests at the base of the statue, but she did not introduce all the other statues or reminders of Fatima. She couldn't have made all of the associations or known all the details at Fatima, for she died only sixty-nine days after the last apparition of October 13, 1917, on December 22nd, 1917. It could only be Lucia's work. No one else knew the contents of the Crusade or the content of the apparitions held secret.

There are stairs leading from the parking area to the statue of the Sacred Heart of Jesus. It is a short hike to the top. An important part of this walk up the mountain to the statue, are the Stations of the Cross, off to the right side along the flight of stairs. The Statue of the Sacred Heart by virtue of the Stations of the Cross is another Icon of the Risen Christ. It is a beautiful white, tall figure of Jesus, so large it is actually visible to the naked eye from some areas of Denver for anyone looking with a keen eye. The statue is very tall; it could well be "the big man" who her mother said rescued Lucia from the crowd after the Third Apparition on July 13, 1917. He rescued her from everyone. He is another of the "Hidden Jesus" Jacinta spoke about being in the Eucharist, but with this parallel meaning.

From the statue of Jesus to the east there are some trees planted by Mother Cabrini. To the north and below is the chalet building and chapel. Lucia must have designed this and had built to her exact specifications, modeled to aid, in conjunction with the map of Fall River, Massachusetts, finding her secret location.

At the very foot of the statue of Jesus, there is a mysterious case that is inset two feet deep, covered by a sheet of glass, and surrounded by an iron fence. Inside this mystery case are white stones, laid in the shape of a heart by Mother Frances X. Cabrini.

In front of the entrance to the chalet was a small flower and rock garden that is said to have been designed and made by Mother Cabrini herself, (the new Mother Cabrini seen in the images of Sr. Maria Lucia). Right above the garden is the building's peak, which has four areas of stained glass, one on each face. Just inside the door of the chalet is a small gift shop. Everyone is invited to look about the chalet building at dolls and items of interest about Mother Cabrini in the display cases. Mother Cabrini's death being in 1917, she didn't direct construction more than where the Stone House should be built, but did set the Sacred Heart of stones and located the miraculous spring. Though the garden before the chapel may have been her doing, it is more likely that it was actually built to Sr. Maria Lucia's exact specifications and not those of St. Frances X. Cabrini.

The chapel is on the second floor, up a flight of stairs from the gift shop. It can be reached by going up the slope directly from outside. Leading from the back of the chapel at the sanctuary is a center altar with the tabernacle behind it.

Chapter 18

The Stairway to the Sacred Heart as the Presage and Reasons for September 11, 2001

The Steps to the Sacred Heart

Lucia wrote to her mother from the convent asking her to help begin a devotion to the Immaculate Heart of Mary. "Everything you need to know is on the back of this enclosed little stamp,"[182] she told her. It sounds as though she meant the stamp placed on the letter. Lucia included an image of the envelope in the *Crusade* in a special way. The stamp is on the back of the envelope pictured in the photo on page 205. In the photo, there is a triangular arrow pointing at Lucia's eye (Iria). Lucia is looking at the garment Our Lady is wearing. On it, beginning beneath Her collar are pictured the twin towers with the letters, WTC, and a face. This location is of strategic import you shall see. The page is a collage of words telling the story of 9/11. She is told Our Lady wants people brought back into the "fold." Folding the page through the arrow creates what looks like the back of an envelope. On the back of this tiny envelope, the other side of the page where a stamp might be placed is the expression, "Good-Bye". Perhaps a good-bye to the twin towers. This is but one of hundreds of stamps to be found in the *Crusade*. The US has the unusual "Liberty Stamp". Once purchased, it can still be used even if the cost of postage is raised.

182 Ibid., Chapter XIV, p 204

Many more stamps are found at Mother Cabrini too. Beside the staircase leading up to the Sacred Heart of Jesus statue at Mother Cabrini shrine, as mentioned, are the Stations of the Cross and the Mysteries of the Rosary. They have been placed along the path up the mountain to show the easy way to eternal life with Our Lord in Heaven.

Each step up to the monument has a small stamped plate honoring some of the many contributors to the Shrine. They could fit in an envelope. The names, however, are either a mystery or a miracle designed to help Lucia's mission to increase a devotion to the Immaculate Heart of Mary. Whether these nameplates represent the names of true contributors or are names Our Lady told Lucia to use, they could have a purpose and a special meaning, and they are stamped, so they were checked. They each have a message of a sort and seem relevant to Our Lady's greater peace plan. If they were unintended, providence has taken a part in them being there.

"Even to this date there are important words of Our Lady, yet undisclosed."[183] They provide part of her mission's message—the key to finding the secret proper holding secret the presage of 9/11. They are prophetic evidence, enough to say that the events of September 11, 2001, were an act of God.

The names on plaques and stamped plates on the steps up the mountainside as well as those in the garden include the names of Lucia's family members, in particular, of her father Antonio L. Santos. These provide more signs that she, and also the Marto children were at the shrine. Though they are said to have died in Fatima, Jacinta's breath "like a flower" and rosy cheeks in her casket, which was later closed in private, and the fact of the

183 Ibid., Chapter XI, p 145

location of the Queen of Heaven Orphanage, say otherwise. For example, the word *Taytay* is the heartwarming word for "Dad" or "Papa" in Portuguese.

Figure 46

This identifies Lucia. The list of stamped nameplates is long and includes support of the fact that Lucia spent time at Cabrini. The hidden meanings in the words give instruction, telling us what we must overcome to reach the Sacred Heart of Jesus and Heaven, and include more signs that the day 9/11 was presaged—all part of Lucia's mission.

The presages of Fatima are recorded history at this point, but in her book, Lucia reveals she received further apparitions from Our Lady and Jesus after leaving Fatima. I assume she received more presages and visions as well. The secret message she held should be found here at Cabrini, in plain sight, on the "stamp"[184]

184 Ibid., Chapter XIV, p 204

put on brass plates on each of the steps, in the architecture, and on the grounds of the complex. Did she receive the 9/11 presage here in Golden, Colorado, or down in Denver? It is not disclosed directly. What is clear is she wrote the prediction of September 11, 2001, before it took place. By specifying the time and place of the attacks and attributing the information to Our Lady, she literally exposed the miraculous and proved not only the divinity of Our Lady and Jesus Christ as Lord, she actually proved the very existence of God!

No harm is intended, only a retelling what Lucia said in *Mother of Christ Crusade*. Remember the source of this information; Lucia received it from Our Lady, and by it she is telling the world what Our Lady wants of us. No one's eyes were opened to this information until now; the lack of its discovery before the events of September 11, 2001, consider an act of God! No one is to blame for not knowing about it or not finding it. This is presage, what the Immaculate Heart of Mary had prepared for the world. By the Will of God it stayed hidden. *Mother of Christ Crusade* was written with divine help and stands on its own as a miracle, holding the secret presage of 9/11. The presage is also written at Cabrini Shrine. This was Lucia's mission, to record the presage of 9/11 and the reasons for it in both the *Mother of Christ Crusade* and did again at the Mother Cabrini Shrine, to prove to the world the divinity of Our Lady and to show Jesus Christ is Lord. It explains why she hid herself in seclusion and wrote her message in secret, so it would not be discovered until the presage came to fruition.

Sister Maria Lucia mentioned "spell" several times in *Mother of Christ Crusade* while at the same time misspelling words. It was a hint. The misspellings are the "important words of Our Lady,"

Lucia said were as "yet undisclosed." When a dictionary[185] is used to help decipher the message of the stamped plates on the steps, the results are amazing. The definitions are informative concerning the cause of 9/11. Suggested meaning is offered as well. Read the list as it develops. They tie the song "Only the Good Die Young" and its mocking, demeaning attack on the Catholic Church and the mistreatment of women in general, to September 11, 2001. They also refer back to the Cathedral of the Immaculate Conception in Denver. This list is long, there being 373 steps to the Sacred Heart. If you see the trend and purpose of the definitions, it is all you need to advance to the presage.

Tony A. Notary

Notary: a person registered to represent in notation a message, empowered to certify documents, take affidavits and depositions. This is the first nameplate at the bottom of the stairs.

The sworn truth, Notarized: Lucia's guarantee that the presages and supporting arguments of her message to the world on the steps and in the *Crusade* is truth. These messages include knowledge of how we offend Our Lord Jesus Christ—offenses that need attention and change. It is a life and death message for us, given to her by Our Lady, Immaculate Mary. We must comply with the commands Jesus demands.

To NY, A Not, ary

"To New York a not," are why: "This is why 9/11 took place." The letters *ary* may help to understand the reasons why this happened,

---

185 *Tormont Publications Inc., Webster's illustrated Encyclopedic Dictionary,* Tormont Publications Inc. 1990 edition. 338 St. Antoine St. East, Montreal, Canada, H2Y 1A3. 514-954-1441. ISBN 2-921171-32-5. *Webster's Seventh New Collegiate Dictionary,* G. and C. Merriam Company, Publishers, 1972 Edition

and carry over to the next home of the miraculous presage of 9/11, where the "ary" is written in stone. "Ary", are the last letters of the word sanctuary and reference were the note is written. Lucia leads to her concluding directives, those listed in the Crusade as the purpose for her work. Abortion, pornography, adulterous sex, terror, war, and the abuse of Catholic religious rights are all brought forward.

Ernest Bordigon

Bordure: a border around, or a shield to protect; to bore, to make a hole through.

Jina Florida

A Jingle: to make a repeated tinkling or ringing metallic sound, or a repetitious catchy rhyme or song. This could reference "Jingle Bells" and "Santa" in Lucia Santos. It shows that music is the subject.

Jingo: one who vociferously supports their foreign policy; an uncritical patriot; a chauvinist; by Jingo perhaps euphemistic for "by Jesus." It draws further attention to the Cabrini sanctuary.

Florida: one of the fifty states of America located on the most southeast corner of continental United States; a peninsular appendage of the continental United States that forms the eastern border of the Gulf of Mexico.

Flordina: Flordina and Teresa were Francisco and Jacinta's sisters, who were also asked to become nuns. Their mother objected. Soon after, Our Lady came to take them to Heaven also.[186]

Larry Federico

Larrigan: a moccasin with knee-high leggings of leather.

---

186 De Marchi, *Mother of Christ Crusade*, Chapter XII, p 176

Larrup: to beat or a blow.

Larum: an alarm or emergency signal.

Lars Porsena: an Etrusscan, who in roman legend attacked Rome.

Federico Pena: the first name of a Denver Mayor instrumental in developing the Denver International Airport (DIA). *O' Dia* was the name of a Lisbon newspaper that reported the events of the Sixth Apparition in Fatima.

Fed up: out of patience, irritated, tired of waiting.

Fee: a fixed charge by an institution or law, an inherited estate, an estate or land granted by a lord to a vassal on condition of homage and service.

Fedora: a soft felt hat with a brim that can be turned up or down, with a fairly low crown. A tipped, red fedora can be seen just right of the copper colored halo of the Risen Jesus, on the Cabrini chapel sanctuary wall. It is a tip or clue.

Federation: united under a central government.

Bosilio Oliveri

Bosh: meaningless talk or nonsense, or empty or useless words, directed by the above, meaning the empty rhetoric and false promises of politicians or legislators.

Basky: covered with bushes, shrubs, or shaded by trees.

Bosnia: a Balkan Provence joined with Herzegovina in 1946 to form Yugoslavia.

Olive: one of the types of trees that grew on Antonio Santo's property. Olive tree branches are considered a sign of peace. Olive branches and arrows are grasped by the bald eagle on the Great Seal of the United States as illustrated on the back of the US one dollar bill. Extending an olive branch is the symbolic offering and request for peace. An edible fruit.

Olivary: ovaries or shaped like an olive, or pertaining to two olive-shaped bodies of nervous tissue on either side of the Medulla Oblongata.

Mount Olives: garden of Gethsemane.

Olive drab: military uniform color.

Ernest Bordigon

Erne: a sea eagle (American Airlines?).

Max Ernest: a German painter and sculptor, a leading figure in the surrealism movement and exponent of collage and photo montage.

Erode: to wear away at or destroy.

Border: margin, verge.

Bordure: the border around a shield.

Bore: to create a hole especially by drilling, to advance steadily, the caliber of a firearm, to tire with repetition or dullness.

In memory of Mr. and Mrs. Felix Pomponio

Felix: to fell, to cause to fall. *To fell* is a term often associated with a tree, to cut it down (to fell a tree). On Sept. 11, 2001, the twin towers at the center for World Trade were felled.

Felicitate: to make happy, to congratulate.

Felicitous: well-chosen and in an appropriate pleasing manner.

Felicity: great happiness or bliss.

Feline: suggestive of a cat including lions, tigers, jaguars, lynx, and other wild and domestic cats. A reference to the miraculous images (shown later) found on the marble walls at St. Thomas More Church that include a lioness and lion, appearing very recently, long after Cabrini was built.

Fidelity: the behavior expected of married couples not to engage in relations with anyone besides their own spouse with whom real marriage belongs. Jacinta mentions it when she says, "Many marriages are not good; they do not please Our Lord and are not of God."[187]

Pompous: characterized by an exaggerated show of dignity or self-importance, people who feel others are lower for a multitude of reasons, such as sex, race, and religious practice.

Ponce: Ponce de Leon, an explorer who sailed with Christopher Columbus. A reference to the Knights of Columbus, longtime supporters of the Cabrini Shrine, and a reminder of the Fourth Degree knight with the candle on his head in the photo of the Shrine at Valinhos in the *Crusade* prompting the use of a night-light to view the images.

A Ponce: a man who lives off the earnings of a prostitute, a pimp.

Capolungo

Cap: Cover ones mouth to keep them quiet. Cap over lungs.

---

187 Ibid., Chapter XII, p 177

It speaks to rock and roll, and especially the song "Only the Good Die Young" if abduction and rape are involved. Put a cover over the song mistreating women.

Capo: a small, movable bar placed across the fingerboard of a guitar, altering the pitch of all strings simultaneously.

Capo: the head of an organized crime syndicate.

Capon: a rooster castrated when young to improve the quality of the flesh for food.

Capitulation: to surrender, a document signed containing the terms of the surrender.

Capitulum: a dense, head-like cluster of stalk-less flowers, a small knob or head-like part, such as the end of a bone or the tip of an insect's antenna. Antennae were atop the WTC, which ID rock-and-roll music.

Capone, Al: an Italian-born US gangster, he ruled the Chicago underground ruthlessly. In the St. Valentine's Day massacre, he gunned down seven members of Bugs Moran's gang.

Cosasco

COS: cash on shipment, the payment arrangement in the prostitution business.

Cosa Nostra: a crime syndicate active throughout the United States, hierarchic in structure in locally independent units.

Carmon and Louis Ciano, Welby Colo.-

*The A*s: on the plaque, reading CArmon And Louis CiAno, the *A*s are all a bit taller than the other letters. Each *A* looks like the Eiffel

Tower in Paris, France. The phonetic pronouncement, "I fell tower," provides a clue to the towers being felled. The Lord may be accepting responsibility for doing so. This is the second "to fell" (see "In memory of Mr. and Mrs. Felix Pomponio"), completing the Two Twin Towers, that were to fall. The fact that there are three "towers" represented in this name, lends credence to the idea that the third tower would have been the Sears Tower in Chicago had it not been for two words: "Let's roll." It was also implied by virtue of the repetitious mention of the "three seers" in reference to the three children of Fatima: Jacinta and Francisco Marto and Lucia Santos.

Car-man: a person in a car, taxi driver.

In loving memories of Pasquale and Angelina, Maria

Pasquinade: a lampoon, especially one posted in a public place, or publically broadcast by media. To ridicule, with pasquinade. Also the nickname of a Holy Statue in Rome.

Pasquino: the nickname of an ancient statue in Rome on which lampoons were posted in the sixteenth century. In this circumstance, the public ridicule of all Christian statues in general, by art museums and media.

Pasque Flower: any of several plants of the *Anemone patens* variety, especially the Eurasian species, *genus A. Pulsitilla* (From Old French: Easter). The words of Sister Lucia at the beginning of chapter 3, equating multicolored flowers to children.

Pompous: characterized by an exaggerated show of self-importance, pretentious, arrogant superiority.

Angelina: angel in.

Maria: Sister Maria Lucia of Fatima, a duplicate, a twin.

C. Kane

Citizen Kane: this is Sister Maria Lucia's direct reference to the film *Citizen Kane,* a movie produced in the 1930s. Lucia reveals the meaning of "Rosebud". "Rose Bud," the last words spoken by Mr. Kane as he drops a snow globe to the floor, before he dies at the films start. These words are made the subject of much inquiry, and the viewers are asked to figure out what "Rosebud" really means. In the opening scene is when Charlie Kane is informed of his inheritance, it shows him as a child sledding. He holds a sled named rosebud. His sled hills were also the terrain in the snow globe. In the movie, Charlie Kane a righteous man of new wealth, has a passion for and collects statues. He builds a newspaper empire and uses it to fight corruption by exposing it in business and politics.

At the beginning and at the end of the film, a dead frozen "Rose Bud," is shown on the roof of the "sun" room, of the famous El Rancho restaurant that happens to be near the Cabrini Shrine. The *rosebud above,* directs attention at Mother Cabrini's Shrine, situated nearby in the mountains above the El Rancho restaurant and the budding devotion to the Sacred Heart growing at the Cabrini Shrine. There are many other statues at Mother Cabrini honoring Jesus and the Virgin Mary and other sacred statue icons in addition to the huge Sacred Heart statue. They are the main feature at the shrine. Mr. Kane's empire and his plentiful statue collection is Hollywood's analogy of the Catholic Church and the statues at Cabrini Shrine. The scene in the snow globe and the early scene when young Charlie Kane was found sledding, is a place looking very familiar. The Rose is Jesus. The red and white Jesus in the sanctuary exposes Hollywood's target in the film, the sled named rosebud is just to mislead the naïve, since they keep asking what it means while knowing the name of the sled as it and his statues are being thrown into a huge fire at Mr. Kane's mansion. The growing devotion to the Sacred Heart of Jesus, is the real *Rose bud.* It is also a signal for others who know the true meaning of "Rosebud". The movie is a clear attack on the Church for its trying to promote fairness in business and politics. False promises and corruption are simply sinful the Church points out. Lucia determined while being at the Shrine, perhaps with knowledge gained from Our Lady that the movie exhibits a violation of the religious liberty afforded to all religions in the First Amendment of the United States Constitution, but it is subliminal and could not be proven either way without an admission. Why anyone would desire to squelch social justice and the moral code promoted by the Catholic Church is up for individual interpretation. Hollywood is referenced in another way in how Lucia presented the word holmoak as one word, instead of holm oak. This holmoak is Holywood. Lucia associates it with offensive magazines and all forms of religiously abusive media. By putting C. Kane on the steps she is identifying the Cabrini Shrine as Rosebud. You need to decide for yourself.

It can also reference Mother Cabrini's cane she used to find the miraculous spring, and determine where the stone house should be built.

Michael Marsico

Marscionism: the agnostic movement of the second and third centuries that rejected the Old Testament, and emphasized the teaching of St. Paul.

Lucille Ponzio and Vincent Ponzio

Ponzio: Major contributors to Children's Hospital in Denver and Mother Cabrini Shrine.

Luciferin: a bioluminescent chemical, such as found in "fireflies", that produces a bluish-green light when oxidized;

Luciferous: bringing light or insight. This will be shown to be of great significance, an important reason for condemning "OTGDY". 1978, the year the song came out and 9/11, will be directly related when seen together in what can only be described as an regularly repeated miraculous mirage of presage.

Vincible: capable of being overcome or defeated, surmountable. This name may reference to the radical Supreme Court decision known as "Roe v. Wade," which makes it legal for men to kill a woman's unborn child, at the public's expense. A translation used as an aid to study.

Vinculum: a bar drawn over algebraic terms to indicate they are to be treated as a single term. Any connecting band or fold, such as the umbilical cord, or the connecting ligament below the tongue. A bond or tie. I take this to reference abortion when the fetus and mother are considered one life. The fetus is considered only an organ of the mother, not a separate life, thus not afforded any right to life, justifying abortion as a noncriminal offense; yet the death of the unborn is considered murder and the death of the mother and unborn in a crime makes the perpetrator guilty of two murders and eligible for the death penalty under some state laws. Combined with *vincible*, this says Roe v. Wade can and must be overturned.

Cocasco

Crime syndicate: sounds like "cause" and "ask"; the message becomes, the illegal act of abortion is a cause for 9/11 listed in the *Crusade* and needs to be stopped immediately.

Ponzio

Pony: a racehorse, "a crib," also a translation used as an aid to study. A reference to babies.

Ponzi

Ponzi: a scheme to borrow from one investors own funds to pay another instead of investing the funds. Knowingly entering a Ponzi scheme, even at the last round of the scheme, can be economical if there is an expectation that government will bail-out those participating in the ponzi scheme by defrauding the common taxpayer. Cheating people of their hard-earned money becomes another cause of 9/11. There's plenty of recent news about financial brokers getting in trouble for ponzi schemes.

In memory of Fred E. Padilla By: Mary E. Padilla

Padishah: formerly the title of the Shah of Iran; former title of a Sultan of Turkey. Perhaps an indirect reference to 9/11 and how it was brought upon us, using the unconscious instrument of God of Isaiah 47.

E. Padilla: epact, the excess of time, about eleven days of the solar year over the lunar year. (We are taking too long to eliminate Roe v. Wade decision.)

Eparch: the chief administrator of an eparchy, a bishop or metropolitan. The catholic bishops have always been pro-life and of the belief that laws forcing Catholic doctors and hospitals to perform abortions against their will and faith doctrine, strips them of their right to religious freedom as guaranteed by the First Amendment to the US Constitution. Similar would be forcing patients to see a doctor who they feel is morally incompatible with their faith. As written, the First Amendment puts religious freedom before any other.

In memory of Anna Shrubas and Walter Shrubas

Shrove-tide: three days, the Sunday, Monday, and Tuesday before Ash Wednesday.

Shrove Tuesday: the day before Ash Wednesday. Mardi Gras is a party before Ash Wednesday.

A Shrub: a bush or bushes, in this case maybe referring to the two President Bushes, George H. W. Bush and George W. Bush, who was president of the United States at the time of 9/11.

DEDICATED TO WORLD PEACE

Peace: Lucia writes in the *Mother of Christ Crusade* that Our Lady said "Continue to say the Rosary everyday in honor of Our Lady of the Rosary to obtain peace for the world and an end to the war; for only she alone can save it.[188] Our Lady came to bring peace to the world and the fountain of peace is the possession of grace. Wars are only punishment for the sins of the world. Grace makes man only and pleasing to God. Only when grace illumines man's soul is there peace between God and man. And when peace reigns between god and man, Mary will reward the world with peace.[189] Our Lady's peace plan to restore religious liberty has been outlined.

Loving son Frank John Garcia; (8-18-44–2-24-96)

Garcia: dictionary search leads to Marrakesh, a major Islamic port and tourist city.

In memory of Mary Yacovetta

Yackity-yak: slang for *yap*, the mouth, noisy, scolding talk. All talk and no action. Describing the insincerity of politicians and parties negotiating settlements.

Yafa: leads to Jaffa, an ancient city in west central Israel. Founded by the Phoenicians, it was taken by the Israelites in sixth century

---

188 De Marchi, John, Saint Sr. Maria Lucia, *Mother of Christ Crusade,* Chapter V, p 64

189 Ibid, Chapter XIV, p 216

BC, fell to the Arabs in 636, and fell again to the crusaders. It is now part of Tel Aviv.

Eugene and Isabelle Piro

Pirarucu: a fish, Portuguese.

Pirate or pirate ship: one who robs at sea or plunders the land near the sea without commission from a sovereign nation. One who makes use of or reproduces the work, especially the copyrighted work of another illicitly, without authorization, for example, a video pirate.

Piro: sounds like pyro or fire.

Pirog: a large Russian pastry made with meat, fish, rice, eggs, or vegetables.

In Memory of Donato & Victoria Pietraroia

Piety: religious devotion and reverence to God.

Pieta: a painting, drawing, or sculpture of the Virgin Mary holding or mourning over the dead body of Jesus.

Piezo: indicates pressure, to squeeze or press.

In Memory of Cisco & Maria Iacino

Cisco & Maria: this is probably a direct reference to Francisco and Sr. Maria Lucia.

Iacino: in absentia, absent. In this position on the steps it reminds us of the *Mother of Christ Crusade*, which indicates avoiding TV programs, CDs (music), and DVDs (movies) that are licentious, implicating pornography, and the absence of morality including abuse of women.

Iacocca, Lido Anthony: US business executive, served as president of Ford Motor Co., later president and CEO of Chrysler Corp. As chairman of the Statue of Liberty-Ellis Island Foundation, he organized the campaign to restore and refurbish the statue for its centennial in 1986. He received a government bail-out.

Liberty: the condition of not being subject to restriction or control, of not being in confinement; the right to act in a manner of one's choosing. Authorized leave from Navel duty. There are differing types of liberty. Whereas life, liberty and the pursuit of happiness is in the Constitution, the right to it is clarified in the First Amendment. Religious liberty is specifically protected by the US Constitution, placed before Free Speech in the First Amendment. It reinforces the idea that when Catholics are being forced to perform abortions against their faith, their conscious religious liberty is being violated.

Renewing liberty: restoring it to what it was intended to mean is required of us. The last page of *Mother of Christ Crusade* says Our Lady needs "YOUR" dime too. The dime at the time was a Mercury Dime with a wing headed Lady Liberty on it. She is talking about the restoration of my religious liberty.

Taking liberty: a statement, attitude or action not warranted by conditions or actualities. Could be not occupied or in use. A step, indicating a further need to demand a return of religious liberty for the Catholic Church that was lost to the song "Only the Good Die Young." The final goal of this book is to defend the religious liberty for the Catholic Church and to protect it from Anti-Catholic slurs, innuendos, false accusations and ruin.

Libertinism: sexual promiscuity.

Libertine: one who acts without moral or sexual restraint; a dissolute person; one standing in defiance of established moral precepts.

Liberty cap: a magic mushroom; known as a symbol of "liberty" during the French Revolution, a brimless cap that fits snugly around the head with a soft conical crown.

Liberty hall: a place in which one can behave in a manner of one's choosing.

Liberty Bell: as shown in *Mother of Christ Crusade*. Liberty Bell in Philadelphia is cracked. Accept this break as reasonably miraculous, an act of God performed for this moment in time, associating the cracked bell with the presages of Our Lady in Fatima. Lucia included it with the presages and did so to encourage working toward the goal of religious liberty for the Catholic Church now.

Licentious: lacking moral discipline or sexual restraint, having no regard for accepted rules or standards from freedom.

Liberty Island: located in the Upper New York Bay, Southwest of Manhattan. The Statue of Liberty was placed on it, using the star-shaped Fort Wood as a base.

Libidinous: having lustful desires.

Libido: psychic or emotional energy associated with the instinctual biological drive, the manifestation of sexual drive.

In the Denver area: James Iacino was grandson of Moses Iacino, president of Seattle Fish Company.

Cisco: part of Francisco, his name frequently hyphenated in the *Crusade* to Fran-cisco. "Cisco" means white fish.

Joseph Fiore

Fire: destroying or consuming of an object with fire; luminosity or brilliance.

Mary Piccoli

Mary: Virgin Mother of Jesus Christ.

Piccolo: a flute, one octave higher; flute or small trumpet. Francisco Marto carried and played a flute when the girls enjoyed sing and dancing.

In Loving Memory of Antonio L. Santos; we love you Tatay

Antonio Santos: a plate with Lucia's father's name, confirming Lucia's presence.

Tatay: "daddy" in Portuguese.

Tatar: any of the Turkish Languages of Tatar.

Allen Tate: US Poet, critic, editor, and biographer; included in his works of criticism, *Reason in Madness*.

Santos: a seaport on Sao Paulo State, in southeastern Brazil. It was founded on the Tiete River by Portuguese Jesuits in 1554. Independence from Portugal was achieved in 1822. It is the biggest financial, commercial, and industrial center in South America, according to the source. [190] Sounds like *Santa Claus*.

Cafferata Gandolfo

Caffeine: a bitter white alkaloid.

Gandolfo: a game, a calculated plan or action for attaining an end; a retreat of the pope of the Catholic Church.

In memory of the Vasquez and Verdusco Family

Vassal: a person who held land from a feudal lord and received protection in return for homage and allegiance, one that is a subject or subservient to another.

Verdant: green in color, inexperienced or unsophisticated. A greenhorn or novice.

Steven Chiolera

Wallace Stevens: US poet, distinguished by his poetry's tight construction and its intellectual and lucid content, whose works include "The man with the blue guitar."
Robert Louis Stevenson: novelist, essayist, and poet. His works include "Virginibus Puerisque," *Treasure Island*, and the *Strange Case of Dr. Jekyll and Mr. Hyde.*

Chiolero: chintzy, gaudy, trashy, cheap, bright, fizzy, flowery style that attempts to evoke an old-fashioned atmosphere.

Chin-wag: a gossip or conversation; "OTGDY" with reference to 9/11 and virgins in the *Crusade*.

---

190 *Tormont Publications Inc., Webster's illustrated Encyclopedic Dictionary,* Tormont Publications Inc. 1990 edition. 338 St. Antoine St. East, Montreal, Canada, H2Y 1A3. 514-954-1441. ISBN 2-921171-32-5.

Cholera: the disease; the epidemic of abuse of virgins in "OTGDY," young deaths have become an epidemic. If this was presage, it has come true. Lucia wrote this thirty-two years before the song was released.

Chippendale: a type of furniture with smooth, flowing lines. Also a name for a group of men, who strip for the entertainment of women.

The Francisco M. Rodriguez and Family

Francisco M. Rodriguez: perhaps Francisco Marto's new name. He, too, would need to change his name after leaving Fatima, Portugal, if he faked his death and later became a priest in Denver or wherever.

Fr. Marlon Rodriguez: a priest at St. Thomas More parish in Centennial, Colorado until November 2011. His place of service to Our Lady at St. Thomas More, Sr. Maria Lucia could never have known.

Mr. and Mrs. Joe Vendegnia Jr. Family

Vendetta: hostile malicious campaign, feud perpetuated by retaliatory acts motivated by vengeance. To get back at, for mistreatment or physical harm done.

Vendible: capable of being sold.

Veneer: a thin finish or surface layer of wood and plastic, referencing guitar wood; implication of rock-and-roll musical instrument.

A gift of Theresa Pilo

Teresa: Teresa was Lucia's sister. According to *Crusade*, on August 19, 1917, as part of the Fourth Apparition, Our Lady promised the children she would perform a miracle all could see so they, too, might believe.[191]

> As the apparition began, Teresa and her husband were coming into the village of Fatima, when they noticed the "sudden cooling of the air, the paling of the sun, and the pattern of different colors over everything."[192] When the apparition ended, the children watched helplessly as the older people stripped the holmoak of its foliage and broke off the little branch, which the resplendent robe of Our Lady had touched. This is the little branch Jacinta took home. It had a magnificent fragrance. First, Jacinta showed it to Lucia's unbelieving mother smelled it, and then the entire family gathered around and smelled the beautiful odor. It was not perfume or roses or incense—they could not describe it. Leave it hear, Jacinta, someone will come along who can tell you what kind of odor it is. From that moment on, Lucia's mother and the whole family began to modify their opposition to the apparitions. Jacinta then took the branch and hurried home. Ti Marto said when Jacinta entered the room carrying the little branch he "sensed" a magnificent fragrance he could not explain; when he smelled the branch the odor had gone.

The smell is of a baby, perhaps the new baby of Lucia's older sister Teresa and her husband. It does not say. They would be arriving home about the same time as Lucia and Jacinta. Lucia's family smelled the beautiful fragrance of the baby; Ti Marto sensed the magnificent fragrance of his own baby girl. Our Lady need not prove anything to him, for he had his miracle in Jacinta. Children and babies are beautiful to Our Lady and are not to be aborted.

191 Ibid., Chapter VIII, p 112
192 Ibid., Chapter VII, p 103

Magnifi-cent: "cent," or to find the scent, or rather or pick up the trail. Our Lady has her foot on a twig in the picture on the cover of *Crusade*. The scent of a baby is a warning not to abort children; Our Lady says so. You can see the twig Our Lady stood on when you look at the picture on the cover of *Mother of Christ Crusade*. Examine it with a magnifying glass. The copper halo on the Risen Jesus on the sanctuary wall is Magnifi-cent.

Mother Teresa: an Indian nun who dedicated her life to the desperately poor and dying. She founded the Missionaries of Charity.

Pilot: one who operates an aircraft or spacecraft in flight or steers a ship in and out of port or dangerous waters; something that serves as a test, trial, or model; to control the course of.

Rocco and Elizabeth Garramone

Roc: a legendary bird of prey, a hawk, rock and roll, robust, full of health and strength, down-to-earth, boisterous and rough.

Elizabeth: to eliminate; to get rid of, reject, omit; mother of John the Baptist, Elizabeth II, Queen of England and Northern Ireland; Elizabeth I (1558) succeeded the Catholic, Mary I and returned England to Protestant. She survived many plots to murder her and place the Catholic Mary, Queen of Scots, back on the throne; the mother of the Virgin Mary, Mother of God. This is a message that the Virgin Mary is under attack by the anti-Christian movement in America that dismisses Mary as insignificant and unworthy of honor, contributing to the anti-Catholic attitudes and sentiments in society.

Elijah: a prophet (900–800 BC)

Garret: a room on the top floor of a house, or the “penthouse”; *Penthouse* is a pornographic magazine, and pornography was the reason Lucia Santos used bullet points in *Mother of Christ Crusade*; a turret or watchtower to defend or protect, a reference to the watchman or a gun turret. “Bullets” are ammunition for firearms, sometimes loaded in magazines, thus implicating pornography. If you have large amounts of ammunition, they bullets are carried in “pill boxes,” noting the involvement of drug abuse contributing to addictions and perhaps associating drugs to pornography. The bullet points could be the presage of Woodstock and the widespread drug use and sexual revolution of the sixties.

Figure 47

Carousel tent at the Cathedral of the Immaculate Conception cross-referencing the Cathedral with Cabrini Shrine and the holmoak tree.

Anthony Michael Carocella

Umbrella: the Cathedral of the Immaculate Conception has a carousel-like tent, umbrella, or canopy near a statue of Our Lady. In front of it there is a small tree that has been stripped of its leaves, resembling the description of the little holmoak tree. Umbrellas were used during the Sixth Apparition. Both the tree with the green base and the umbrella tie in *Mother of Christ Crusade* to the Denver Cathedral and the Cabrini Shrine. This statue is nearly an exact replica of the statue at the Shrine at Valinhos in the *Crusade* book.

Caroche: a carriage used in the sixteenth and seventeenth century, a reminder of the magistrate's abduction of the children at Fatima.

Carob: an evergreen tree, with compound leaves and edible pods, also called, "algarroba," and "locust." *Locust* is a word contained in the Book of Joel. The Sacred Heart of Jesus directs us to yet another destination, also rich with information and prophecy. Evergreen is a city just south of Mother Cabrini Shrine Complex.

Carol: a song of praise and joy, especially one celebrating the birth of Jesus Christ; to celebrate in song, to sing in a joyous manor; an old round dance, often accompanied by singing. In *Crusade*, Lucia Santos was the first to put a pink ribbon on the holmoak tree.

Caroucel: a tournament in which knights or horsemen engage in various exercises, drafting the Knights of Columbus to help in Lucia's cause.

A merry-go-round: a canopy looking like that of a carousel stands before Our Lady at the Cathedral of the Immaculate Conception

Carousal: a riotous drinking party.

Carouse: to drink excessively, go on a drinking spree.

Guiliano and Donata Caruso

Guidon: a small flag or pennant, carried as a standard by a regiment or other military unit, the flag of baseball teams and name for winning the World Series.

Giuliani, Rudolph: mayor of New York City when the terrorist attack took place at the World Trade Center.

Guild: an association of people of the purpose, maintenance of standards, or furtherance of some purpose.

Donata, Dona: a Spanish gentlewoman.

Donate: to present as a gift, especially to a fund or cause, contribute.

Caruso, Enrico: an Italian opera singer whose final performance was at the Metropolitan Opera in New York, where he ruptured a blood vessel in his throat while singing and later died from related complications.

Carotid: two major arteries in the neck.

Eucene J. Veraldi

Eucharist: the Christian sacrament instituted by Jesus Christ at the Last Supper in which bread and wine are consecrated into the Body and Blood of Jesus Christ then eaten and drank in memory of Him. "He who eats this Bread and drinks my Blood shall have everlasting life." Jesus said these words. The Body and Blood of Christ are referred to as Holy Communion or the Sacrament of the Eucharist instituted at the Last Supper. The establishment of the Eucharist at the Last Supper is a new Mystery of the Rosary, the final decade of the Luminous Mysteries.

Euchre: a card game in which each player gets five cards and the player making the trump is required to make three tricks to win.

Euchromatin: chromosome material that stains most deeply with basic dyes when the cell is dividing and represents the major genes involved in protein synthesis.

Veracity: habitual adherence to the truth.

Veranda: a porch or balcony; a tie to *Mother of Christ Crusade* with the balcony of the priest's rectory where the children showed up after their abduction by the magistrate.

Jake Schleger

Friedrich von Schlegel: German writer and critic, a Sanskrit scholar, he was the leader of the *romantic* movement formulating its aims and publishing his poetry and philosophy in the magazine *Das Athenaeum.*

Schemial: is an unlucky and habitual bungler.

BEWARE OF DANGEROUS SNAKES,

Devil: made into a snake because of its trickery in the Garden of Eden; the Antichrist, in the smoke of 9/11.

Tiofila Gomez, Jose E Gallegos, Mrs. Orland Gallagos and Gallagos Family

tiny: extremely small, or minute.

Gomorra: a city in ancient Palestine near Sodom. Homosexuality is a serious sin, referred to in the small print in *Mother of Christ Crusade.*

Galla: a member of a pastoral Hermitic people of southern Ethiopia and Somalia.

Gallant: courageous, daring, valorous, amorous, and attentive to women.

C. C. Morley

Orle: an inner border not quite touching the edge of a shield.

Morally: behavior considered appropriate, a set of ideas based on right from wrong, regulating personal or societal behavior to ensure their continued existence.

Moral rearmament: an international movement advocating spiritual revival and the consolidation of morality or Christian principles.

Mormon: a prophet, warrior, and historian of the fourth century AD, was revealed to founder Joseph Smith in 1830.

John Berry and Mary Berry

Marriage vows: stay married until you are buried, "until death do us part." Divorce is an epidemic.

Chuck Berry: one of the first singer/songwriters to evolve a rock-and-roll style. It is an indictment of rock-and-roll music for abuse and assault on the dignity of women.

Berry: a fleshy fruit, such as a grape, date, or tomato, with two or more seeds that does not split open when ripe; any of various seeds or dried kernels, such as that of a coffee plant to produce or bear berries.

Berretta, Biretta: a stiff Roman Catholic cap or hooded cloak, which of a priest is black, of a bishop is purple, and of a cardinal is red.

J. O'Brian Tolve

Job to Solve: Lucia's clue that these steps and the grounds of the Shrine are a "job to solve."

Toluidine: used to make dyes; may be related to dies.

Judith A. and Donald Svaldi

Judiciary: of or pertaining to courts, judges, or judicial decisions. Lucia has included the implementation of the law to fight for religious freedom.

Don: to put on, to dress.

Dona: a Spanish gentlewoman, a title of courtesy placed before a woman's Christian name.

Svelte: slender or graceful in figure or outline.

Svengali: a person with an uncanny power to compel another to do his will.

Lucia, Alfonso, Minella, and George

Lucia: an obvious reference to Sr. Maria Lucia.

Lucid: easily understood, clear, rational.

Lucifer: an archangel cast from heaven for leading a revolt of the angels.

Al Fatah see Fatah: minelayer, a ship or aircraft, equipped for laying underwater mines.

George W. Bush, US President (2004–2008) during 9/11.

Mr. and Mrs. James J. Varone and family

Marcus Terentius Varro: Roman encyclopedist, the first universal scholar of Roman civilization. His highly influential works include *History of Human and Divine Antiquities* .

Mr. and Mrs. Chas Wedow

Wedlock: the state of being married, pledge-giving marriage vow, widowed. Until death do us part.

Florence M. Hussey

Florid: flushed with rosy color, the result of embarrassment.

Hussy: a sexually promiscuous woman.

Concetta Mazzotti Marino

Concessionary: of the nature of or granted by concession.

Giuseppi Mazzini: an Italian Revolutionary Nationalist.

Mariology: the body of belief pertaining to the Virgin Mary.

Mr. and Mrs. Fred Turilli

Turin: a city in northwestern Italy.

Shroud of Turin: the burial cloth of Jesus with the face of Jesus on it.

John and Ellen Stefanac

Step: indicates a relationship through the previous marriage of a spouse, through the remarriage of a spouse rather than by blood.

Stepchild: the child of one's spouse by a previous marriage.

Step down: to take a lower position.

Step fault: a series of steps along a fault line after an earthquake.

Stephanotis: suitable for a wreath.

Steffens, Lincoln: a US journalist editor who exposed corruption in city government and began the era of muckraking journalism, who was later interested in revolutionary Russia and Mexico.

Fred and Mary DeNave

Nave: central part of a church, extending from the narthex to the chancel and flanked by aisles; the hub of a wheel (like the one found at Cabrini Shrine); wheels stuck in the mud of pilgrims coming to see the Sixth Apparition in Fatima, referral to the cathedral.

John B. Martina

G. L. Martin: a US airplane manufacturer who established one of the first airplane factories in America.

Delores Louis Lesch, of Canoga Park, Calif.

Dell: a secluded valley.

Delouse: to rid of lice by physical or chemical means.

Lice: a parasite.

Louis d'or: a 20 franc gold piece issued before the Revolution.

Letch: characterized by a strong craving, especially of a sexual nature.

Lecher: a man given to excessive sexual cravings or indulgence, such as a pedophile, also lasciviousness in acting on this craving.

Lesbian: a female homosexual.

Lese majesty: a crime committed against a sovereign power.

Carmen and Louise CiAncio and Family of Welby, CO

Car-man: a man who drives a car or cart, or a driver or conductor of a streetcar.

Carlsberg Caverns: in southwestern New Mexico, in the Guadeloupe Mountains, limestone caves discovered about 1900 that began to form 60 million years ago.

The most notable aspect of these names was the way the letters were made. The "A" in CArmon, CiAncio, and fAmily, were made especially tall and are shaped like the Eiffel Tower, presage of the World Trade Center towers. This presentation gives credibility to using the names as unfound words Lucia suggested we find with urgency. "CIA" prompts a person to take a closer look.

Carmelite: a monk or mendicant friar belonging to the Order of Our Lady of Mt. Carmel, founded at Mt. Carmel in about 1155. Our Lady dressed in the robes of Mt. Carmel is in the Cabrini sanctuary.[193]

Carmichael, Hoagland: a US songwriter, who moved to New York City in 1920 and dedicated himself to music. He wrote "Stardust," "Georgia On My Mind," and "Riverboat Shuffle."

Welcome: received with pleasure and hospitality into one's company. Cordially permitted or invited to do or enjoy. Freely granted one's courtesy.

193 Ibid., Chapter X, p113

CiAncio: an Italian fascist statesman who became influential after marrying Benito Mussolini's daughter. Having urged Italy to join the Axis powers, he later favored a separate peace with the Allies and was one of those who forced Mussolini's resignation.

Richard Chavez III-

Chávez, César: US Labor organizer, founded the National Farm Workers Association in California's prime agricultural areas.

Josephine Stracina Delina of Buffalo, New York-

Joe Blow: the average Joe, the man in the street.

Joel: a book of the Old Testament containing Joel's prophecies of the judgment of Judah.

Joey: a young kangaroo, or a young child.

Straddle: to sit, stand, or be in a position astride; shots fired behind and in front of to determine range; to fall on or take in parts; to fall or lie on either side of; or to sit or stand with the legs apart. Speaks to "OTGDY."

Delina: to deliberate, to take careful thought of, or to consult with others as a process of reaching a decision, or a premeditated and intentional choice. Also speaks to the lyrics of "OTGDY."

John and Adele Tosi, of New York, NY-

A phonetic warning: John and Adele To-see of New York, or you'll see!

Toss: to throw out. Infers tossing out, a remembrance of the victims of abortion. The fate of children abducted and raped.

Toss it out: the music.

Mr. and Mrs. Felice Pomponio-

Fell: to cause to fall.

Pompous: characterized by an exaggerated show of dignity or self-importance.

Ponce de Leon: an explorer who sailed with Christopher Columbus, a duplicate.

Hazel Mae Subalo-

Subalpine: growing or living in mountainous region below the timberline.

Subaerial: located on or near the surface of the earth.

Nanay, Carmencita, Baldonado Ramos from Nenita and Sidney Jensen-

Nance: is an effeminate man, especially a homosexual.

Carmel: a village in western California on Carmel Bay at the southern end of the Monterey Peninsula, known as a writer's and artist's community and popular with tourists.

Ramjet: a jet engine using compressed or heated air, an aircraft propelled by such a jet engine. Partial presage to 9/11.

Ramose: having many branches, like the holmoak tree at Fatima.

Nemesis: retributive justice in its execution and outcome; another reference to courts.

Neo: new or revived. A recent formation or change. The goddess of retributive justice or vengeance. I believe Lucia earmarks "Only the Good Die Young" for retributive justice to regain religious liberty in the Supreme Court.

Siege: surrounding or blockading a town or fortress by an army intent on capturing it.

Jenny: a female donkey or ass, a hand operated machine for bending sheet metal at an angle, a monetary unit.

Tatay, Ambrocio Ramos from Nenita and Sidney Jensen-
Tatay: Portuguese for "Daddy," in memory of Lucia's father.

Ambo: either of two pulpits or raised stands in early Christian Churches from which parts of the service were chanted or read.

Ambry: a niche near the altar to keep sacred vessels and vestments.

Ambrose: Saint Ambrose, Bishop of Milan and leader of the early Christian Church, he was influential in imposing Orthodoxy on the early Church and strengthening the power of the Church against the State. A pending dual of Church and State looms because of prior knowledge of 9/11. This refers back to the Cathedral of the Immaculate Conception and the pulpit that parallels visiting the Saints that Lucia said she had on her final tour of Fatima before leaving for the convent school.

Ramjet: a jet engine using compressed or heated air; an aircraft propelled by such a jet engine. A partial presage of 9/11. The second time Ramos is used and therefore a second jet, and the second tower.

Joe L. Sanchez-

Sanctify: to reserve for sacred use, made Holy or purify, to make productive of holiness or blessing, to give religious sanction or legitimacy.

Sanctimonious: making a pretense of sanctity or piety, hypocritically virtuous and high-minded, pretentious.

Flora Loggins and Mary Jean Sunquis-

Flora: Roman Mythology, the goddess of flowers, suggestive of flowers.

Floppy disc: a thin, flexible disc with magnetic coating used to store computer data.

Loggins: loggia, a roofed open gallery or arcade along the front or side of a building often at the upper level, an open balcony in a theater.

Log-in: the computer entry password. Change the Internet to eliminate pornography.

Maryland: an Atlantic state of the United States, founded in 1634 by Lord Baltimore as a refuge for Roman Catholics. A State named after and in unity with the Virgin Mary.

Sunnite: a Muslim of the Sunni. "Son Quiz." Our Lord Jesus Christ is asking us to mend our ways.

Mrs. Christini Frazzini

Queen of Heaven Orphanage

Mother Cabrini Shrine is summer residence of Queen of Heaven Orphanage

Shrine plaque placed by the Knights of Columbus in honor of the charter founders of the Mother Cabrini Shrine. The word *supremely* and *Supreme Lucia* used many times suggests the Supreme Council of the Knights of Columbus is involved.

John B. Martina

John: a man seeking a prostitute.

John: a section of the New Testament of St. John.

Martial: of or pertaining to war.

Martial law: rule by military imposed on civilians in time of war when civil authority is unable to maintain public safety.

Alexander and Minna E. Phannenstiel

Phantasm: something apparently seen but having no physical reality, an illusory mental image, objective reality as perceived and distorted by the five senses, to make visible, such as mental images produced by listening to music.

Phantasmagoria: a fantastic sequence of haphazardly associated imagery, as seen in dreams or fever; a fantastic imagery as seen in art, such as the image of Our Lady of Guadeloupe or the Sacred Heart.

Joseph P. Scavo Family

Scavenger: to collect or remove refuse, to collect by searching, to search through discarded material for edible or useful material.

Concetta Mazzotti Marino

Concert: an event attended by the public where music is played live for listeners.

Mazurka: a lively Polish music for dancing, such as a polka.

Mazzini: Italian Revolutionary Nationalist, exiled in 1830 for joining a secret society, the Carbonari, and lived mainly in London after 1837. He began the newspaper *Thought and Action*, stirring Italian nationalist opinion.

Maria: a dark area on the moon, yet considered Holy to Christians, representing the Virgin Mary. It also would help identify Sr. Maria Lucia.

Mariachi: music performed by a Mexican street band.

Mr. and Mrs. Turilli

Turk: the Turin Shroud, by some believed to be a fraud and not the image of Jesus Christ.

Livia Cinocco

Livid: ashen or pallid with illness or rage; extremely angry, or furious.

Cinnamon stone: referring to the "world" beneath the feet of the Risen Christ in the sanctuary of the Cabrini Chapel.

Jimmy O Brian

A repeat of J. O'Brian Tolve. Lucia's clue that these steps and the grounds of the shrine are a "job to solve," or from Lucia's perspective, she has a job to do. The Book of JOB.

J. M. Rosa

Rosary: A Roman Catholic form of devotion to the Virgin Mary; similar to beads of other religions.

Rosary Pea: a black spotted poisonous seed used as beads, sometimes called Indian licorice.

Maria Rosa: Lucia's mother's maiden name. She may have visited the Cabrini Shrine.

Eleanor M. Neurath of New Britain, Connecticut-

Eleanor of Castile: died 1290, Queen consort of Edward I of England, daughter of Ferdinand III of Castile. In her memory, Edward had crosses erected at twelve stages of her funeral procession from Nottinghamshire to London.

New Britain: Near New Haven, Connecticut, headquarters for the Knights of Columbus Catholic men's organization. Long live the Queen.

Neurasthenia: a condition marked by abnormal fatigue, loss of energy, loss of memory, or feelings of inadequacy; once thought to be from exhaustion of the nervous system; "Nervous breakdown" or "nervous prostration."

New wrath: a coming day of the Lord

Eleanor Antonio Giantonio

Elenchus: refuting by proving the opposite, as Lucia attempts by the narrative about the divinity of the Virgin Mary through the publically seen miracle of October 13, 1917, and other presages given her by Our Lady in Fatima and after presented in the Crusade and at Cabrini Shrine.

Angelina Florentine-

Angelico Florentine: artist painter famous for his frescos and religious subject. Named Guido di Piedro,[194] he became a Dominican Monk. His most famous work is a cycle of thirty-five paintings that decorate the sanctuary of the church S. S. Annunziata (The Annunciation) depicting the visit to Mary by the Angel Gabriel, of the incarnation that She is to bear the Son of God. The Festival Day of the Annunciation is March 25.

Maria

Maria: the name of Our Lady the Virgin Mary whose name most often precedes the given name of new member of any Order of Nuns, as an example Sister Maria Lucia, the name given to Lucia de Jesus dos Santos of the Immaculate Heart of Mary. Lucia's mothers first name.

Mari: An ancient Amorite City in Mesopotamia, now Tel-Hariri, Syria, on Euphrates River.

Marie: pleural of mare (a dark area of the moon).

Salvadore Delina

Salvage: to save from destruction, to rescue a ship from disaster, to save imperiled property from loss.

---

194 http://www.britannica.com/EBchecked/topic/24542/Fra-Angelico

Delineate: to draw or trace, to represent pictorially.

Delinquency: failure to do what is required.

Josephine Strascina Delina-

Joseph of Arimathea: Israelite who provided a tomb for Jesus out of which He rose from the dead.

Strass: a type of leaded glass; stained glass.

Stratagem: use of deception or trickery.

SAM A. CARPENTER (1968) on the stamped nameplate of the statue of Our Lady along the ramp leading up to the Cabrini chapel reads

SAM: the "SAM," the initials for a surface-to-air missile; makes a hissing sound when fired. It warns of the dangers of cruise missiles and is a call for the United States to take up the Cross of Christ. This "rocket" of the Resurrected Jesus is a striking feature of the Cabrini chapel. Jesus is the SAM. The light in the stained glass window could be viewed as the warhead. Jesus is in control.

Carpenter: one who repairs wooden structures. Joseph and Jesus were carpenters. Joseph taught Him the trade before He began His Glorious Self, revealing Himself as the Son of God at the wedding feast of Cannas, where He turned water into wine.

Carpentum: a two wheeled vehicle like a chariot, a reminder of the Book of Joel.

Figure 48

The rocket spoken of in "The hissing of a rocket" of the Second Apparition

They will have rockets: one of the incentives Mrs. Santos reminded Lucia of to try to get Lucia to attend the St. Anthony's Church Feast Day celebration instead of going to the Cova da Iria as Our Lady requested of her in *Mother of Christ Crusade*.

In Thanksgiving from Cordova, Sanchez, and Ta Foya families

Cordovan: fine leather from Spain made from goatskin.

Cordon Sanitaire: a chain of buffer states organized around a nation considered ideologically dangerous or potentially dangerous, any physical or figurative barrier devised so as to keep off some potential danger.

Sanchez: to reserve for sacred use, made holy by blessing, to give religious sanction or legitimacy; sanctimonious, making pretense of sanctity or piety; hypocritically virtuous, high-mindedness, pretentious. A gold cross and the Holy Rosary of Mary are two examples of Catholic artifacts deemed sacred, not to be desecrated.

Taffy: a sweet, chewy candy.

A Taffy: used as an address to another, and considered offensive.

Dafydd: the Welsh version of David, patron Saint of Wales.

Isuada and Tiofilo Gomez-

Issue: a point of contention; an act or instance of passing out; the act of circulating, distributing, or publishing by an official group. An item or set of items, such as coins or stamps, made available at one time by a government or organization; all copies of a periodical printed for publication at the same time; a point of dispute in a legal action of essential importance. I reference the booklet of the US Constitution published by the US printing office that has a prayer by Thomas Jefferson stating "God comes before all." It is entered on the inside cover, before the body of the Constitution. Evidence the US government should accept freedom of religion taking precedence over free of speech.

Tip: the end, or the extremity of something, to tip off, to bring to a slanting position. Such is the case with the official US Constitution having a prayer written in before the body of the document itself.

Gomez, Juan Vicente: a Venezuelan soldier, politician, and president after gathering an army of guerrilla forces to help him win the presidency.

Goliath: a giant Philistine warrior who was slain by David with a rock and a sling. courageous, daring, valorous, and attentive to women, chivalrous, courteous, and amorous, an act or instance of gallantry in speech or behavior.

Orle: an inner boarder not quite touching the edge

Jose E. Gallagos and Mr. and Mrs. Orland Gallagos

Gallant or gallantry: courageous, daring, valorous, attentive to women, chivalrous, courteous, and amorous, an act or instance of gallantry in speech or behavior.

Orle: an inner boarder not quite touching the edge of a shield.

Vasquez and Verdusco

Vassal: a person who held land from a feudal lord and received protection in return for homage and allegiance, one that is subject or subservient to another.

Verdure: lush green vegetation.

Verge: the extreme rim or margin of something on the brink; the point by which an action, state, or condition is likely to begin or occur; the area of jurisdiction of the Lord High Steward, especially the surroundings of the royal court.

Verger: a person who takes care of the interior of a church and acts as an attendant during ceremonies; the male reproductive organ of an invertebrate.

In Memory of: Joe L. Sanchez

Joel: the Book of the Old Testament containing Joel's prophecies for the judgment of Judah.

Joel: the letters of this first name and middle initial spell "Joel," a point made about him or the Book of Joel.

Sanchez: to reserve for sacred use, made holy or blessing, to give religious sanction or legitimacy.

Sanctimonious: making pretense of sanctity or piety, hypocritically virtuous and high-minded, pretentious. This is a description of exactly what is wrong with in the Book of Joel and with today's media imposing on the Catholic public the anti-Catholic song, "Only the Good Die Young." It is a violation of religious liberty, allowing freedom of speech to demean and mock the Catholic Church to the world, inferring it is a third-rate false religion unworthy of respect.

The Knights of Columbus Plaque: lists the following names of the charter members of the shrine complex dedicated to St. Frances X. Cabrini. It was placed there courtesy of the Knights of Columbus, Fourth Degree. It was a Fourth Degree Knight that had a candle on his head to illustrate how to find hidden presages by looking through the pictures.

Alcorn-

Corn: the peak of the Cabrini chapel has stained glass windows that may look like ears of corn. What Lucia may have meant is that what you will see here is *amazing*.

Louisa May Alcott: A US novelist, her most famous work, *Little Women*.

Alcove: a recessed or partly enclosed area connected to or forming part of a room. Any arched niche or recess, as in a wall. This describes the small Cova where the Statue of Maria Lucia Santos stands facing over the convent church.

Beckius

St. Thomas Becket: an English cleric, appointed archbishop of Canterbury in 1162. He fell into disfavor for misappropriation of crown funds, and fled the country and remained in exile for six years. Upon his return he became involved in controversy, as King Henry had appointed his son archbishop of York. At Henry's behest, *four knights* of the royal household murdered Becket in Canterbury Cathedral on December 29. He was canonized in 1173.

Beckon: to signal or summon another by nodding or waving.

Max Beckmann: an artist who developed an expressionist manner, under the influence of Edvard Munch, and in the 1920s came to his most lasting style, the painting of brutal, often grotesque, large figurative canvases. Persecuted by the Nazis, he fled to Amsterdam in 1937 and in 1947 settled in the United States.

Becloud: to darken with clouds, to confuse, obscure.

Creamer

Creamer: a machine or device used for separating cream from milk.

Cream cups: a plant *Platystemon Californicus*, having a long-stemmed cream-colored or light yellow flowers.

Creamery: an establishment where cream products are bought or sold. Jacinta was brought milk as she lay dying that she found so hard to swallow.

Crematory: a crematorium for a funeral cremation, to dispose of dead bodies without burial.

Campbell

Campbell's: the name of a popular and well-known soup company. The children and Ty Marto had soup with the pastor.

Donald Campbell: (1921–1967) set the land speed record in a gas turbine four-wheeled car with a top speed of 403.1 mph on July 17, 1964, in Lake Eyre salt flats in Australia. Later that year, he achieved the water speed record of 276.33 mph at Dumbleyung Lake, Australia. During his final attempt on a water speed record, his jet-powered boat reached a top speed of 527.8km/hr or 328mph.

Dumbbell: free weight for exercise. Is a reference to a person who did a dumb thing or foolish act—like writing or promoting the song "OTGDY."

Camp David: the official country retreat used by the president of the United States in the Appalachian Mountains of Maryland. President Jimmy Carter mediated a peace treaty between el-Anwar Sadat, the Egyptian president, and Meacham Begin, prime minister of Israel, which became known as the Camp David Agreement. This is a call for the world to secure peace.

Dooling

A duel: a gun challenge with life or death consequences.

James Harold Doolittle: US Army officer and aviator, who became involved in aviation development in World War I. In World War II, he led a daring bombing raid on Tokyo and other Japanese cities (1942).

Doom: a predestined end or ruin or tragedy; a terrible fate; the last judgment; condemnation to severe penalty.

Eakins

Thomas Eakins: a US artist, his paintings and portraits and starkly realistic art created using his knowledge of anatomy has contributed to his reputation as one of the foremost US painter of all time.

Eager: a tidal flood.

Kilcourse

Kilauea: active volcanic crater in Hawaii.

Kildare: county in the Republic of Ireland, a market town that was founded by St. Bride in AD 490.

Legg

Leg: an appendage of animals for locomotion or movement; any part of a garment especially a pair of trousers; in cricket, the right side of the field when the batsman is right-handed; to assist by boosting or providing support.

Not a leg to stand on: to have no justifiable or logical basis for defense or proposition.

Pulling your leg: to tease, make fun of, or fool someone.

Shake a leg: to hurry.

Little

Small: an enduring name for children of a lesser age who have not grown yet into adulthood, such as a teenager; more vulnerable in strength, physically and emotionally.

Mills

Miller: one who grinds grain.

Millstone: a heavy stone rolled to mill grain.

Mason: a builder who uses stone and mortar.

Masonic: of or pertaining to Freemasons. The Magistrate of Ourem in *Mother of Christ Crusade* was Catholic but later left the church.

Masochism: the deriving of pleasure, especially sexual arousal, from having physical or emotional pain inflicted on one; loosely the practice of deliberately undergoing unpleasant experiences, usually in pursuit of some higher satisfaction.

Nelson

Half-nelson: putting one's arm around the neck of another to hold or choke; in wrestling, to put one's arm under his opponents arm and applies pressure on the opponent's neck.

Noone

Noon: the time set by Our Lady for the start of the public Sixth Apparition of October 13, 1917. [195]

Noose: a loop secured in a rope or cord by means of a slipknot so that it tightens if pulled, a snare or trap. Indicative of a hanging or shown to intimidate or threaten death.

Noodle: to improvise music in a haphazard fashion.

Walsh

Waltz: a smooth flowing ballroom dance in triple time with a strong accent on the first beat.

Wamble: is to move in a weaving, wobbling, or rolling manner. I add rock-and-roll music as the intent. This could be referencing the rolls of the feast at St. Anthony's in the *Crusade* or the roll of an aircraft turning.

Mr. and Mrs. George T. Toto

George W. Bush: US president on September 11, 2001

T: the Sign of the Cross[196] found on the rubble

Toto: Dorothy's faithful dog in *The Wizard of Oz.* The name Toto from the movie *The Wizard of Oz* matches up with the name for: "the Order of the good sisters who had taken care of her, the Sisters of St. Dorothy. They were happy to welcome this sweet and holy girl into their midst."[197]

---

195 Ibid, Chapter IX, p 128
196 Ibid, Chapter X, p 130
197 Ibid, Chapter XIV, p 201

PETE LA GUARDIA

LaGuardia: the name of one airport in New York City, a reference to aircraft.

Much of the inferred meaning of the names on this list, like the content of *Mother of Christ Crusade*, is intended to target rock-and-roll music and its negative effects on women when the lyrics are intent on achieving sexual satisfaction at all cost. One song that is the most harmful and probably in part responsible for the epidemic of abduction, assault, rape, and murder of children, specifically Catholic children, according to Lucia and Our Lady is "Only the Good Die Young." It demeans the Christian faith and all its sacred elements, as well as endangers Catholic children. Lucia condemns the song, while Our Lord is thoroughly outraged.

Some of the signs and nameplates on the site and presented in this list are duplicated, but Lucia had a reason for this. For example, 9/11 involved more than one airliner.

Lloyd and Jennifer Acree "Jesus Christ is Lord"

Jesus Christ is Lord! This is the whole point. By proving there is a miraculous prediction of September 11, 2001, in the *Crusade* and at Cabrini Shrine, the divinity of Our Lady and Jesus as Lord of all is proven.

There are more names in the memorial garden than those I have included. These names from the steps to the Sacred Heart seem enough to persuade everyone to believe Lucia did come to Mother Cabrini's Shrine and spent some time down in Denver at a convent school, focused on documenting the secret presage of 9/11 to be found at a later date.

The topic of mistreatment of women was clearly outlined in these definitions, with music involved. These were the names found on the steps at the time they were recorded. They may be what Lucia included with other unfound words. The names may or may not be real people, but are believed to be contributors to the Cabrini Shrine. If real, it appears Our Lady brought them here for a greater purpose.

Chapter 19

The Apparitions at the New Cova da Iria on the Cinnamon Stone Are the Presage of 9/11.

Figure 49

The Cabrini Shrine chapel and the cinnamon stone

There is a true miracle going on at Mother Cabrini Shrine. On the thirteenth of the designated months, the same dates Our Lady told the children to meet at the Cova da Iria for the apparitions in Fatima, little miracles occur at the *new* Cova da Iria at Mother Cabrini Shrine. There are apparitions you can experience for yourselves. As if by magic; words, initials, and images appear on the cinnamon colored earth of the mosaic sanctuary wall beginning at the hour of the sun, from about noon until four o'clock. They tell the story of 9/11.

Placed long before 9/11, the presage of 9/11 is literally spelled out on the stone wall of the earth on the thirteenth of the months. In the course of a year, the numbers and letters included 911, 2001, "OTGDY," JOEL, WTC, JET, 78, even OSAMA. They are written in bubble letters. There are also the miraculous mirages of transparent images, including an image of the twin towers, a little girl confronted by adult men and men face-to-face confronting each other. There is no error, signs of the prediction of 9/11 were available long ago on this wall, though understanding what 911, WTC, JOEL, and "OTGDY" meant would have been impossible before 9/11. Like the hidden words and images in the *Crusade,* it provides a valid prediction of 9/11, so does the sanctuary wall at Cabrini, powered by the Son of God through the stained glass windows above it. Truly it is miraculous. Who says the stained glass you have been hiding behind never lets in the sun? This is what the song OTGDY claims.

The "cinnamon stone" of the world were alluded to when researching the names on the stamped plates of the steps to the Sacred Heart. This refers to the "world" beneath the feet of the Risen Jesus on the Cabrini chapel sanctuary wall. When the sun is shining through the four stained glass windows on the peak of the Cabrini chapel, another miracle of the sun takes place on this cinnamon colored stone, on the thirteenth of the same months as the apparitions in Fatima.

Beginning May 13 through October 13, new images and words show up in the new Cova da Iria. It is different each month. Over the course of the year you can see 9/11, "OTGDY," JOEL, 1978, JET, the initials WTC, and pictures of the WTC towers. Like in the *Crusade,* these signs reference "OTGDY" specifically and serve as a call for its condemnation. The message demands a challenge and a decision in favor of Catholic religious liberty from the Supreme Court. A refusal would be antichrist.

During the Sixth Apparition in Fatima, the miracle of the sun was visible to everyone in Fatima. On October 13, the cinnamon stones are lit by the sun, putting on an incredible, rather unbelievable miraculous display for everyone to see.

The images and information are constantly in motion like in a movie. Between each set of pictures, a penny appears to flip over then disappear. The penny has a face on it that looks a bit like President Lincoln. However, the copper colored halo around the head of Jesus on the sanctuary wall tells you it is Jesus' face on the coin and may have something to do with The Head described on p. 2 of the *Crusade*. The Risen Jesus stands on the world taking responsibility for what is written on the wall, endorsing the images. *God himself condemns "OTGDY."* The prediction of September 11, 2001 is seen reviewed every year on the 13th of the months over the course of a year.

Oddly, though the mirage[198] images are best seen through a camera lens, photographing them simply does not capture what the human eye can see. At times, there are two people appearing face to face, scowling. One is in a three-cornered hat like an American patriot; the other is Arabic. This is a clear sign 9/11 was an act of God, just as the cross in the rubble of September 11, 2001, would suggest. You need to see it in person to get the full effect. You won't be disappointed with what transpires on October 13. July 13th, the Vision of Hell and the secret Lucia never told is revealed as 9/11.

The word *sun* is a verbal homonym: *sun* and *son*, as in Son of God. The Son of God is mocked in "OTGDY." The songwriter of "OTGDY" states the stained glass window Virginia is hiding behind never lets in the Sun.[199] This miraculous production of images proves that insulting

---

198 Ibid, Chapter VIII, p 113

199 Billy Joel, Only the Good Die Young, 1978

remark is exactly wrong. The sun shining through the stained glass windows of the Cabrini chapel does let in the Son of God to create a miracle on this cinnamon world, for the world to see. Henceforth, the song "OTGDY" is an anti-Catholic lie. It is the antichrist, the devil in the smoke. Cinnamon sounds like "sin of man".

Figure 50

This table in the meeting room at the Cabrini Shrine appears to be in the shape of a Pentagon another clue to 9/11

Hopefully we will all agree with the resurrection of Jesus Christ, in time. It is possible. Jesus loves everyone in the world. Religion is a sensitive issue, a difficult topic. Some people are not interested in Jesus and the resurrection, but the facts of the miracles presented prove Jesus is Lord of all the earth. Some have yet to believe in a Supreme Being—God— at all. The time has come for all to believe in the truth made evident through the devil in the smoke, the cross of Christ at ground zero, the *Crusade* book, and the signs at Mother

Cabrini Shrine. On September 11, 2001, "God in Heaven had called the people of the world to join in praying honor and glory to His Blessed Mother, Mary."[200] Consecration to Her Immaculate Heart is strongly recommended by the events of 9/11. Her protection is worth it, yet it does not seem to be just a request.

Jesus has set a course for all to believe in Him. In the chapel at Cabrini, He stands with open arms, gathering everyone unto Himself. Let the *Mother of Christ Crusade,* written by Lucia de Jesus dos Santos, do the convincing. It is true what Lucia reports and hides in the *Crusade*; it cannot be dismissed or ignored. Once you see with your own eyes the hidden messages in the *Crusade* and the miracle of the sun on October 13 on the sanctuary wall, you have to believe Jesus is the Son of God and has been raised from the dead. Once you know Jesus is Lord, you cannot knowingly go back. You may find yourself becoming Catholic, as the three children were.

The shrine is a quiet and serene location, at peace with man and nature. It needs to stay this way, unmolested by evildoers; it's sacred ground. There is a chance the Marto children, most probably Lucia, and Mother Cabrini all walked the grounds; if so four Saints have lived at the shrine. It is hallowed ground.

---

200 Ibid, Chapter XI, p 144

Chapter 20

The Miraculous Marble of the Sanctuary Marble at St. Thomas More Catholic Church in Centennial, Colorado, Condemns "Only the Good Die Young" and Media

Before the marble is shown there is the important icon mentioned in the Crusade found at St. Thomas More that has just one fold. Lucia said fold as is everyone coming to be in one flock in Christianity into one Church. The parallel message is a reference to the official registered image of Our Lady of Guadeloupe. In it you can see the presage of 9/11 given to Juan Diego in 1531[201] by Our Lady.

201 www.catholic.org/about/guadeloupe.php

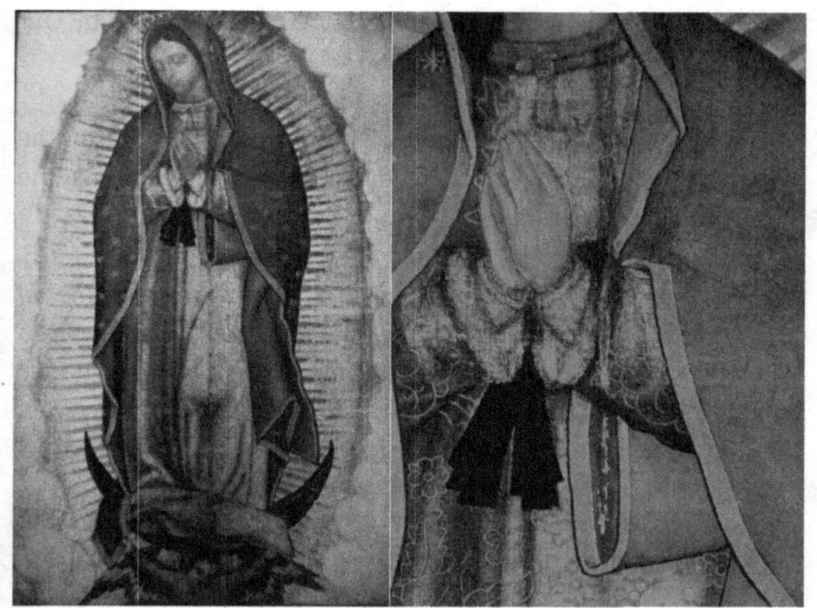

Figure 51 Our Lady of Guadeloupe[202]

Figure 52 an isolated view of 911.

In this image beginning at our lady's collar, written vertically along the fold, are the numbers 911.

The vertical "fold", perhaps created when it was stored or held, can be seen in the center of the image. The edge of her gowns collar is the top of the 9 in black. The ones are in the fold below first in white on Her cuff, then below it in the loop of Her outer garment. It has the myriad of stars mentioned in the first apparition in the *Crusade*. Our Lady's knee rests on the back of a man being pressed into service. You should examine an authenticated copy of Our Lady of Guadeloupe in great detail to determine your own findings. What looks like the World Trade Center tower can be seen in the upper

202 *Our Lady of Guadeloupe*, of the year 1531 AD, at St. Thomas More Catholic Church, 8035 S Quebec, Centennial, CO 80112,

right corner. The presage of 911 was given 480 years ago by Our Lady, once again proving Her divinity.

Behind her folded hands is the face of a young woman, her arms the narrow band on the edge of Our Lady's star spangled garment. She is the defender of all virgins.

Lucia had personal reasons for doing so when she wrote *Mother of Christ Crusade*. Our Lady asked her too. You should be convinced already that the *Crusade* book takes to condemning OTGDY, and the steps at the Cabrini Shrine are conclusive, but this will convince you. The best is last, and this next exposition tells all.

The Marble Walls of the Sanctuary

The following photographs are of the remodeled sanctuary wall at St. Thomas More Catholic Church. The wall and its surroundings are constructed of green and beige marble. When the large tiles were first placed, the marble seemed to have no particular features, no patterns. Over time, images of characters could be seen. The marble appeared to transform into a collage of many images, each bringing with them a story; historical events and elements of prophesy are recorded in these amazing images. Many of the images seen have a common theme. The marble includes images of a Billy goat wearing a robe, and a young girl on her knees. In front of her is a penis, above it a ghoulish man is looking at her, face to face.

Our Lady is depicted on the wall. She stands tall, two-thirds the height of the green sanctuary wall. Her arm is bent at the elbow and Her hand rests on the kneeling child's shoulder[203] just like it

203 De Marchi, *Mother of Christ Crusade*, Chapter XIV, p 201

did during one of Our Lady's visits to Lucia. It is a direct tie in with the *Crusade*, a miracle created by God long after the *Crusade* and Mother Cabrini Shrine. Our Lady's face is joined with the face of a rocking horse, both of which are in the open mouth of a lion. The number of images is simply amazing. The story they tell is even more astonishing.

Figure 53

St. Thomas More Church, Centennial, Colorado

From the baptismal font to the sanctuary, the white panels are stained glass windows

Figure 54

The miraculous marble can be thought to condemn "OTGDY" and antichrist media

As it happens, St. Thomas More is where the copy of the Mother of Christ Crusade was made available, being given away to Knights of Columbus and anyone else who wished to have one.

There are no appropriate words to define the marble patterns on the sanctuary wall at St. Thomas More Catholic Church except one: miraculous. The existence of these images in the marble is simply impossible without divine intersession. They were not planned; the tiles weren't chosen to piece together a picture puzzle, they were simply quarried, polished, and inserted. The images would be impossible to create from quarried marble and striking enough that even an atheist would have to admit the images in the marble are simply not natural—they must be of supernatural origin. Given some of the images, it would be doubtful the church would even want to place some of the tiles.

From a distance, you can see the letters *PS* on the lower right quadrant of the marble. A kneeling little girl has the hand of Our Lady on her shoulder, fitting the description Lucia gave of Our Lady putting her hand on her shoulder in the apparition of December, 10, 1925, eight years after leaving Fatima.[204]

On the left side lower quadrant, along the edge, is a Billy goat. It is, in a way, half beast and half man, with the horned head of a goat, but a man's shoulders and wearing a robe. Slowly the eyes and minds of parishioners were opened to see these images, to see what God, Jesus Christ, and the Immaculate Heart of Mary has done. Even though their purpose and meaning remains a mystery to many, people do see them. By exhibiting a Billy goat and a little girl on her knees with a penis in front of her chest while a ghoulish man looks her straight in the eyes, you have to believe divine intersession has come to protect the reputation of the Virgin Mary and all Catholic

204 De Marchi, *Mother of Christ Crusade*, Chapter XIV, p 201

virgins from the song "Only the Good Die Young", adding to the list of miracles that condemn it. With the Crucifix of Jesus Christ hanging on the sanctuary wall, and the nature of the images, you should be able to accept that God personally has delivered his own condemnation. The sanctuary wall can only be regarded as a divine mandate to act on behalf of Catholic virgins and the Catholic Church harmed and damaged by the anti-Catholic song. With a crucifix hanging on the sanctuary wall, one must conclude Jesus casts a yes vote for a court challenge, and to condemn "OTGDY" and its media broadcasters for violating the rights for Catholics equal religious liberty. The Mother of Christ Crusade, the Mother Cabrini Shrine and the sanctuary wall have already condemned the song. With 9/11 visible with each, rejection of the challenge is unacceptable, the potential divine consequences, up in the air.

The Billy goat and the little girl wearing a white dress (the marbling is white) with a penis in front of her at the level of her chest and the ghoulish man staring her down, are all representations identifying the song. Many images in the marble are pictorial representations of 9/11 or of imagery used in the book of Joel. Together, the major reason for the 9/11 attack is drawn in stone at St. Thomas More, to help to get this thorn, "OTGDY," removed from the foot of the lion and restore religious liberty to the Catholic Church, success thereby diminishing God's outrage, generated by media's public broadcasting of abuse of all faiths especially Catholics. This challenge is not to be dismissed. This challenge is in truth only the beginning of Our Lady's peace plan for the world and living as God expects us too.

In the right quadrant, there is a rocking horse. It has its head in the face of Our Lady, while Her own head is in the mouth of a Lion. The union of the smiles on the faces of the rocking horse and that of Our Lady form a perfect V, for Virginia, the target victim of OTGDY. These miraculous images concern the very song Sr. Maria Lucia herself identifies as needing to be challenged in court in order to restore the religious liberty of the Catholic Church. When Jesus and Our Lady perform miracles to support a cause asking for assistance, it is not a choice but a convincing mandate—one can hardly say no when God calls the nation to legally reject a specific song on the grounds it obstructs the Catholic Church and endangers the lives of its most vulnerable members. God is calling on all Americans to defend Jesus Christ, Gods only Son, for the common good of all. For those who recognize it as their calling, feel free to defend the faith, it is your God given right.

After the images of a Billy goat, a penis, a girl kneeling, suggested she is doing so to receive the sacrament of Confirmation by the image of a "seal" (the left part of the PS image, and a word used during the anointing with oil, "Be sealed with the Holy Spirit", the song's lyrics now can be said to insult God, the Holy Spirit. You will need to get the significance of this insult from a priest, like Fr. Andrew Kemberling, current and long time pastor at St. Thomas More, or the other priests and deacons.

You have to see the marble to get the full avalanche of art. When viewed from different locations in the church—up close, from the back, from the right or left—different images are accentuated. There are easily twenty-five different images throughout the marble in the church, and many of them have relevance to "OTGDY." For the purpose of condemning "OTGDY," we will need to only consider those directly involved with "OTGDY", and the book of Joel.

Only through an act of God could this collage, with its multitude of images on the sanctuary and adoration chapel walls and the pulpit, include the story of the Book of Joel, the events of 9/11, and those signs identifying the song "OTGDY." The song must end, abortion must end, and the persecution of clergy and nuns in the Sisterhood must end *now*. This message in the marble is nothing new; Lucia had been giving the same message ever since she left Fatima, writing it into *Mother of Christ Crusade* and again in messages on the stamped plates of the steps at the Cabrini Shrine. Lucia warned us about how God was outraged. We were reminded again by the devil in the smoke of 9/11. They should have recognized and known sooner that anti-Catholic, anti-Christ broadcasting would bring on the promised punishment. Where is public broadcasting media when our need is for more faith in God rather than less morality.

The Holy name of Our Lady the Virgin Mary must be preserved. She has through the apparitions in Fatima, the images found in Mother of Christ Crusade, in the sanctuary at Mother Cabrini Shrine and now again at St. Thomas More Catholic Church, proven Her Divinity.

Figure 55

The sanctuary marble at St. Thomas More reveling images of a Billy goat, virgin, prick, Virgin Mary, lion, and a rocking horse

See Joel 2: 4–5

Our Lady's work with Lucia has been extrapolated upon by Jesus Christ Himself. He has drawn on stone His desire to end the abuse of the religious liberty of the Catholic Church. What is God's intention, decide for yourself. "Free Speech" has now become the cowardly cover used by those who attack Jesus, His Sacred Heart, the Immaculate Heart of the Virgin Mary, the Apostles of Christ and the dignity of all Catholics. Worst, it is even being used to endanger the lives of young children.

Entering the St. Thomas More Church from the narthex area, plainly seen in the lower left quadrant of the sanctuary wall are the letters *PS*,[205] shown at the center of the image of the little girl. Refocus to see an A. It is the seal. When you mock the Sacrament of Confirmation, you denounce the Holy Spirit, and doing so is a mortal sin.

The *PS* in the marble images can be taken as a "postscript" to the *Mother of Christ Crusade* and Mother Cabrini Shrine. Because the *PS* also stands for the Psalms, it must mean that songs are factually one of the topics under consideration in the marble. The Psalms, which praise God combined with the rocket and rolls of the *Crusade*, the rocket on the sanctuary wall at Cabrini Shrine and the rocking horse image in the marble, should be conclusive enough evidence to believe some rock and roll has been deemed offensive enough that God is outraged with what it has become.

205 Fig. 57

Figure 56

PS, -ARY,* and *A

PS: remember Tony A. Notary from the signs on the steps at Cabrini? The individual letters *A, R,* and *Y* share the same lines and are all visible in the *ARY. ARY,* and *PS* are visual isomers when you refocus with your eyes. The *PS* letters are fused, part of the white dress worn by the little girl facing right, who is on her knees as if in prayer or like she was receiving the Sacrament of Confirmation. Looking at her—almost touching her—is the face of a Neanderthal-looking man. Believing this wall is also a reminder of 9/11, this Neanderthal's face looks like the nose and cockpit of an airliner.

This ties in the pictures of the children praying with hands folded in the *Crusade*[206], where the shape of the fingers of the children when seen under magnification appear as penises. It also infers that it is correct to use a dictionary to figure out the meaning of the important misspelled words in the *Crusade* and those found on the steps leading up to the statue of the Sacred Heart of Jesus at Cabrini Shrine. *ARY* also happen to be the last three letters of "sanctuary."

206 Ibid, Chapter II, p 15 and 16

It was Jesus who opens our eyes to understand the hidden message in *Mother of Christ Crusade* and who leads us along Lucia's path to find traces of her at Mother Cabrini Shrine. The reason Our Lord needed to draw on the church sanctuary walls was in part to provide further proof 9/11 was punishment of the antichrist actions. It connects St. Thomas More to the *Mother of Christ Crusade*, also containing the presage to 9/11 and the condemnation of the song. The face of the Billy goat seems an ID of Billy Joel and "OTGDY", not unlike what was written into the *Mother of Christ Crusade*. The images provide a telling addition to the child abuse theme Lucia began in the Crusade using of the large hand placed on Lucia's breast in the photo of the children chapter II, p 15 as a clue.

Figure 57

The head of a Billy goat with a donkey above, found in the lower left hand quadrant of the sanctuary wall

For several reasons, St. Thomas More is an extension of Cabrini. The locations are close, about fifteen miles apart. One image on the St. Thomas More marble sanctuary wall is of Lucy, the *Peanuts* character, a name once used for Lucia in the *Crusade* in the image where her house was shown on page 13.

Figure 58

The little girl on her knees is wearing a white dress, as in the lyrics of "OTGDY." There is a prick in front of her suggestive of an ultimatum: do or die. Also visible are the letters *PS* that help to form her dress.

Figure 59

The Mother of Christ, the Virgin Mary, Immaculate Mary, stands center behind the crucifix, Her profile facing right, as tall as the wall, her hand rests on the child's shoulder. The face of a rocking horse is in Her face, while Her own face is inside the mouth of a lion. A stallion's nose is shared with that of the upper jaw of the lion. Both are just above Our Lady's face. Two sets of antennae are seen in the center of the middle left and right side—all are imagery from the Book of Joel. The singer/songwriter's name being the same as the prophesy identifies "OTGDY" as the outrage against our Lord Jesus Christ who hangs on the Crucifix, reiterating what Our Lady has already made known in the *Crusade*.

Figure 60

The north and west side of the pulpit

The pulpit at St. Thomas More Catholic Church also depicts elements of the Book of Joel: a lioness; and the nose of a horse doubling as the cockpit of an aircraft, has human teeth. The partial image of the Hindenburg hydrogen blimp exploding is analogous to the explosion and fireball created when the jets impacted the twin towers

Many of the images are of imagery found in the Book of Joel. The *Crusade* book tells of the sins offending Jesus. Terrorism is not only a result of sin but a sin in itself. The final page of the *Crusade* claims that abortion, war, pornography, and adulterous sex are all also condemned.

Figure 61

The pulpit at St. Thomas More Church

On the front of the pulpit you can see in the lower half of the left side, the pontiff wearing white, sitting in a chair. Above him is a nude woman bent forward facing upward and left,—reasonably a pornographic image. You can't say the pope didn't tell you pornography was wrong; now here it is straight GOD, and His Son, the Lord Jesus Christ.

In the upper right quadrant of the front of the pulpit and extended onto the west side, the Hindenburg hydrogen blimp aircraft is again seen, appearing to have a fist thrust into it, exploding, an event that looked similar to the impact of airliners into the WTC towers. Combine this with the image of a soldier, found on the lower right of the sanctuary wall at the foot of the tree of the Crucifix, gives the impression that the Hindenburg disaster was actually a warning from God that if Hindenburg lost the election to Hitler, it would be a catastrophe. No doubt it was, creating a holocaust for all. This ties Our Lady's presage of World War II in *Mother of Christ Crusade* to St. Thomas More. The marble images confirm Lucia's memoirs that Our Lady's prediction of WWII to follow WWI, was a True Divine Presage, all further proof of Her divinity.

Figure 62

This image of a soldier in a WWII uniform suggests World War II was presaged by Our Lady and that this soldier at the foot of the Crucifix was the unconscious instrument of God. There could well have been a message in the loss of the Hindenburg, a warning sign. Is it a sign from God, ignored? In Fatima, the Virgin Mary warned that if men don't mend their ways, a greater war would break out. She said wars are just punishment for the sins of men. That being the case, Germany was an unconscious instrument of God, just like the Muslim extremists seem to have been in 9/11. It is just another repeat of people being the unconscious instrument of God like in the book of the Prophet Isaiah.

This image proves the divinity of Our Lady, as She had presaged World War II, "another worse war,"[207] as She said, to take place after

207 Ibid, Chapter V, p 66

World War I, for the sins of men. Our Lord was obviously greatly offended back then if He brought on a world war, twice. Moreover, the image reveals Germany was not the villain they continue to be made out to be, rather only another case of being the unconscious instrument of God, and under God's spell, used for His purpose. It is history, but the effect it has had on Germany's image still lingers. It need not linger any longer.

Figure 63

This image of a shark can be found in the marble beneath the statue of the Immaculate Heart of Mary in the St. Thomas More sanctuary.

Chapter 21

The Condemnation of "Only the Good Die Young"

Events Like 9/11 Hang in the Balance

Lucia presented the case for Our Lady's peace plan, expecting efforts will be made to condemn the song "Only the Good Die Young" and media who promote it when it was found.

The song about the little Catholic girl named Virginia when written in the *Crusade*, and now more recently pictorially represented on the sanctuary wall at St. Thomas More, identify how and what changes are required to prevent another coming catastrophe. God relented for Nineveh, why not us if we too repent. All that is necessary is acknowledgement of our sins to God.

Sr. Maria Lucia and Our Lady have identified Joel. The Joel prophecy is a historic and contemporary warning. It depicts Jesus' death and resurrection and describes 9/11, making the cross of hope, of Jesus Christ standing atop the rubble at ground zero, the grounds for tying the antichrist acts of today to the responsibility for 9/11. The Joel prophecy is catastrophe, but it is followed by forgiveness and the restoration of God's favor, but only if repentance occurs. That is a big if, but it is what we are called to and must do now. The fact that the good is included in the prophecy should mean it will happen sooner or later.

Denial and slander of Jesus is antichrist. If the outrages and slander continue, it is sure to bring with it further catastrophe – "If they do not amend themselves, punishment shall come.[208] The worst being the antichrist acts being promoted publically. There is still opportunity for everyone to recognize Jesus as Lord.

Mr. Joel admitted his song is anti-Catholic himself.[209] It is the paramount example of the antichrist in action—worse than the gay Last Supper painting or feces thrown on the image of Jesus and the Virgin Mary, then put on display in the Brooklyn museum—the reason being, according to Lucia and Our Lady, it has cost innocent lives. Our Lord and Our Lady have said it must be challenged with the pictures in the *Crusade* revealing the initials "OTGDY", made visible by magnification and trans-illumination. The stamps on the paper in the margins of some pages have the same initials, and serve as corroborative evidence. God has responded in kind to the loss of young Catholic virgins caused by media's insistence on playing this song globally for over thirty years. God wrote the same message in the smoke of 9/11 and drew it in the marble of the Sanctuary wall at St. Thomas More just so there was no mistake about the intended meaning. Who knows, it just may be that the song is responsible for as many deaths as suffered on 9/11.

The song "Only the Good Die Young" has drawn a lot of attention since it was released in 1978. Citizens, Catholics, Clergy, Bishops and the Pope have all condemned this song and have asked for the song to be taken off the airwaves. Media has ignored the plea. Thirty three years is a long time, as long as Jesus walked the earth, for this Anti-Catholic song to be imposed on the world by public broadcast media. Virgins, little Catholic girls have had to listen to Joel trashing their faith, while instilling in them a sense of fear that

---

208 De Marchi, Mother of Christ Crusade, chapter XII, p 175

209 Song Facts on the www., Wikipedia Quotes, 2011

their resistance to the unwanted sexual advances of strangers, rape in all legal and practical terms, could very well spell death for them if they are unwilling to surrender their principles of faith.

The song psychologically sensitizes virgins to be fearful of resistance to sexual assault and rape, and desensitizes them to being raped, as if because they are Catholic, they are unworthy of protection and should expect it could happen. OTGDY's message must be true they may conclude, since it has been allowed to be broadcast to the world for 33 years by anti-Catholic media unchallenged. By threatening children with death for sex, while at the same time liberating pedophiles of their guilt if they rape or murder a Catholic child, OTGDY has terrorized all young children. Every little virgin, Catholics and non-Catholics alike get the message being sent out from radio stations around the world, that if encountered by a man who wants to rape you, it would be smart not to resist, just to remain alive.

There is no good in the song what-so-ever. Media makes it out to be a joke, just a mockery, but it has become persistent part of anti-Catholic culture, an effort to delegitimize and abolish the Catholic faith, promote Catholic genocide, and get people to change their faith, so as not to burden their children with being "Catholic". It is anti-Christ. Some may have already changed or are reluctant to become Catholic afraid of the potential threat this song encourages. Joel and the anti-Christ media think Catholics are a joke it seems, their faith unworthy of protection under the U.S. Constitution. They had gotten away with it, until 9/11, but still they insist on continuing to broadcast the song.

When people first heard the song in 1978, some people hated it, the song, not Billy Joel. This book hopefully extends Sr. Maria Lucia's mission and helps in condemning Billy Joel's song, and will end Public Broadcast Media's thirty three years of arrogance in imposing upon all Catholics and the general public a message that demeans the Catholic Church, the Sacrament of Confirmation and most everything the Church holds sacred. It is clearly intended to lower the status of the Catholic Faith in the eyes of the general public, is a deliberate attack and a violation of the God given Right to "Religious Liberty" of specifically Catholics. Religious Rights are guaranteed to all Americans in the First Amendment of the United States Constitution which places first, before all else, the Freedom of Religion, notably before Free Speech.

The extrapolated interpretation is that some other rock-and-roll music, that also abuses women and virgins is being served notice to clean it up. It is not the Catholic Church that is asking; it is Gods Will that it happens. Media should voluntarily filter it out of station playlists. If they continue to disrespect Our Lady and the Rosary, and most of all, God, we can reasonably expect more catastrophes. Everything presented thus far supports the cause to restore religious liberty to the Church by eliminating the antichristian persecution media now imposes on Jesus, His Church, its followers and the general public.

"OTGDY" is a special case however. Our Lady condemns it directly in the Mother of Christ Crusade. It is worse than all other rock-and-roll music. It mocks and demeans the Church and its sacraments and rejects its teachings. The song, in unity with the anti-Catholic media since 1978 have publically broadcast their message around the globe, trying to convert the public to see things their way; that Catholic virgins are undeserving of sexual respect, even of life itself, because as they must teach from generation to generation, Christianity is a false religion unworthy of constitutional protection as written in the First Amendment. It is the basis on which they feel free to promote Catholic genocide. By playing OTGDY for more than thirty three years, is media asserts it is so politically powerful that they are actually above the law of the land, untouchable.

These miraculous images concern the very song Sr. Maria Lucia herself identifies as needing to be challenged in court in order to restore the religious liberty of the Catholic Church. When Jesus and Our Lady perform miracles to support a cause asking for assistance, it is not a choice but a convincing mandate—one can hardly say no when God calls the nation to legally reject a specific song on the grounds it obstructs the Catholic Church and endangers the lives of its most vulnerable members. God is calling on all Americans to defend Jesus Christ, Gods only Son, for the common good of all. For those who recognize it as their calling, feel free to defend the faith, it is your God given right.

Lucia had personal reasons for doing so when she wrote *Mother of Christ Crusade*. Our Lady asked her too. You should be convinced already that the *Crusade* book takes to condemning OTGDY, and the steps at the Cabrini Shrine are conclusive.

Figure 64

A man points down at a man holding a knife assaulting a young child

For Christians, they are not amused by this song. It appears Jesus hates it too, enough to perform miracles to condemn it. This accusation may bring an outrage of its own, but Lucia, a Catholic Saint, defends this position in the *Crusade*, and Our Lord here has backed her up with images on the adoration chapel wall.

Catholic Church is intentionally being lowered in status to a third-class religion by the media. The current attacks on the Church for the acts of a few wayward priests are viscous and fueled by greed. Media gleefully promotes child abuse then scornfully financially feeds off it. With other religious denominations untouched by scandal, what other conclusion is there? Claims are filed for hundreds of millions against priests who have been dead for thirty years. Curiously, only the Catholic Church is under attack. Who gets the greatest deal in these settlements, lawyers. One successful case means easy street. It is quite unbelievable that left wing media are so eager to attack the Catholic priests and report as many alleged cases available yet they eagerly broadcast the anti-Catholic song sung by a man with the lyrics promoting an attempt of seducing, or if resistant, raping a child as young as twelve years of age using the threat of death. The antichrist have been encouraging sexual abuse of specifically Catholics for over thirty years, promoting pedophilia, yet then when the lyrics are acted upon, they pretend to be outraged.

The evidence in the marble walls of St. Thomas More Church have, through an act of God, reasonably and convincingly condemned the song “Only the Good Die Young”, and media’s antichrist insistence on broadcasting it.

As if everything so far is not enough to convince you 9/11 was caused by the antichrist, on Holy Saturday, at the Vigil Mass of Easter, the Ceremony of Light takes place, during which a cauldron of fire is lit. When this cauldron was burning in the narthex of St. Thomas More

Church, an amazing revelation was visible on the overhead screens shown by the cameras filming the ceremony. Like a hologram, the image of an airliner, cockpit and fuselage is seen on the projection screen. To the right of it was a turbine engine, as if you were looking straight into the turbine from the front. It looks just like the silver disc described during the Sixth Apparition. This image should be miraculous and convincing enough to be recognized as relating all other evidence to 9/11. Its sheer existence is an additional act of God associating 9/11 with "Only the Good Die Young. This makes a new connection of the Denver airport with the newspaper *"O' Dia"* in Portugal, still in business today. Denver's airport is named Denver International airport, commonly referred to as "DIA". The Cathedral of the Immaculate Conception, Mother Cabrini Shrine and St. Thomas More are part of the greater metropolitan area of Denver. Miraculously, 91.1 FM on the Denver radio dial is for the Christian broadcasting station. It all comes together, to confirm Denver was Lucia's secret destination, that God is in fact outraged and that Jesus truly is the Son of God. It is also recommended we venerate the Sacred Heart of Jesus and consecrate ourselves to the Immaculate Heart of Mary soon.

Chapter 22

The Fight for Religious Liberty

The cross was delivered to the World Trade Center site by a very unlikely source. It is undeniable—not a mystery of science, but a miracle—and the point, given all else, seems to be this: the Lord God is outraged that Jesus is being taken down by the antichrist in America and something must be done to defend Catholic religious liberty.

The last page of *Mother of Christ Crusade* text reads, "She very much needs Your dime too."[210] The *Y* of "Your" is stressed and capitalized, which begs the question why.

Jacinta reports Our Lady said "that there are many wars and discords in the world. Wars are only punishments for the sins of the world. Our Lady cannot stay the arm of her Beloved Son upon the world anymore. It is necessary to do penance. If the people amend themselves, Our Lord will come to the aid of the world. If they do not amend themselves, punishment shall come."[211] She also makes known specific personal sins besides antichrist acts. "...the sins that bring most souls to Hell are sins of the flesh. Certain fashions will be introduced which will offend the Lord very much. ... Many marriages

210 de Marche, Mother of Christ Crusade, epilogue p 220
211 de Marchi, Mother of Christ Crusade, chapter XII p 175

are not good; they do not please Our Lord and are not of God."[212] On an international scale, she asserts only one major and most ominous sin; the violation of the religious liberty of the Holy Church, the Catholic Church. The pending consequence is just reason to pray for all governments. She informs the Mother Superior of this, "Pray a great deal for governments. Pity those governments which persecute the religion of Our Lord. If governments left the Church in peace and gave liberty to the Holy Religion, they would be blessed by God."[213] With this statement she makes aware Our Lords demand for religious liberty for the Holy Church and the reason for doing it. The Church has been trying to overcome oppression for years. This issue must be addressed by the world. The Lord expects and intends to restore religious liberty to the Church eventually to establish world peace. The events of 9/11, by virtue of the divine signs presented, are the consequence for failing to believe that the warning Jacinta recorded for us from Our Lady was serious. As disagreeable as it might sound to some, the obvious must be said directly. All evidence supports the conclusion it was the action of those promoting their antichrist policy who failed to amend their ways that we the people, the entire nation, had to pay the consequences. They continue unrepentant to this day, the evidence is provided by media's public broadcast of OTGDY, unrelenting even in the wake of 9/11 being regarded as merely the emergency wake-up call to warn us of greater impending catastrophic consequences. Given this, we can no longer afford to deny God's will when 9/11 was our warning. Those representatives with an antichrist record were elected. Examples are legislating to promote abortion and redefining marriage as other than between and man and a woman. They are just two offenses. Those who legislate away the conscious religious rights of Christian healthcare professionals, rights Thomas Jefferson declared as endowed by God, are essentially stating Christianity, specifically Catholicism,

212 de Marchi, Mother of Christ Crusade, chapter XII p177
213 De Marchi, Mother of Christ Crusade, Chapter XII, p 175

is a fraudulent faith unworthy of constitutional protection. When challenged, if upheld, the political ruling class alone will control government, the new rules of law they write and pass, we will have ourselves allowed. Understand, it is our own fault, we have no one to blame but ourselves. However, at least so far, it remains our right and responsibility to uphold each others right to religious freedom, and appropriately vote our response.

Meanwhile, the Holy Religion's liberty is being trampled—literally trashed. Free speech is desensitizing the public to killing Catholic children, reducing them to the status of unworthy of life. When the public broadcasts are not prevented, they start to believe these sentiments are widely accepted, actually true in the eyes of the public. It's anti-Christian, it's against the law, and considered criminal, it's anti-American, and it's time "OTGDY" came to an abrupt broadcast end. Doing so, is the real Crusade of the Mother of Christ. It is Our Lady's peace plan. Only by the power of Jesus Christ can the injustice and harm to Catholics done by the antichrist end and religious liberty be restored for all. His attentive interest is well noted. The existence of impending consequence has already been reported. It is unbelievable that media insists on being so self-righteous that it takes an act of God to get their attention. Ignoring and refuting the meaning of the signs at ground zero and Lucia's testimony are sure to anger God even more.

You can research the song lyrics of "Only the Good Die Young" and assess the damage it has caused to Catholicism and the fear it instills in the hearts of not only young Catholic girls, and how it endangers all young girls. You can see why Jesus Christ would be outraged by this trashing of His Church and the threatening His children. The young virgin Catholic girl named Virginia in ""OTGDY" and the Catholic faith together have rights, and they should be constitutionally protected, equally with all faiths, from the abuse and mockery the lyrics of "OTGDY" imposed on the world by public broadcast media. "Not so much anti-Catholic as it is pro-lust,"[214] the song writer says, but a little anti-Catholic is still against the law, it is illegal, yet no one has done a thing, maybe because the singer makes clear he hangs with a dangerous crowd, a defensive threat all its own to discourage a challenge. It is not an innocent song, and it isn't funny. Heavy fines should be imposed and paid to the Church and government, for what media has done by promoting the anti-Catholic attitude and sentiments of the song around the world. Criminal charges should even be filed. The "Virginia Declaration of Rights," written by Thomas Jefferson and commonly referred to as the "Bill of Rights," sounds as though it was written specifically with young Virginia in mind.

Figure 65

Washington and the antichrist

214 Song Facts on the www., Wikipedia Quotes, 2011

In this photo, the Antichrist looks down from the upper right corner. A man looking like George Washington is gazing up at him. His eye is in the center of the top center tile, his face the size of the wall. It speaks for itself. This message written in stone, indicate those antichrist, have engineered power over Washington. This sign is bad news for Christians expecting equal religious liberty. Restoring it will be an uphill battle, but it must be won. The entire point of Our Lady's message is to stop the outrages, sacrileges and indifferences that offend Our Lord Jesus Christ. The evidence presented is testimony that Jesus is the Son of God and an invitation to worship Him. If not, stop persecuting Him. The antichrist are the worst offenders of God, "OTGDY" is the benchmark example of acts against the Catholic Church and its members, in addition to being the vehicle by which Our Lady's Peace Plan is to begin. A challenge of it and the reestablishment of religious liberty of the Catholic Church by the US Supreme Court and its enforcement, should stop media propaganda, radical nations and government attacks on all faiths, a sure step toward world peace. Religious opposition will be outlawed and peace given to us through Jesus Christ. We have already seen the Lord God impose His own justice for our failure to interrupt the antichrist acts of some. There is no reason to believe the case against "Only the Good Die Young" won't be successful. Religious liberty is already protected, written before free speech in the First Amendment to the US Constitution, it only needs to be reaffirmed; then effectively enforced. Virginia clearly has her religious rights well documented by the author of the Constitution, in Thomas Jefferson's, Virginia Statute of Religious Freedom. The outcome rests in your hands.

The Virginia Act For Establishing Religious Freedom[215]

Thomas Jefferson, 1786

Well aware that Almighty God hath created the mind free; that all attempts to influence it by temporal punishments or burdens, or by civil incapacitations, tend only to beget habits of hypocrisy and meanness, and are a departure from the plan of the Holy Author of our religion, who being Lord both of body and mind, yet chose not to propagate it by coercions on either, as was in his Almighty power to do; that the impious presumption of legislators and rulers, civil as well as ecclesiastical, who, being themselves but fallible and uninspired men, have assumed dominion over the faith of others, setting up their own opinions and modes of thinking as the only true and infallible, and as such endeavoring to impose them on others, hath established and maintained false religions over the greatest part of the world, and through all time; that to compel a man to furnish contributions of money for the propagation of opinions which he disbelieves, is sinful and tyrannical; that even the forcing him to support this or that teacher of his own religious persuasion, is depriving him of the comfortable liberty of giving his contributions to the particular pastor whose morals he would make his pattern, and whose powers he feels most persuasive to righteousness, and is withdrawing from the ministry those temporal rewards, which proceeding from an approbation of their personal conduct, are an additional incitement to earnest and unremitting labors for the instruction of mankind; that our civil rights have no dependence on our religious

215 Library of Virginia, Historic Virginia, Documents, www.lva.virginia .gov/public/guides/Historical Documents, 12/201

opinions, more than our opinions in physics or geometry; that, therefore, the proscribing any citizen as unworthy the public confidence by laying upon him an incapacity of being called to the offices of trust and emolument, unless he profess or renounce this or that religious opinion, is depriving him injuriously of those privileges and advantages to which in common with his fellow citizens he has a natural right; that it tends also to corrupt the principles of that very religion it is meant to encourage, by bribing, with a monopoly of worldly honors and emoluments, those who will externally profess and conform to it; that though indeed these are criminal who do not withstand such temptation, yet neither are those innocent who lay the bait in their way; that to suffer the civil magistrate to intrude his powers into the field of opinion and to restrain the profession or propagation of principles, on the supposition of their ill tendency, is a dangerous fallacy, which at once destroys all religious liberty, because he being of course judge of that tendency, will make his opinions the rule of judgment, and approve or condemn the sentiments of others only as they shall square with or differ from his own; that it is time enough for the rightful purposes of civil government, for its officers to interfere when principles break out into overt acts against peace and good order; and finally, that truth is great and will prevail if left to herself, that she is the proper and sufficient antagonist to error, and has nothing to fear from the conflict, unless by human interposition disarmed of her natural weapons, free argument and debate, errors ceasing to be dangerous when it is permitted freely to contradict them.

Be it therefore enacted by the General Assembly, That no man shall be compelled to frequent or support any religious worship, place, or ministry whatsoever, nor shall be

> enforced, restrained, molested, or burdened in his body or goods, nor shall otherwise suffer on account of his religious opinions or belief; but that all men shall be free to profess, and by argument to maintain, their opinions in matters of religion, and that the same shall in nowise diminish, enlarge, or affect their civil capacities.
>
> And though we well know this Assembly, elected by the people for the ordinary purposes of legislation only, have no powers equal to our own and that therefore to declare this act irrevocable would be of no effect in law, yet we are free to declare, and do declare, that the rights hereby asserted are of the natural rights of mankind, and that if any act shall be hereafter passed to repeal the present or to narrow its operation, such act will be an infringement of natural right.

Virginia has a right to religious freedom

Virginia's rights could not have been spelled out any better than in these profound words by Thomas Jefferson. The Catholic girl named Virginia has religious rights that are being violated by ever expanding anti-Catholic acts by media that were thoughtfully recognized by Thomas Jefferson, and the great State of Virginia, as rights given to everyone, by God. Although other dictatorships have outlawed Christianity, and Christians have been attacked and murdered in foreign countries, Americans allegiance and concern is with America. Patriotism is one motivation for every American to be concerned, it is our duty to defend our nation and preserve our government and its founding principles. If as a Catholic, we are denied our Constitutional rights to practice our freedom of religion, the abolition of Christianity altogether is sure to follow. In the United States the process of rejecting what the founding fathers of our nation found the most important right of everyone, including its Catholic and Christian citizens; the right of freedom to work while maintaining their religious conscience. This freedom is being abolished, made illegal with legislation, and some congressional representatives are approving it! Law has been written attempting to take away the right of Catholic doctors and healthcare professionals who on the basis of their faith, refuse to perform abortions or distribute "morning after" drugs. It would make Catholics "equal" with them, legislating against the Doctrine of the Catholic Church and forcing its member doctors to act against their faith with their license to practice, and their careers on the line. This antichrist legislation and is not only immoral, it outrages God.

It could actually be a devious, reprehensible attempt by antichrist legislators and lobbyists, both in State Houses and especially in the US Congress, who act unified yet vote independently, to personally cast their votes, as your elected representative, to deny the foundational foresight of our great leaders, and Catholics their Constitutional and God given rights. Abortion is specifically offensive to the Lord God according to the Catholic Church and an inseparable message in *Mother of Christ Crusade*. Why else would God intervene to present signs of the devil and the cross of Jesus Christ on the date 9/11? Consequences are at stake? We are headed down a dangerous slope. It is up to us, "We the People", to read the signs and vote appropriately to preserve our nation.

Renewed religious freedom can prevent them if enforced. Other nations have been forced into worship of a national religion. It appears efforts are being made covertly to dismiss Christianity and legally remove it from America. It is near unbelievable that even in America, representatives are actually uniting to legislate against God Himself, and take down His Son Jesus Christ with Him. This was part of the urgent emergency warning sent during 9/11 from God Himself, intended especially for Americans, yet serving notice to the whole world. We are still free to elect representatives who will abide by

Gods law, respecting His Word as written. "Marriage" for example is a word coined and used by the Church, a sacrament instituted by the Church, established to represent the union between a woman and man. It is Gods natural law, it is intuitive, and the State should not be allowed to adopt it as their creation then change its definition. It is legislating against the Church. Our Lady presaged through Sr. Maria Lucia of the Immaculate Heart, 9/11, and thereby made fact, the words Jacinta spoke about punishment in chapter XII prove true.

God Has Mercy on His People

God has blessed the world with knowledge of Him and His law. You must recognize that by telling us of this major event ahead of time, whether discovered before the disaster took place or not, we have been blessed by God and rightfully ought to give Him thanks and praise. Our Lady should be honored and respected for Her presages. Take heed of this notice Lucia printed in *Mother of Christ Crusade*. It is part of the "exact truth" that Lucia writes in her *Crusade* book. We should give thanks and praise to Jesus Christ for showing us the way to religious freedom and peace on earth. He gave this generation these miraculous gifts of insight. Praise the Lord Jesus Christ for His mercy on us.

This presage of Our Lady, given to St. Sr. Maria Lucia, was recorded in *Mother of Christ Crusade*; granted, it is difficult to find since it was hidden in the text, but that needed to be done to prevent those who would destroy all traces of the book and the presages attributable to Jesus and Our Lady, from doing so. Lucia was asked to further a devotion to the Immaculate Heart of Mary. The Mother of Christ Crusade is a successful masterpiece. Lest we forget, the miraculous world at the Mother Cabrini Shrine, on the sanctuary wall remains a miracle in progress, presaging 9/11, year after year.

The *Crusade* should prove the divinity of Our Lady, making Her worthy of worship, praise, and honor she deserves. The everlasting life, a real life with Jesus for eternity is available to anyone who believes in him, not myth, and He was then and is now the Son of God. To Him we can give worship and praise, honor and glory together with the Holy Spirit, and God the Father Almighty.

The Mother of Christ Crusade, Mother Cabrini Shrine and St. Thomas More parish begin our quest for peace. Maintaining the sacred nature of any scripture, religion, or prophet is your God given religious right.

However, this is the case for defending the religious liberty for Catholics. The signs presented only condemn the antichrist actions of those attacking Christians, for they have intentionally imperiled the safety and demeaned the dignity of Catholic children. They condemn the acts, not the people themselves. The media and rock and roll music lyrics, some not all, who continue to mock Jesus Christ, the Virgin Mary, and the Rosary of Mary and work against everything good the Church holds sacred, intent on propagating their agenda and destroying the validity of Jesus Christ as Messiah and Christianity altogether, have been singled out as the offenders, but also as the stepping stone to renewed religious liberty and the promise of world *peace*. It comes to us courtesy of Jesus Christ the Son of God.

The Book of Revelation 9:11[216]

Lucia's work prompts the reader to examine the Book of Revelation by formatting the word Revelation two different ways: at times it is capitalized, on others not. The former refers to the Book of Revelation, and the latter refers to the revelations of presage found in *Mother of Christ Crusade*, the where she went, and the important words and their interpretation she left behind, waiting to be discovered.

---

216 *The Holy Bible of the Old and New Testaments, Translated out of The Original Tongues.* New York: American Bible Society, 1850.

Revelation infers disaster and catastrophe that transpire because men will not repent of the work of their hands and will not give up the worship of demonic acts and idols made from gold, silver, bronze, stone, and wood, which cannot see or hear or walk. People had fallen victim to greed, seeking pleasures of the flesh instead of the spirit, or so the prophecy says.

In Revelation, there are seven angels holding trumpets prepared to blow them, initiating events to come.

The "abyss" spoken of in some versions of Revelation 9:11, is a great fiery furnace, not the depths of the ocean as some may fathom. This great furnace of the abyss could be thought of as analogous to Hell or the blaze inside the WTC with the explosion of the jet fuel. It may be the "vision of Hell" the Children of Fatima were privileged to see and report, the final secret they never told out loud to anyone was entered into the Mother of Christ Crusade. It is 9/11. Revelation maybe upon us now.

Revelation 9:1-12

King James Version (The Holy Bible of the Old and New Testaments, Translated out of The Original Tongues. New York: American Bible Society, 1850.)

Revelation 9

1 And the fifth angel sounded, and I saw a star fall from heaven unto the earth: and to him was given the key of the bottomless pit.

2 And he opened the bottomless pit; and there arose a smoke
out of the pit, as the smoke of a great furnace; and the
sun and the air were darkened by reason of the smoke of
the pit.
3 And there came out of the smoke locusts upon the earth:
and unto them was given power, as the scorpions of the
earth have power.
4 And it was commanded them that they should not hurt the
grass of the earth, neither any green thing, neither any
tree; but only those men which have not the seal of God
in their foreheads.
5 And to them it was given that they should not kill them,
but that they should be tormented five months: and
their torment was as the torment of a scorpion, when he
striketh a man.
6 And in those days shall men seek death, and shall not find
it; and shall desire to die, and death shall flee from them.
7 And the shapes of the locusts were like unto horses
prepared unto battle; and on their heads were as it were
crowns like gold, and their faces were as the faces of
men.
8 And they had hair as the hair of women, and their teeth
were as the teeth of lions.
9 And they had breastplates, as it were breastplates of iron;
and the sound of their wings was as the sound of chariots
of many horses running to battle.
10 And they had tails like unto scorpions, and there were
stings in their tails: and their power was to hurt men five
months.
11 And they had a king over them, which is the angel of the
bottomless pit, whose name in the Hebrew tongue
is Abaddon, but in the Greek tongue hath his name
Apollyon.

12 One woe is past; and, behold, there come two woes more hereafter.

Abaddon and Apollyon mean “destroyer”.

Revelation 9: 11, states they had as their king, the angel of Hell.

[The king of the abyss is the fallen angel Satan, the Antichrist, the angel of Hell and was represented by the devil in the smoke of 9/11. We do not really know where we are in Revelation, but this seems to apply.

Glory Be to God the Father, the Son, and the Holy Spirit, now and forever. Thanks Be to God. Blessed are we, the world, the Lord God has visited His people.

Bibliography Page:

The Holy Bible of the Old and New Testaments, Translated out of The Original Tongues. New York: American Bible Society, 1850.

Mother of Christ Crusade, Saint Sr. Maria Lucia, of the Immaculate Heart of Mary and Father John de Marchi, *1947.*

Webster's Illustrated Encyclopedic Dictionary, Tormont Publications Inc., 1990 Edition

Webster's Seventh New Collegiate Dictionary, G. and C. Merriam Company, Publishers, 1972 Edition

Fig. 1 The Cross at ground zero, New York, NY; *"A picture of Hope at 911"*. Photograph by Anne Bybee, available from BGEA, the Billy Graham Evangelical Association, viewed 10/20/2011. Also, www.charismamedia.com.

FIG. 2, *"Satan in the Smoke?"* Photography by Mark D. Phillips, markdphillips@markdphillips.com and Stellarimages.com Photo taken on September 11, 2011. Viewed 10/20/2011

Fig. 3 Spain and Portugal, from CIA Maps. Found at www.cia.gov/library/publications/theworldfactbook/maps/maptemplate/sp.html

Webster's illustrated Encyclopedic Dictionary, Tormont Publications Inc.. 1990 edition published by Tormont Publications; 338 St. Antoine St. East; Montreal, Canada; H2Y 1A3. 514-954-1441. ISBN 2-921171-32-5.

Fig. 4 Fall River, Mass. Ask.com Encyclopedia 788 x 466 jpeg. Wikipedia, Ask.com. 10/23/2011

Fig. 5 The Denver Cathedral Basilica of the Immaculate Conception, Photo by Dr. David Randolph

Fig. 6-14 from the Denver Cathedral of the Immaculate Conception

Fig. 15-56 Photos taken on location, at St. Frances Xavier Cabrini, Mother Cabrini Shrine, Golden Colorado, David R.Randolph

Fig. 57 "Our Lady, the Virgin Mary", on location at the Denver Cathedral Basilica of the Immaculate Conception. By David Randolph

Fig. 58-61 On location at the St. Frances Xavier Cabrini, Mother Cabrini Shrine, Golden, Colorado.